America
1900

Visiting day aboard the U.S.S. Oregon.

America
1900

The Turning Point

Judy Crichton

HENRY HOLT AND COMPANY · NEW YORK

Henry Holt and Company, Inc.
Publishers since 1866
115 West 18th Street
New York, New York 10011

Henry Holt ® is a registered trademark of
Henry Holt and Company, Inc.

Due to limitations of space, illustration credits appear on pages 341–42.

Library of Congress Cataloging-in-Publication Data
Crichton, Judy
America 1900: the turning point / Judy Crichton.—1st ed.
p.   cm.
Includes bibliographical references and index.
ISBN 0-8050-5365-4 (alk. paper)
1. United States—History—1865–1921. 2. Nineteen hundred, A.D.
I. Title.
E711.C75 1998
973.8—dc21   98-19909

Henry Holt books are available for special
promotions and premiums. For details contact:
Director, Special Markets.

First Edition 1998

Designed by Paula R. Szafranski

Printed in the United States of America
All first editions are printed on acid-free paper.

1 3 5 7 9 10 8 6 4 2

This book was informed by five generations of Americans—by my great-grandparents who connected me directly to the days of the Civil War, by my grandparents who came of age in 1900 and whose memories are now my own, by my parents who helped put the past into context, and by my children and their children who are daily reminders that the past is the present and the future is always closer than it seems.

Contents

America
1900

"*Looking Foward*—A.D. *2001: Broadway, New York, as it may appear a hundred years hence, when modern inventions have been carried to the highest point of development*" (Collier's Weekly, *January 1901).*

Prologue

———◆———

It was snowing on New Year's Day, 1900, across much of the country, from the coast of Maine, where the snow was blinding, down through New England, where great fat drifts blocked the trolley cars, and as far south as Savannah, Georgia, where the telegraph and telephone lines were heavy with ice. On the prairie, even the sturdiest horses found it hard going; trains were stalled and small towns were running low on coal. Across the broad northern tier of America, New Year's celebrations were tempered by the weather, but no matter. The snow was a comfort. The night before, Theodore Roosevelt, the governor of New York, had promised his children it would snow on New Year's Day, just as it had snowed one hundred years before. To Americans trying to divine the future, the snow was seen as a positive omen.

Older folk confessed they had prayed since childhood to live to see this day. Crossing the divide between 1899 and 1900 was almost a mystical experience. But on the streets, in homes, saloons, and newsrooms that night there was sharp division over what was called the "century question"—whether January 1, 1900, was the first day of the new century, or simply the beginning of the last year of the old. President McKinley, Queen Victoria, and Pope Leo XIII were all quite certain that the twentieth century was still one year away, but in Berlin on New Year's Eve, the German emperor, the willful Kaiser Wilhelm, hailed the birth of the new century with a thirty-three gun salute. No one considered 1900 just another year.

In the weeks leading up to January 1, there was a flood of books and essays, news columns, sermons, and lectures summing up the wonders of the nineteenth century. It had been a period of such momentous change that there was a visceral need to take stock, to mark the moment and put the past into perspective. *The New York Times* reported that "The 19th century had been marked by greater progress in all that pertains to the material well-being and enlightenment of mankind than all the previous history of the race." *The Washington Post* declared that "in every department of scientific and intellectual activity, we have gone beyond the wildest dreams of 1800."

In just one hundred years, America had grown from a small and fragile republic into a nation *The Times* declared the envy of the world. In 1800, five million Americans had lived in thirteen states. Only the most adventurous—a few hundred thousand people—had pressed beyond the Allegheny Mountains. By 1900, seventy-six million people in forty-five states were sprawled across a continent three thousand miles wide. America was such a young country its entire history could almost be measured by the life span of its oldest citizens. Those caught in the exercise of remembrance tried to describe the changes they had lived through, and often failed.

The pioneers who first settled the Plains—and many were still alive—had spent months, sometimes years without a visitor to break the isolation or the reassurance of a letter from home. They had suffered a loneliness the young could not imagine. For them, crossing the continent had been a "matter of life or death"; now, as the *Atlanta Constitution* noted, it was "a matter of a $100, and take your ease as you go." Americans whose grandparents had fought in the Revolutionary War were reading about the use of X rays to cure cancer. In Philadelphia, Elizabeth Cooper McIntyre, who had recently celebrated her ninety-ninth birthday, had been born the year Philadelphians lined the streets to watch President Adams, his wife, Abigail, and congressional leaders leave the city for the new unfinished Capitol on the marshy banks of the Potomac.

She could remember when there were no fireboxes or friction matches, no postage stamps or envelopes, when communication was as slow as it was uncertain and signaling was done from town to town by means of fires on mountaintops or waving flags. In her youth it had taken six weeks to get news from Europe; now it took six seconds. Mrs. McIntyre had seen the coming of the cable, the telegraph and telephone, trolleys and high-speed trains. "In the span of a single life," wrote John J. Ingalls for *The Examiner* (San Francisco), "the humblest artisan enjoys what kings could not purchase with their treasures a century ago." Many Americans now had ice in the summer and heat in the winter and artificial light—kerosene, gas, or electric—which could be summoned any time of night or day. There were modern coal stoves and bathtubs with running water and water closets that flushed waste away.

By the end of the nineteenth century extraordinary discoveries in medicine, such as the germ theory and antiseptic surgery, had greatly extended life. The horror of operations without anesthesia was still within memory. American men could expect to reach forty-eight years of age, women could count on reaching fifty-one—if they had money and access to modern care. Many of the most important scientific theories were little understood, but they turned up on all the New Year's summations, anyway. Spectrum analysis, electromagnetism, the atomic theory in chemistry, the molecular composition of gas, the measurement of the velocity of light were phrases that seemed to suggest the mysteries of heaven and earth were on their way to solution.

That a single lifetime had embraced such revolutionary change was almost beyond comprehension. "If time and space signified what they did in 1800," Ingalls wrote, "the United States could not exist under one government. It would not be possible to maintain unity of purpose or identity of interests between communities separated by impassable barriers." The nation was now bound by hundreds of thousands of miles of rail, telegraph, and telephone lines. "The continent has shrunk to a span. The oceans are obliterated. London and Paris and Peking and New York are next-door neighbors."

In January 1900, in the hills of Oakland, California, a young writer named Jack London composed a meditation called "The Shrinkage of the Planet":

> . . . What a playball has this planet of ours become! Steam has made its parts accessible and drawn them closer together. The telegraph annihilates space and time. Each morning every part knows what every other part is thinking, contemplating, or doing. A discovery in a German laboratory is being demonstrated in San Francisco within twenty-four hours. The death of an obscure missionary in China, or of a whiskey smuggler in the South Seas, is served up with the morning toast.

The progress of the past inspired soaring visions of the future—and there would be many more by the end of the year. Publisher William Randolph Hearst predicted the twentieth century would see "the barbarous races of the world civilized. The powers of the wind, the sea, the rivers, and the sun will be chained, so that the air will no longer be fouled with smoke for which men have worn out their lives in coal mines. The deserts will be the seats of vast manufacturing enterprises, carried on by electric power developed directly from solar heat." An ostrich farm in Southern California was already producing solar power. Change had come so fast and been so radical that no one seemed certain where reality stopped and fantasy began.

The Reverend Edward Everett Hale envisioned a time when people would be shot by pneumatic tube from Texas to Georgia. In Pennsylvania, Frank Stockton, a wood engraver, was composing fairy tales for adults about a wonder-worker named Toland Crewe who invented an "artesian ray" that could reveal the inner structure of the earth, a submarine that could travel under ice to the Pole, and a new metal, "shadrach," that had the potential of cooling off men's minds and hearts. Stockton understood that for all of the astounding leaps of progress, the human heart and mind still had a ways to go.

John Ingalls questioned whether a writer in the year 2000 would be able to tell his readers that "the encroachments of capital have been restrained and that labor has its just reward; that the rich are no longer afflicted with satiety nor the poor with discontent; that we have wealth without ostentation, liberty without license, taxation without oppression, the broadest education, and the least corruption of manners." He concluded with the words, "Perhaps not." It was easier at the start of 1900 to predict advances in technology than expansion of the spirit.

Between the summations of the past and the prophecies of the future appeared stark reminders that progress had a price and the bright promise of America had a dark side. In 1900, the reverence for God and the Constitution seemed more than matched by a reverence for money. Expansion had been profitable beyond measure, but too often one man's triumph led to another man's defeat. America had never been more prosperous, but the disparity between rich and poor had also never been greater. Racism and sexism were rampant. But the possibilities of America were as great or greater than they had ever been. And if the country had yet to live up to its democratic ideal, the ideal had survived.

Across America on that snowy New Year's morning there was a soaring sense of confidence and tremendous curiosity about the days and years to come. Without the gift of foresight, what no one understood was that the forces of the future were closer than they seemed. Issues that would surface over the next twelve months would be much the same as those their grandchildren and great-grandchildren would struggle with in the year 2000.

1900 would be a remarkable year.

New York City in the winter of 1899.

In 1900, the greenhouse, or conservatory as it was called, on the west side of the White House, opened up onto the State Dining Room. Dinner guests were able to look through French doors into a tropical paradise of plants and palms and potted fruit trees.

CHAPTER ONE

New Year's Day

I

On January 1, in Washington, D.C., a fresh fall of snow about an inch deep was brightening the city. Skaters were out on the Potomac and in Rock Creek Park, horse-drawn sleighs moved through the woods in splendid isolation. At the Capitol, where the old gaslight posts had finally been removed, cinders were being scattered on the icy steps. With Congress in recess and the federal bureaus closed, the city was even quieter than usual. But midmorning the Sabbath-like stillness was broken by the warning gongs of trolleys as crowds crammed on streetcars heading for the White House.

The diplomatic corps was out in full regalia; there were more women wearing tiaras in the morning than even the oldest reporter could recall. Elegant carriages, their wheels creaking on the hard-packed snow, with coachmen and footmen on the box, jockeyed for position on Pennsylvania Avenue. At the edge of the city, in a curiously shaped modern studio, Frances Benjamin Johnston, the idiosyncratic, cigarette smoking photographer, was preparing for President McKinley's New Year's Day reception. On Johnston's calendar was the simple notation, "WH."

America's court photographer, she had been in and out of the White House for years, but this morning she would leave her cameras home.

Down the Mall, on the second floor of the crowded Executive Mansion, President and Mrs. William McKinley, surrounded by friends and aides, were greeting cabinet members and their wives in the presidential library. The reports from the Philippines that morning had been unsettling. A rebel plot had been uncovered in Manila and native spies were reporting that two thousand armed insurgents were strengthening artillery placements outside the city. But as the presidential party waited for the signal to make their way down the central stairs and into the Blue Room, McKinley seemed unperturbed.

Two thousand citizens were already standing by the gates in an arctic wind, waiting to pay their respects. The president had never been more popular, and the reception this morning promised to be as splendid as any ever held in the White House. As the diplomats and their wives were ushered into the East Room, it was clear their attendance was more than just a courtesy call. America was no longer an upstart republic; it had emerged from the Spanish-American War as one of the richest and most powerful nations on earth. If there were misgivings among the Europeans over this shift in world affairs, and indeed there were, the mood among the Americans was triumphant.

When Senator Chauncey Depew of New York declared, "There is not a man here who does not feel four hundred percent bigger in 1900, bigger intellectually, bigger hopefully, bigger patriotically that he is a citizen of a country that has become a world power," he reflected the feelings of millions of people. In the year-end roundups published in newspapers that weekend, one state after the next reported an unprecedented level of well-being. And the staid *New York Times* reported a "prosperity panic on Wall Street."

At the start of this election year the Republican party had an enormous advantage. But on New Year's Day, no one knew for sure, not even McKinley, whether he would run for a second term. It was the great question of the day. As the Marine band played "Hail to the Chief," the president and his wife, following the cabinet, threaded their way past favored friends into the Blue Room where thousands of tiny electric bulbs were woven through the smilax and jungle of palms. Ida McKinley, in a new, mauve-colored brocaded gown with diamond ornaments on the bodice, settled into a chair by her husband's side.

The president's wife was a pale and fragile woman, given to seizures and nervous complaints. Over the past three years Mrs. McKinley had stood up to the demands of the White House better than expected, but there was speculation now

At twenty-six, Major William McKinley was a dashing horseman, but a straight-laced fellow. Brought up in a strict Methodist home where dancing, cards, wine, and tobacco were considered the snares of Satan, McKinley later developed the politician's vice—a passion for cigars.

among Republican leaders as to whether she had the strength to face another term. The president himself was uncertain. After thirty years of marriage, Ida remained at the center of his life and he would do nothing to jeopardize her health.

When the McKinleys first met, Ida was a great beauty, rich and headstrong and somewhat spoiled, but McKinley didn't notice. He was a Civil War veteran just starting out as a lawyer. One year after they married, Ida gave birth to a baby girl, Kate, who was said to look much like her father. But Kate died when she was only four, and a second child lived only five months. Ida never really recovered. In recent years she had grown exceedingly nervous and only the president seemed able to settle her down.

New Year's Day, however, as the receiving party moved into place, the press noted that Mrs. McKinley's face was flushed with pleasure. She loved these state occasions. For all the talk about the democratic spirit, there was widespread fascination in 1900 with the American equivalent of court life and the prerogatives of privilege. Newspapers around the country carried in detail exquisite descriptions of the women's gowns, their jewels, the feathered aigrettes worn by congressional wives, the spangled black net dress worn by Mrs. Elihu Root, the wife of the new secretary of the War Department—all was news.

The popular Russian ambassador, the Count de Cassini, arrived monocled and pomaded in a fur-trimmed tunic and high, polished boots. He was, as usual, accompanied by the mysterious and exotic

This photograph of Ida McKinley was taken on her wedding trip to New York in 1871. The daughter of a prominent Canton, Ohio, business-man, Ida Saxton was educated at a girls' finishing school and sent on a grand tour of Europe. She briefly worked in her father's bank in Canton, but her training as a business-woman ended when she met Major McKinley.

eighteen-year-old, Mlle Marguerite Cassini. Marguerite served as the ambassador's official hostess and was the subject of great capital gossip. She was always presented as Cassini's beloved niece, when in fact she was his daughter. The Chinese minister, Wu Ting Fang, said to be the cleverest and wittiest after-dinner speaker, appeared in a hat of green and crimson silk, while his elegant wife wore a headdress of black, held in place with magnificent diamond pins. It would be a difficult year for the minister.

The president greeted the large American military contingent led by General Nelson Miles, the commander of the army. McKinley knew full well that Admiral Dewey, the small and truculent hero of Manila Bay, was furious that he had not been placed at the head of the line, but the president refused to break with tradition. Protocol required naval officers to follow the army, and the admiral found himself in the wake of the youngest army lieutenant in line. The president was bemused by Dewey's discomfort. There was little love between the two and there would be less before the year was over.

After Alexander Graham Bell and his friend Samuel Langley, the inventor of a fantastic flying machine, had paid their respects, Mrs. McKinley, clearly fatigued, retired to the cramped private quarters on the second floor. The mansion now had electric lighting, a steam heating system, bathtubs with hot and cold running water, an elevator, and a few telephones. But the house had been built as the home and office for the president of a small republic. The country had expanded but the White House had not. The second floor was a jumble—the presidential offices and the McKinleys' private quarters were side by side. Ida rather liked the arrangement. Her husband was seldom out of her sight.

Eleven secretaries meandered through the halls, often working into the night, and sometimes on Sunday. Next to the telegraph room, the map room, and secretarial offices lay the president's office and the oval library. Down the corridor were five bedrooms, two dressing rooms, and one full bath. In the presidential bedroom, where Mrs. McKinley spent much of her time crocheting, stood two brass postered beds beneath a portrait of Kate. The family dining room and kitchen were on the first floor of the house and officially out of bounds to all but family and personal staff, but aides regularly had to shoo tourists away.

Tradition required American presidents to remain accessible to the people, and every weekday McKinley was in Washington hundreds of citizens arrived expecting to meet him. In the great East Room, where Mrs. John Adams had once dried the family wash, they gaped at the crystal chandeliers and frayed upholstery and hoped for a casual chat with the president himself. McKinley was a cordial man

The McKinleys' bedroom, the largest of the five bedrooms in the private quarters, was no grander than that of a small businessman. The spindle-back rocker was similar to those on sale for $1.95. The picture of the McKinleys' daughter, Kate, can be seen hanging over the beds.

By 1900, the presidential offices, right next to the McKinleys' private quarters, were greatly overcrowded. All the men, excluding messengers, wore formal morning attire : a black cutaway coat, gray-and-black-striped trousers, and a silk tie. The president received about a thousand letters a day; many were simple requests for autographs. Some letters included threats, which were never publicly disclosed.

who seemed to enjoy his role as national host. On New Year's Day, as the official guests were heading off to private receptions, the general public was finally admitted for a presidential smile and handshake. Two hours later, when McKinley left the Blue Room and headed up the stairs to join his wife, aides noted he had greeted 3,354 people.

Security at the White House was casual, and for the most part had always been so. In all of the Executive Mansion, there was only one guard on duty at night, and he retired early. One of the doorkeepers, Thomas Pendel, was an older man who had served at the White House for over thirty-five years. He had the curious distinction of having seen President Lincoln off to his carriage the night Lincoln left for Ford's Theater and had been working in the White House when President Garfield was assassinated. Pendel would serve for the remainder of McKinley's time.

A few years back, Senator Mark Hanna, the president's closest advisor, became alarmed when anarchists murdered the Empress Elizabeth of Austria, the president of France, and the premier of Spain and were said to be plotting to assassinate every head of state of a Western country. Hanna had added several Secret Service guards to the White House staff, but that winter the anarchists were quiet and the extra guards were gone. Over the course of the coming year, the president's security would again become a concern, and not without reason.

But if the president worried about security matters he certainly didn't show it. He would continue to take his daily constitutional alone or with a friend. In a New Year's homily, McKinley's pastor had spoken of the promise and splendor of the future. "The radiant angel of Hope," he said, "points to a prospect as glorious as any that greeted the eyes of Moses when he looked upon Canaan, or any that filled St. John with holy rapture as he dreamed of the City of God."

January 1, 1900, Americans were optimistic and so was the president.

II

In Boston that New Year's Day, the nor'easter that had struck the city early was slowing down the loading of ships in the harbor. Americans had come to depend on reliable weather predictions, but the Weather Bureau had been closed for the holidays, and down at the docks the teamsters had been caught unawares, without time to sharpen the shoes of the horses. Dragging heavy loads up steep and icy inclines to the piers, horses were losing their footing; many slipped and fell.

Around the hotels that morning, old-time cabbies and hackmen waiting for holiday fares had an unnerving glimpse of the future. The new automobile broughams, enclosed machines from the Cyclorama Electric Vehicle Station, had surprising traction on the snow. Only one out of the dozen working that day broke down, and that was because its battery had run low. When the storm started, drivers were instructed not to fill orders for long-distance duty. Running in snow required extra power and the auto batteries needed to be recharged after every three or four calls. There were still only about eight thousand cars in the country, but as coachmen covered their horses against the chill wind, there were predictions that their days were numbered. The National Biscuit Company's electric wagon were on duty as usual, and so were the Edison Company's two light electric carriages.

But there was far more dramatic evidence of change in Boston that weekend than a few automachines running in the snow. As long as anyone could remember, Boston had been the city without a New Year's Eve. Traditionally, church services had marked the turn of the year, quiet affairs that ended just after midnight. Bostonians might read about celebrations in New York and all those other noisy cities, but then they would go about their circumspect ways. The Lodges and the Cabots and the Lowells and the Adamses were not about to indulge in raucous display or give license to those who would. At the end of 1899 it was assumed that Bostonians would greet the New Year in the time-honored fashion they had greeted those that came before.

But as in so many of America's older cities, the population of Boston had changed radically. The old families were now outnumbered by new Americans from Ireland and Italy and eastern Europe, who were transforming the demeanor of the city as well as its demographics. On this New Year's Eve, some hours before midnight, tens of thousands of people were out in the streets. Pope Leo XIII had decreed 1900 a "Jubilee Year"—a holy year, to be celebrated with a midnight mass. Every Catholic church in the area complied. As if caught in some heavenly competition, a more than usual number of Protestant churches scheduled evening services, and New Year's Eve in Boston became a festive occasion.

So many people came out to church, hundreds had to be turned away. In the Catholic churches, Christmas decorations were still in place, altars were ablaze with lights, choirs sang Haydn's First Mass and the St. Cecilia Mass at midnight services. In the North End, an overflow crowd, mostly Italian, stood in the cold narrow street outside the church door. All over town there were feasts following the services, and Boston streets had never been more lively at two-thirty in the morning. Spoilsport antiquarians, try as they might, could not shut out the sounds; neither heavy damask drapes nor closed shutters quite succeeded.

The next day, an editorial writer for the *Boston Evening Transcript* wrote: "We have managed to ignore new years with a characteristically Puritan stubbornness, but we can't rest in any condition forever. The introduction of the midnight mass will prove the entering wedge by which customs that prevail everywhere else in the world may get a footing here."

In Boston, on January 2, thousands drove down Beacon Street for the opening of the sleighing season.

Out in the historic town of Concord, evidence of change was less dramatic. Stone walls marked fields that had been cleared in the seventeenth century. And the elm trees in town were so large that in places their trunks blocked the sidewalks. The roots of the trees had yet to be amputated by the laying of water pipes or sewage lines. But a municipal sewer system was coming and the oil lamps, now tended by two lamplighters every evening, would soon be replaced. Along the snowy roads outside of town, young men appeared for the first time traveling on skis. The custom had just been introduced by Norwegian immigrants who had made and sold the runners to a "progressive" sporting-goods shop in Boston. On meadows that had been neatly shorn were acres of clear ice, where the more adventurous were taking advantage of the wind for "skate sailing."

In town, in a large wooden house set back from the street on a small rise, the gregarious Democratic congressman from Boston, John F. Fitzgerald, was preparing to return to Washington for the opening of Congress. A Boston paper reported that Fitzgerald and the powerful ward boss from East Boston, P. J. Kennedy, had just attended a Democratic party caucus together. The two men, both sons of Irish immigrants, were longtime friends and political allies. Their families summered together at Orchard Beach, in Maine, a popular seaside resort for Boston's Irish Catholics. It was at Orchard Beach that John's daughter Rose first met Joseph Kennedy. He was seven at the time; she was five.

Now serving his third term, the ambitious Fitzgerald was well liked by his constituents. For the rest of the year he would do what he could in the Republican-dominated Congress, but after that he would be moving on. He hoped to become mayor of the city. An immigrant's son, he could speak to the new Bostonians. He was one himself.

III

For nine million Americans the first day of January was more than the turn of another year—it was the anniversary of Lincoln's Emancipation Proclamation.

From New England down throughout the South, African Americans were holding the annual Freedom Day celebrations. In Franklin, Louisiana, three thousand people, most of them country folk, attended services in the new Odd Fellows Hall. One reporter wrote of "the old mothers and fathers bending toward the graves," who had come "from far distance walking on sticks, to hear things concerning their freedom and the struggle they underwent during the days of slavery." They had held these services for thirty-seven years now.

Mrs. Hendrix, the wife of the town barber in Black River Falls, Wisconsin.

In Savannah, Georgia, in spite of frigid weather, a grand procession made its way down Liberty Street. Black military units in full dress, carrying arms, and aging black veterans from the Civil War were escorted by students and faculty members from Georgia State Industrial College. In the speeches and the prayers that morning was the sad reflection that while slavery had ended, racism was growing. Captain J. J. Durham, speaking of the new laws designed to keep black men from voting, declared: "Any policy toward the Negro that does not take into account his citizenship is doomed to failure." But Durham also urged black Americans to "seek by all honorable means to live on good terms of peace with their white neighbors."

In Wilberforce, Ohio, Professor W. S. Scarborough responded to the government's failure to protect her black citizens. There had been over one hundred lynchings the year before and most of the victims had been black men. "Mob law, mob violence, reigns supreme throughout the South. . . . Our future," Scarborough said, "depends largely on ourselves." In Atlanta, Georgia, at services sponsored by the Negro Literary and Historical Association, a prominent young sociologist, Dr. W.E.B. Du Bois, spoke on "The Problem of Negro Crime." Du Bois pointed out the limitations of life for black Americans, the frustrations among young men locked out of the workplace because of the color of their skin.

The closing prayer at the service in Atlanta was listed on the program as "a proclamation of victory." While it was not an easy matter, most African Americans that day were struggling to share in the optimism of their country.

Other Stories of Interest

The New York Times,
December 31, 1899

CHICAGO—The plan of the Jews to purchase the Holy Land for the occupation of their race has been much discussed in Chicago during the last week. . . . A number of leading Jews of this city are deeply interested in the scheme of purchasing Palestine for purposes of colonization, feeling it . . . would be a haven for the oppressed of their race from all countries.

The Kansas City Star,
December 31, 1899

The physical requirements in girls who are given positions in the telephone exchange are almost as stringent as those insisted upon in men enlisting in the army. To become a "hello" girl the applicant must not be more than 30 years old or less than 5 feet 6 inches tall. Her sight must be good, her hearing excellent, her voice soft, her perception quick and her temper angelic. Tall slim girls with long arms are preferred for work on the switch boards . . . to reach over all of the six feet of space allotted to each operator. . . . It is said that girls of Irish parentage make the best operators. They are said to be quicker with their fingers and their wits and control their tempers admirably.

Boston Evening Transcript,
December 31, 1899

LONDON—The year opens very gloomily for Great Britain, with the operations of her armies in South Africa brought to a standstill. . . . A long struggle, one costly in blood and treasure is to be anticipated.

The New York Times,
January 1, 1900

NEW YORK CITY—The 100th anniversary of the death of George Washington. Services were held in St. Paul's Chapel of Trinity Parish, where funeral services had been held on Dec. 31, 1799. Washington's pew was unoccupied and draped with the national flag.

The New York Times,
January 1, 1900

William J. Witt and Anna Waddilove, of Jersey City, were married at Liederkrantz Hall, one minute after midnight last night. . . . The couple selected that time for the ceremony because they desired to be the first couple married in the new century.

Like most Americans in 1900, Mrs. Wetzel—seen here reading her Bible in Junction City, Kansas—was still using a kerosene lamp. Gas light was too expensive, and it would be decades before homes in rural America were wired for electricity.

CHAPTER TWO

January

I

In the Middle West in 1900, old-timers were trying to confirm what their eyes could see but their minds would not accept. Square in the middle of America, or close enough, was a large modern city. Two cities, really—Kansas City, Kansas, and Kansas City, Missouri. Two hundred and fifty thousand people lived on the Missouri side of the line, another fifty thousand lived in Kansas, but few could tell where one city began and the other left off. As late as 1880, the city had been so poor it was said that "the hogs trotting down main street were fitter for the racetrack than the pork barrel." In the course of just twenty years, a cluster of improbable frontier villages had evolved into a sophisticated urban center with concert halls and formal parks, libraries and music teachers.

The first wave of settlers had come on the backs of "river turtles," steamboats that plied the Missouri and Kansas rivers. Settlements had grown at the junction of the rivers, but the rivers did not generate enough work to sustain a proper town and the land immediately around the settlements was too hilly to be profitable. The townsfolk were said to be "an unpromising mix of renegades, demoralized soldiers, and wrecks from the Civil War." Charles S. Gleed wrote that "a billion frogs in the green ponds at the bottom of the choicest city lots saluted the sun with croaks of despair. In wet weather the townsite was a sea of mud, and in dry . . . a desert of dust. The water supply made whiskey drinking a virtue and the gas was not of much better use than to facilitate suicide."

And then in 1880, Jay Gould, the railroad tycoon, chose Kansas City as the center for his rail operations and the city was transformed from a rough river town into one of the busiest rail hubs in the country. By 1900, there were great modern buildings, hotels with lobbies said to be as large as wheat fields, and a few homegrown millionaires living in private palaces. Miss Barstow's School was preparing young women for Wellesley, Smith, and Vassar.

In the pecking order of cities, Kansas City did not compare to St. Louis, any more than St. Louis could compare to Chicago. But lying smack in the middle of one of the richest farming areas in the world, Kansas City had become the great way station on the Plains. Charles Gleed wrote, with only modest hyperbole: "All the people of the earth could be fed from the land within a circle of a thousand-mile radius." The abundance of America's farmland was astounding. Farmers who were once penalized for producing more than the nation could consume were now shipping produce all over the world. Over a third of the nation's wheat, 10 percent of the corn, and two-thirds of all American cotton were being sold overseas.

In 1899, in the heart of the city, over two and a half million swine had been herded down an incline into vats of hot water, and over six million head of bellowing livestock were "rendered unto the packers the things that are the packers." Nothing was wasted—the offal, the bristle, the hooves all had their uses. The city's prosperity rested "on things material and unpoetic." But the grime, the noise, and the stench from the stockyards intruded into every corner of the town. The horse traffic—the unending parade of delivery wagons—left the streets in perpetual filth.

Those new to city life found the noise unbearable; the battering of horseshoes on ill-paved streets, the sounds of clumsy unbalanced wheels on overladen carts, the constant sounds of overburdened animals complaining of their lot. On the steep bluff overlooking Union Station, where city fathers hoped to expand the park system, stood a clutch of squatters' shacks surrounded by refuse and smoky, evil-smelling fires. The shacks could go, that was easy, but no one knew what to do with the people. In December, the cold weather had driven the destitute to the Provident Association for fuel and food and clothing. Now the Weather Bureau was warning of cold weeks ahead, with heavy falls of snow. Money was being raised for the Orphan Boys' Home, and the Free Unemployment Bureau dispatched a circular letter asking help in finding work for the unemployed.

At the start of the year, members of the Woodmen's Club had set out on their great annual rabbit hunt in quest of game for the poor. Hiring a special railcar, the hunters were taken to a location ten miles north of town, where the fifty-two men split into two teams, captained by Oliver Hast and Ora C. McGoon. The men spent the day and had a jolly time, but the slaughter of rabbits was slim: only 115 were bagged. On the way home, the Woodmen determined they would keep the rabbits for themselves and take up a collection for the needy instead. But Kansas City was going broke and rabbit hunts were never going to solve the city's problems.

The city had grown so fast that its makeshift tax system had not kept apace, but the mayor seemed unable to goad voters into action. A number of "white-wings" had already been laid off, and the dirty streets would be even filthier by spring. The fire department had been forced to borrow a chemical fire-wagon from a nearby town, street lighting was reduced, work on the hospital had been postponed, and cutbacks had all but wiped out the music program in the parks. Crime was up, "the ruffian population" was growing, and *The Kansas City Star* was recommending "ridding the city of idle and dangerous characters by the prompt and simple process of banishment." Idlers and beggars would be led out of town.

While tickets for Jan Paderewski's concert in February were selling pretty well, civic pride would not pay the electric bill or the $300 a day being spent to stamp out smallpox. The only way of raising additional funds at the moment was to lay off more city employees.

A half-hour trolley ride away from Kansas City, in the small town of Independence, Missouri, the local post office had yet to sell enough stamps to qualify for home mail delivery, the fire chief boasted that he had seldom been beyond the sound of the town clock, and the horses he used to pull the fire trucks were still getting their regular summer vacations, being sent to pasture for two weeks at a time. In 1900 Independence relied on gas lamps; the one small electric plant in town had burned down. Change came more slowly to small towns, but even in Independence the signs were clear.

Like the rest of the state at the beginning of 1900, Independence was working its way out of the economic depression that had begun so suddenly seven years before. On the outskirts of town, barns were being repainted, homes spruced up, and in town there was talk of paving the dirt roads and replacing the old planks that still served as sidewalks. On Main Street, artist Victor Kress would copy classic paintings or create an original, on commission. The best restaurant in town was featuring "Oysters, any style," and one could now order "fancy" groceries by telephone—if one had a phone. Some shops, pressured by the big department stores in Kansas City, were advertising the installment plan. Others kept to the old ways. Hildebrand Bros. continued to accept livestock in payment for furniture and stoves.

There were high hopes for the local baseball team. The Maroons had only one "substitute," but the team was young and strong and their record pretty good. And the Independence Athletic Club was playing basketball. Dr. James E. Naismith, the inventor of the game, had arrived in town a few years back and turned a handful of young athletes into centers, forwards, and guards. The first games were played on the second floor of a livery barn with a hard old medicine ball, until one of Naismith's basketballs was sent up from Chicago. In lieu of hoops, the team knocked the bottoms out of a pair of kitchen chairs, turned them upside down, and hung them on the walls.

Like so many Midwest towns of the time, the social fault lines in Independence were subtle. William Allen White, the editor of a Kansas paper, the *Emporia Gazette,* wrote that "there is in these towns an intense social democracy. There are gradations . . . lines of difference, and distinction between cliques and coteries, [but] wealth plays a minor part in the appraisal of people." On the edge of town on Waldo Avenue, John Truman and his family were carving out a pleasant life. The Trumans had just returned that week from a trip to Texas. A livestock trader and an ingenious man, Truman was doing well and had every expectation of doing even better.

The family now had servants and books and a piano, and Truman's oldest son, Harry, was in his third year of high school at a time when many boys his age had long since gone to work. His friends all rode horses and played cowboys and Indians, but Harry didn't ride. School was the center of his life. He studied hard, was intending to go on to college, and had already read Caesar's *Commentaries* and Plutarch's *Lives,* and all of Shakespeare. He had also acquired a passion for history, and no wonder. The past was ever present in Independence in 1900. There were men hanging around the drugstore or barber shop who had driven mules and oxen across the West before there was a railroad. Pet Parker, who was still

For children like Bessie Turner, leading a donkey caravan in Junction City, Kansas, life in 1900 had changed little. Children were still expected to invent their own pleasures. Even the very young wandered on their own but under the watchful eye of everyone in town.

living out on the old family homestead, had led prairie schooners filled with corn to military outposts.

Harry's own grandfather, Solomon Young, had driven forty wagons to Salt Lake City where he sold his goods to Brigham Young. Independence had been the jumping-off point for those moving west down the Santa Fe Trail. The bloody confrontation over slavery had raged in this area for ten years before the Civil War even started, and for most everyone in town there were daily reminders of the conflict. The vice president of the First National Bank had served with the Southern army and lost his arm at the battle of Pine Ridge. There were even a few veterans of the Union forces, but Independence was still a southern town and reconciliation remained an uneasy business.

Over in Kansas, men from the Union Army were raising money to mark the

In 1900, Harry S. Truman was reading about the great generals in history and hoping to enter West Point. An uncommon young man, steadier than most, in an essay on courage, written in 1899, he said: "The virtue I call courage is not in always facing the foe but in taking care of those at home. . . ." West Point would turn Truman down and circumstance would force him to take care of his family for much of his young life.

graves of Confederate soldiers and there was a move afoot to force the McKinley administration to return captured Confederate battle flags gathering dust in the basement of the War Department. But in 1900, the tension between the North and South would be played out in the political arena. Southerners tended to be Democrats, pure and simple. There was little affection for the party of Abraham Lincoln.

John Truman had strong ties to the local Democratic machine and was active in party affairs. Harry would never forget the night in 1892, after the Democrats had captured the White House, when his father rode a white horse in a torchlight parade. But the Democratic victory had been short-lived. In 1896, William McKinley, the Republican governor of Ohio, had handily beaten the Democrat William Jennings Bryan. Now it was assumed, whatever the rumors coming out of Washington, that both McKinley and Bryan would face off once again. Harry was hoping his father would take him to the Democratic Convention the coming July.

The Democrats knew they were in for an uphill fight. But the story that first broke on New Year's Day seemed to provide the campaign issue the party had been looking for:

The Washington Post, January 1, 1900
Plot in Manila

MANILA—Four explosive bombs, a few firearms and five hundred rounds of ammunition were discovered in a house in the center of Manila this morning. . . . Filipino insurgents were planning an uprising against American forces.

Reliable reports from native spies show that . . . 2000 insurgents massed at Mt. Arayat . . . command steep and narrow trails and are prepared to roll boulders down on advancing troops.

In the steamy jungles of a distant land, American boys were dying in a nasty guerilla war. *The Independence Sentinel* reported that the subject for debate at the coming meeting of the Blue Springs Literary Society was whether the Philippine islands should be retained. It would not be an easy question for the Society—or the country.

The gunboat Oceana, *towing troops, skiffs, and supplies up the Rio Grande River in Candaba, Philippines. Guerilla warfare began in earnest early in 1900. The Filipinos gave up trying to defend cities and towns and took to the bush, cutting telegraph lines, attacking supply trains, ambushing American units.*

II

In the Far West on January 2, a storm blanketed the Cascade Mountains and the Sierra Nevada with snow. On the summit, the fall was fifty-two inches deep and more was expected. In the California valleys the rivers were rising, and in Siskiyou County, a mudslide washed down on the rail tracks. In San Francisco, *The Examiner* reported that the tide was the highest in the memory of the oldest inhabitant. A steamer on its regular run to Oakland was struck by a wave of such immense power that it shattered all the windows on the port side of the vessel. Passengers were demanding that the crew lower the lifeboats when the wind diminished and the crisis passed. In the San Francisco harbor ships were driven onto the mudflats and the schooner *Kodiak* lost its bow when it jammed another vessel.

When the rain began, the ranchers in Salinas Valley, who had suffered several years of drought, were jubilant. Sloshing about town, merchants and farmers and sugar beet growers exchanged joyous New Year's greetings. But the rain continued all of Tuesday; the creeks began to rise and the Salinas river overflowed. By Wednesday the great ranches were five feet under water. Ten thousand acres were flooded. And then on Thursday, as abruptly as it started, the water began to subside and by Friday night was gone. Fifteen hundred acres of beets were destroyed, but the silt deposited on the briefly flooded land was rich in nutrients and all but guaranteed a good harvest. The paper predicted that in the long run, the rain meant "millions for the people of Monterey county, and above all, no mortgage on the farm."

In San Francisco, *The Examiner* announced that "in the history of California there has never been so brilliant an outlook for a New Year as there is now for the year of 1900." The town fathers were euphoric. In 1900, San Francisco was a sophisticated city of 350,000 people spreading up into the hills and along the eastern shore. Fifty years before when the first prospectors had arrived, heading for the gold fields, the town consisted of eighty-two houses, a few scattered tents, one toll road along Mission Street, and miles and miles of all but impassable sand dunes.

The original gold seekers, and those who came in their wake—the railroad men, the lumbermen, and cattle ranchers—had built great universities and stunning parks, art centers and opera houses, creating one of the loveliest and most cosmopolitan towns in the nation. In 1900, there was still a decidedly Mexican and Spanish cast to San Francisco—or Yerba Buena, as it was known back in Mexican days. In the harbor, Italian fishermen launched their brightly painted feluccas—small fishing boats—into the brilliant waters of the bay. One of the old whaling ships, captained by William Shorey, boasted the most heterogeneous crew ever to sail the seas—Europeans, Scandinavians, Asians, Africans, and a man from British Guiana.

In an old business area downtown, twenty thousand Chinese were crowded into an Asian ghetto, where they had managed to build an entire city within a city. There was a small, prosperous Jewish population that mingled with the standard

San Francisco was an important international port of call for merchant ships on their way to Alaska, Hawaii, and China. European and Scandinavian vessels, which had made their way around the Horn, were resupplied here before heading off to Asia.

late-nineteenth-century mix of Anglo-Saxons. San Franciscans were known for their love of food and wine, and down by the waterfront were scores of small inexpensive ethnic restaurants. There were Chinese, Japanese, and Slavic restaurants, and a vegetarian restaurant. In the Latin Quarter, near Chinatown, in a Mexican place called Matias, one could get a five-course lunch, including a bottle of good strong claret, for twenty-five cents.

At Luchetti's, which served ravioli, spaghetti, and "fried cream," fishermen in thigh-high gum boots dropped in to fill their demijohns with claret before setting out to sea. Adding to this mix of people around the docks in 1900 was an unusual number of servicemen. San Francisco was now a designated port for military transports, and ever since the start of the Spanish American War, military vessels had been steaming in and out of the harbor. Nowhere in America was it more evident that the country was still at war, and nowhere was there greater evidence of the change in the nation's fortunes.

The economic turnaround was directly linked to America's expansion following the war. In 1898, the United States had seized the Spanish colonies of Cuba, Puerto Rico, and then the Philippines, and had annexed Guam, Hawaii, and an island in the Samoas. Competing for the rich Asian trade with Britain, Germany, and Russia, the United States had established fueling stations straight across the Pacific. On January 9, Indiana's Albert Beveridge, in his maiden speech in the Senate, declared that China was the "mightiest commercial fact" in America's future. "China's foreign commerce is only beginning," he said. "Her resources, her possibilities, her wants—all are undeveloped."

Beveridge then went on to provide the Republican rallying cry: "We will establish trading posts throughout the world . . . cover the ocean with our merchant marine. Our institutions will follow our flag on the wings of commerce." In the port cities of Seattle and Tacoma, steamship lines were suddenly overwhelmed. Raw cotton from the South, fabric from New England, and flour, iron, and steel from Chicago, Pittsburgh, and Kansas City were piling up on the wharfs. Nine thousand tons of tobacco were awaiting shipment to Asia. Every port in the country was booming. The chief of the Bureau of Foreign Commerce, Frederic Emory, in an article for *Munsey's Magazine* declared, "It seems almost incredible that we should be sending cutlery to Sheffield, pig iron to Birmingham, silks to France, watch cases to Switzerland . . . or building *sixty* locomotives for British railroads."

Having saturated European markets, America turned east and was making inroads not only in China but in Korea and Japan as well. "More markets and

The Sutter Street Line in San Francisco. Without the invention of cable cars, the hilly sections of the city would have been doomed to slow and doubtful growth. However, transportation remained a problem, and in 1900, San Franciscans were lobbying for elevated trains and subway systems.

larger markets" became the national slogan in a country that produced far more than it could consume. But the dispatches from Manila the first week in January underscored troublesome questions about America's new role in the world. When the United States had wrested Cuba, Puerto Rico, and the Philippine islands from the ancient Spanish empire, American forces had moved into Manila bent on building a naval station at Subic Bay to protect commercial shipping. But Filipino nationalists had no intention of allowing one more Western power to move into their country.

President McKinley disliked the idea of "forcible annexation." It did not seem the American way. But when the Filipinos resisted the American incursion, the president insisted "there was nothing left to do but take the [islands] to educate . . . uplift, and civilize" the Filipino people. America would follow Rudyard Kipling's advice and "take up the white man's burden." The Filipinos had declared their independence, but Senator Beveridge had dismissed the Filipino people, calling them "children," incapable of self-government. "God has not been preparing the English-speaking and Teutonic peoples for a thousand years for nothing," he insisted. "He has made us the master organizers of the world . . . that we may administer . . . among savages and senile peoples."

Emilio Aguinaldo, the insurgent leader in the Philippines, considered himself neither senile nor savage. The war had begun in earnest early in 1899. At first American officers believed they would easily subdue their barefoot, spear-carrying opponents with twenty to thirty thousand men. But soon commanders were asking McKinley to increase the force to forty thousand men, then fifty, sixty thousand regulars. The misreading of the Filipino people seemed a curious error for Americans to have made. A war against those seeking their own independence seemed to some a "monstrous perversion of American ideals." Mark Twain, saddened that the American flag was flying over the Philippines, suggested the stars be replaced by the skull and crossbones.

A small but prestigious anti-imperialist movement developed, led in the main by former abolitionists. Andrew Carnegie, the steel tycoon, became an outspoken member. "Is it possible," he asked, "that the American Republic is to be placed in the position of the suppressor of the Philippine struggle for independence?" Carnegie offered to buy the Philippines for $20 million and provide the island nation with its independence. McKinley declined the offer. Throughout 1899, while journalists reported on devastation and horror half a globe away, Americans had been repeatedly assured that the war was all but over, that "the backbone of the insurrection" had been broken and hostilities would end within a relatively short time.

On January 3, with the war moving into its second year and casualty lists running in every paper, an editorial in the *St. Louis Post-Dispatch* accused the McKinley administration of "a deal of lying. . . . Let us have the truth," the paper demanded, "if we are in for a hundred years' war let us know it. Political soldiers and politicians better not try to bamboozle the American people." Senator Chauncey M. Depew, one of the most articulate defenders of the Republican position, spoke for many when he said, "The American people produce $2 billion worth more than they can consume and we have met the emergency, and by the providence of God, by the statesmanship of William McKinley . . . stand in the presence of 800 million people, with the Pacific as an American lake."

For William Jennings Bryan, the election campaign was starting early. At a Democratic rally he told his followers, "If we carry on a war of conquest; if we hold the Filipinos as subjects; if we tax them without their representation and govern them without their consent, we dare not educate them lest they should read the Declaration of Independence. . . . As to the religious argument, that God opened the door of the Philippine islands and pushed us in, it is a potent argument, [but] . . . how many lives have been lost by men who believed God had commanded them to do so? When a Republican tells me that God's hand is in his I demand his credentials."

But at the start of 1900, in the rich valleys that lay beyond San Francisco, with their abundant orange groves and vineyards, walnut and almond trees, and great olive holdings, the arguments for eastern expansion seemed all but overwhelming. *The Examiner* pointed out at the beginning of the year that no state had more to gain from the possession of the Philippine islands or the expansion of Oriental trade than California.

III

Across the bay from San Francisco in the hills of Oakland, Jack London was correcting the proofs of his first book, a collection of stories about Alaska, to be published by Houghton Mifflin under the title *Son of the Wolf*. At the start of the year, Jack would interrupt his work to attend the funeral of Fred Jacobs, a childhood friend, who had died on his way to the Philippines. The sight of the litter bearers carrying the wounded and dead off military transports in the harbor was becoming too familiar. Jacobs had been engaged to marry Jack's friend, Bessie Maddern, and Bessie now needed Jack's support. She had helped him with some of his early work and he was grateful to her.

In January 1900, London was still little known outside California. But after two years of almost steady rejections his fortunes had begun to turn. It looked as though he would now be able to make a living as a writer. He had sold one book, was writing another, and was cheerfully concocting a myth about his life to be used as publicity. The truth would have done as well. London was the illegitimate son of a spiritualist from Ohio—a dwarfish woman named Flora Wellman—and a ne'er-do-well astrologer named John Chaney, who had disappeared before Jack was born.

Flora had given the boy dreams of a better life, taught him to be a reader, but withheld her love. A stepfather named John London gave him his name, but little else. Jack survived a miserable childhood. He had been a truant, a petty thief, done a short stint in jail, worked as a seaman and an oyster pirate, and in 1897 had joined American gold seekers making the treacherous trek to the Klondike in the Canadian Northwest Territories. He was now twenty-four years old. He would draw on these years, somewhat embroidered, of course, for a remarkable collection of stories and novels.

Reflections about the journey to the north country were woven into his essay, "The Shrinkage of the Planet." He had been witness to one of those moments of change that signaled the fault line between the past and the future. When he had gone up to the Klondike just three years back, the trip had been a hazardous six-month journey into the unknown. Now, modern steamship and rail lines were converting the wilderness into just another stop on the tourists' itinerary.

London wrote, "In the fall of 1896 a great gold strike was made—greater than any since the days of California and Australia; yet so rude were the means of communication, nearly a year elapsed before the news of it reached the eager ear of the world. . . ." London described the "passionate pilgrims" on the trail to the gold fields, who "with heavy packs upon their backs plunged waist-deep into hideous quagmires . . . and after infinite toil and hardship, arrived at the Klondike. . . ." Many of the pilgrims "had paid for their temerity the tax of human life.

"A year later, so greatly had the country shrunk, the tourist on disembarking from the ocean steamship took his seat in a modern railway coach. . . . And in a

few hours more he was in Dawson, without having once soiled the lustre of his civilized footgear. Did he wish to communicate with the outside world, he strolled into the telegraph office. A few short months before he would have written a letter and

Jack London at home in Oakland, California. Contrary to appearances, London was a compulsive worker, allowing no more than four and a half hours of sleep. Nights were spent reading—science, history, economics, and sociology—searching for what London called the "scientific basis of life."

deemed himself favoured above mortals were it delivered within the year."

At the end of his invented autobiography for Houghton Mifflin, London explained that he had yet to marry. "The world is too large," he said, "and its call too insistent." But it was a subject that was on his mind; he needed more order in his life, and at a Socialist meeting at the Turk Street Temple just a few weeks earlier, he had fallen in love with an intense young student named Anna Strunsky. He had begun their correspondence:

> Dear Miss Strunsky—
>   O Pshaw!
> Dear Anna—
> There! Let's get our friendship down to a comfortable basis. The superscription, "Miss Strunsky," is as disagreeable as the putting on of a white collar, and both are equally detestable. . . .

When Anna Strunsky and Jack London met at the end of 1899, she was a twenty-two-year-old student, the daughter of Russian-Jewish intellectuals.

IV

As John F. Fitzgerald headed back to the Capitol for the opening session of Congress, carpenters in the basement of the House of Representatives were fashioning pine and cedar chests for members to store their papers and personal goods. The chests would come in handy as shipping crates when Fitzgerald gave up his seat, but he had no intention of making the announcement until closer to the end of his term. One of only three Catholics in the House, Fitzgerald had been outspoken about the anti-Catholic tone in Congress and the wave of hostility that had been building over the "alien immigrants" crowding into Boston and other eastern cities. Fitzgerald was a canny politician, but he was not afraid of controversy.

He seemed to enjoy going head to head with Henry Cabot Lodge, the patrician Republican senator from Massachusetts. Lodge was a privileged member of

Boston society, from an old and revered family. Fitzgerald had grown up in the Irish North End, as far from the Cabots and the Lodges as one could be. The two men could not have been more dissimilar and agreed on virtually nothing. A few years back they had had a classic confrontation. Lodge, believing that the new immigrants—Jews from Russia and Poland and eastern Europe, Italians, Hungarians, Romanians, and Greeks—were threatening "the very fabric of the Anglo-Saxon race," had wanted to end unrestricted immigration.

The Senator had argued that "if a lower race mixes with a higher race, history teaches us the lower race will prevail." In the House, Fitzgerald had fought hard against the legislation, which he believed was an "attempt to set people against people." In an exchange that Fitzgerald described sometime later, Lodge asked him if he believed Jews or Italians had any right in the country. Fitzgerald responded, "As much right as your father or mine, it was only a difference of a few ships." The legislation had been vetoed, but the attitudes persisted. In 1900 an English novelist described America as a melting pot. It was a romantic idea but not very accurate.

Like many other congressmen who left their families at home, when Fitzgerald was in Washington he lived in a rooming house. Few representatives had the means to support two residences. On January 3, *The Courier-Journal* (Louisville, Kentucky) reported that those "members staying at hotels, where an extra charge is made for a bath, usually wait until they reach the Capitol to enjoy this luxury at the expense of the people." Fifteen tubs were available, along with attendants and barbers hired by the government. As the representatives began to assemble that morning, reporters also noted that the House had spent an extraordinary sum of money—$1,776—on gold leaf and labor to spruce up dingy mirrors in committee rooms and lobbies.

But life in the House was not luxurious. The old ceilings were smoky, the frescoes had long since dimmed, and members sat at dilapidated desks in the chamber. The ventilation was dreadful, and only the chairmen of the most important committees had private offices—the rest were forced to meet in the halls or back at their hotels. Over in the Senate, however, nothing was thought of spending a few thousand dollars on deeply upholstered chairs and silver inkstands. The Senate was still the most exclusive club in the country. There was talk of connecting the Senate and the House with a subway in the basement and erecting a new office building near the grounds. But that would be awhile.

As the House galleries began to fill with tourists and reporters, Speaker David

B. Henderson of Iowa called the members to order. Henderson had returned to the Capitol with a new leg, which was said to please him greatly. He had lost his limb at the battle of Corinth in February 1863, and since that time had tried four different artificial legs. The latest, which was made of rubber, had knee and ankle joints similar to those in the human leg. The artificial limb was controlled by bands that passed over Henderson's shoulder and worked so well that the Speaker believed he would soon be able to dispense with the use of a cane.

As the chamber quieted down, the members eagerly took up the matter of Brigham Roberts, the congressman-elect from Salt Lake City, Utah. Ever since his election, Roberts had been the focus of endless editorials and news stories. The Hearst papers depicted him as a threat to the very sanctity of marriage. A handsome man, with a large black mustache and an engaging sense of humor, Roberts was a Mormon, a member of the Church of the Latter-day Saints and an avowed polygamist, with three wives and fifteen children.

While the Mormon Church had outlawed polygamy before Utah became a state in 1896, Roberts refused to desert his wives and children. His constituents argued that he was a good family man and that "men who remained polygamists from motives of honor and husbandly devotion ought not to be excluded from office." But the newspapers were demanding that Congress strike a blow against "this relic of barbarism." One columnist wrote: "It is one thing for a Christian monogamist to fall into sin, as monogamists will; it is quite another for a Mormon to flaunt his polygamy at the nation's Capitol."

There were debates in the gossip columns over how official Washington should respond in the event that Roberts brought any of his wives with him to Washington. A commentator in Salt Lake City found this unlikely; the Misses Roberts were quite reclusive: "They seldom go out with him to functions here or even to the theatre or opera. . . . The night after his nomination he had accompanied Dr. Maggie Shipp, his third 'plural' to the theatre, but he has not been seen in public with her since."

An eclectic coalition of patriotic, religious, and women's groups banded together in a nationwide campaign not just against Roberts but against the Mormon Church, which was described in one petition as "an organized school of immorality." Large sums of money were raised by chain letters asking, "Will you not as a Christian and a patriot help us in the campaign against Mormonism?" In the midst of the battle, Susan B. Anthony, the aging leader of the Women's Suffrage Association, infuriated even some of her own followers when she dismissed the controversy, saying, "Almost all men, as a general thing violate the sanctity of the home." On January 3, at the start of the debate, a petition, which was said to include seven million signatures, was carried into the House wrapped in an American flag.

Roberts argued that polygamy was not a constitutional disqualification for congressional office and, furthermore, that a congressman could not be expelled for an offense committed prior to election. But he was fighting a losing battle. When he arrived in Washington, a local African-American paper noted that he was traveling with one of his older daughters. *The Washington Bee* reported that "Miss Acah Roberts, a young lady of strong dark features," had all her father's pugnacity. "She is intensely interested in his cause and not at all discouraged, although she resented the treatment accorded her as a curious freak." Roberts, under the tension of the moment, was chewing gum incessantly. He told the reporter, "Let polygamy be prohibited by constitutional amendment, once and forever. I will vote for that, but I will not desert those dear to me . . . even though my life were at stake."

When Roberts was finally expelled, he left the House saying, "I have lived in good conscience. . . . I shall leave with head erect and brow undaunted, and walk the earth as angels walk the clouds."

———————

As the Senate went back to work, a nomination arrived from the White House, requesting the appointment of Lieutenant Colonel Arthur MacArthur to brigadier general. MacArthur had been serving in the Philippines for two years and it was rumored he was soon to be given command of American forces in the islands. A Civil War veteran with a colorful past, MacArthur had joined the Union army as a boy of seventeen. At Kenesaw Mountain, he was shot through the arm and chest and, as the story was told, was saved by a packet of letters and a Bible in his breast pocket.

As MacArthur was leaving for the East, his eighteen-year-old son, Douglas, was straining to enlist, but MacArthur warned the boy, "There will be plenty of fighting in the coming years and of a magnitude far beyond this. Prepare yourself."

Written on this photo in 1900: "Just returning from fight—Nag Bayabas—27 hours on march—mud and rain—24 hours without food." U.S. supply lines were stretched thin and soldiers often found themselves isolated, caught without either ammunition or food.

V

In 1900, America was a nation of war veterans and the numbers were staggering. In Washington, the Pension Bureau was grinding out paperwork for a million Americans, including four widows and seven daughters of men who had fought in the Revolution. Checks were being sent to veterans from the Mexican War, the Civil War, the Spanish-American War, and now to those returning from the Philippine campaign. Disability payments ran from two dollars a month for the loss of any one of the smaller toes to one hundred dollars for those completely disabled. In the coming year the bureau would be paying out an astounding $132,000,000, raising talk about the need to cap the budget.

For the sons of immigrants, war was the confirming American experience. When nineteen-year-old Carl Sandburg returned to Galesburg, Illinois, with

Company C, it looked as if the entire county had turned out. Every boy in Company C was embraced as a true son of Galesburg. The men were feted by the Army and Navy League, the Presbyterian Church, and at an oyster supper the president of Knox College saluted them with a poem about their exploits. Carl's father, a

Ten thousand people turned out at the depot when Company C returned to Galesburg, Illinois, after serving five months in Puerto Rico. Private Carl Sandburg later wrote, "They acted like we were heroes. We had our doubts." Sandburg described the conflict with the Spanish as "a small war, edging to immense consequences."

Swedish immigrant, told his son that at last he felt like a proper American citizen. Charlie gave the old man half his mustering out pay of $103.73 and his discharge papers, which August Sandburg framed and hung in the front parlor.

When he left home he carried a pocket dictionary with a Shakespeare quote pasted in the flyleaf: "I have hope to live, and am prepar'd to die." Sandburg had come home alive but twenty-two pounds lighter. None of the Galesburg Company had been killed or even wounded, but all had returned emaciated or ill. Sandburg noted, rightly, that yellow fever had killed more young men than Spanish bullets. His friend Private Lewis Kay had died of the fever. In the colonies of Spain—Cuba, Puerto Rico, and the Philippines—less than two thousand Americans would be killed by enemy fire, but more than eight thousand would die of tropic diseases—malaria or dysentery as well as yellow fever. To some it seemed less glorious to die from the ague than from an enemy bullet, but the boys were dead too young, no matter how they died.

Like other veterans without much schooling, Carl returned to a town full of jobs that went nowhere. He had already tried working on a dairy farm, driving the milk wagon, sanding and scraping as a painter's apprentice, and had watched his father, a blacksmith's helper, "day on day swinging sledges and hammers on hot iron on an anvil." The boy had dreamed of a world beyond while his father dared dream of little more than surviving the next depression.

It was an American phenomenon, this gulf between the two, the psychic tangles between the immigrant and his son—the one seared by deprivations he never wished to speak of, the other nurtured without much money but with "visions and hope." Carl, or Charlie, as he had come to call himself—it sounded more American—loved his stern and brooding father, and his mother, whose own mother had been a gooseherd in Sweden, but he had dreams beyond those they could ever understand.

And then, on what seemed a fluke—a wonderful and very American fluke—he entered Lombard, a small college in the center of town, on a veteran's scholarship. He carved out a study for himself at the end of a hall on the second floor of his parents' home, with a window framed by a tulip tree. Warmed by a small kerosene stove that "smutted the walls with skeins of soot," and by the light of a kerosene lamp, he read a ragged secondhand copy of Walt Whitman's *Leaves of Grass,* "then read it again and read it slowly."

"I had wondering and hopes," he wrote, "but they were vague and foggy."

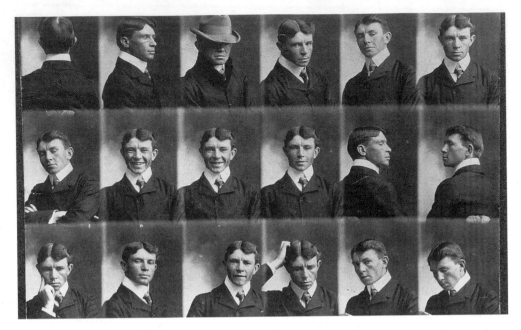

As a student at Lombard College, in 1900, Sandburg considered becoming a newspaper reporter, a foreign correspondent, an author of books, an agitator, or "an independent drifter"—anything but a respectable conformist.

When Barney Dougall came home from the army to the small Mormon town of Springville, Utah, like Carl Sandburg he was facing an uncertain future, although Dougall came from a prosperous family and was among the few in town who had gone to private school and college and acquired a profession. He was a civil engineer and experienced surveyor. But one of the more unsettling problems in America in 1900 was that many small towns like Springville, those that were beyond the comfortable reach of a city—or abundant farmland—no longer were growing.

Springville lay in the valley at the edge of the Wasatch Mountains, smack in the middle of sugar beet country, beyond which lay the cattle ranches. A crushing mill had been built on the edge of town, where the juice was piped to the Lehi refinery to be transformed into sugar. Beets were a good cash crop, but work on these small farms was still done mostly by hand. Life was hard, and the return marginal. At the start of the year, Dougall was not the only one planning to move on. But it was not easy. The Dougall family had been among the founders of the town.

Barney's maternal grandparents were early Mormon converts, who had left Philadelphia for Utah in 1849 in unusually well-appointed covered wagons. They had arrived in the West just two years after Brigham Young had led his followers into the Great Salt Basin. Barney's mother, Kate, an independent-minded girl, had made something of a name for herself when she turned down a proposal to become one of Brigham Young's plural wives. His father, Hugh, had come out from Scotland around 1851. The family embraced an extraordinary sweep of American history.

They had watched as the Great American Desert, as vast and desolate as the Sahara, had been transformed into rich and prosperous farmland. Salt Lake City had quite literally grown up around them. There was also a handful of truly ancient settlers in Springville, a generation older than the Dougalls, the memory keepers, the tellers of the tales of the Black Hawk Wars, men and women able to recall the days before the Mormons had even reached Utah. As they followed the trials of Congressman-elect Brigham Roberts, the anti-Mormon rhetoric was painful, but not unfamiliar.

For Barney and a number of his neighbors now, the future seemed to lie in the minefields of the Pleasant Valley Coal Company, seventy miles south. In the hills where huge herds of cattle had once grazed, surveyors for the railroad had discovered seemingly inexhaustible veins of bituminous coal and, years before, bought up the entire area. The mines had become the largest employers in the region, pulling in men from England, Scotland, and Wales, from Ireland and Italy, who built log cabins on the hillsides of railroad land and worried about title later.

The newcomers joined fraternal orders—the Knights of Pythias and the Odd Fellows—and created a raggedy but proper village amid the slag heaps. As the miners settled in, neat cottages appeared, and a meeting house, and a school with a fife and drum corps. By 1900, there were stores and saloons, a new hotel was under construction, and so was the Odd Fellows Hall. On the side of the canyon, just above Scofield, at Winter Quarters, were two of the richest mines in the state: Number One, which had been open for more than twenty-seven years, and Number Four, open for less than a year. The company had yet to install a watering system to dampen the dust, but the mines were considered relatively safe and the state inspector was due to return in March.

Everyone knew, of course, that a miner took his life in his hands every time he went down into the bowels of the earth. That was the term—*going down into the bowels of the earth*—in the dark with the coal dust clogging your nostrils, with the creaking of the timbers and the moaning of the roof, and the whispers, from those who were superstitious, about the headless man who stalked the coal rooms and sometimes rode the coal cars to the mouth of the tunnel. Miners lived with

Abe Luoma, who posed for this photograph in 1899, was the oldest of six brothers from Finland who had made their way to Scofield, Utah, to work for the Pleasant Valley Coal Company. By 1900, ten men in the Luoma family, including a brother-in-law and three men from the younger generation, were working together in the mines.

the suspicion that if not today or tomorrow, disaster still waited. Each man carried his own explosives down with him, and each understood that his life was in the hands of all the others. But Barney would not have to work as a miner; he would hire on as an engineer and surveyor.

The Pleasant Valley mines were expanding. In 1900, America still ran on coal. Coal fueled the industrial engines, the great fast trains, the international steamers. Every American who could afford it, and millions could, had a coal furnace and a coal stove. There were six hundred men working in Scofield now and more were needed. Among the newcomers were the "Finlanders." A serious and taciturn people, the Finns tended to stick together, to live in their own enclaves—whether by desire or because the men from the English-speaking countries viewed them with suspicion was never clear. But they were industrious and anxious to get on. The Luoma family, six brothers and three of their sons, were doing so well they had persuaded their parents to leave Finland and join them.

Two hundred thousand Finnish people now lived in America. Over the coming months another eight thousand were expected, fleeing from conscription in the Czar's armies. No one could predict how many would head for the coalfields, but in February agents put out word that Pleasant Valley was expecting a major contract from the Navy Department. There would be work for Barney Dougall—and the others—when they came.

Life seemed pleasant for Barney Dougall (right) of Springville, Utah, when he posed with friends after serving for a year in the Hawaiian islands. But like so many ambitious young men of his generation, Barney would have to leave home to further his career.

Other Stories of Interest

The Courier-Journal (Louisville, Kentucky), January 3, 1900
WASHINGTON, D.C.—Society here is engrossed in a movement planned to reduce the number of functions during the official season. There have been on an average two or three luncheons or two dinners and two dancing parties every day. . . . The hostesses are exhausted and many of them sick. . . .

The Russian Ambassador announced that his niece, Miss Marguerite Cassini, was not strong enough to accept more than two invitations a week. Count Cassini added that in no place, even Paris, was the social part of the government carried to such excess.

The Boston Herald, January 31, 1900
New Baseball League Is All But Complete
PHILADELPHIA—Seven cities declared themselves "in it," today at a meeting at the Continental Hotel to form the new American Association of Baseball Clubs. They were Boston, Philadelphia and Baltimore in the East, Chicago, Detroit, Milwaukee and St. Louis in the West. The eighth club will probably be either New York or Providence.

The Washington Post, February 1, 1900
SAN FRANCISCO—The steamer Australia . . . from Honolulu, arrived here today and reports that up to the time of her departure forty-one deaths from the plague had occurred and there was a total of fifty-two cases.

In an effort to stamp out the plague, it was decided to burn one of the blocks in Chinatown. The fire was started and it gained such headway that the fire department could not control it. The flames spread rapidly from one block to another and soon the whole Chinese quarter was in flames. Hardly a house was left standing; 4,500 people were rendered homeless and they are now living in tents.

By 1900, Americans in love with speed had become impatient with trains that could travel no faster than 60 mph. The proposed Brott Bicycle Railway was to run upon a single rail in the center of the track. The lead car was designed to diminish air resistance; it was hoped the train would reach 200 mph.

CHAPTER THREE

February

I

On February 4 in Detroit, a headline in *The News-Tribune* announced: THRILLING TRIP ON THE FIRST DETROIT-MADE AUTOMOBILE WHEN MERCURY HOVERED ABOUT ZERO. SWIFTER THAN A RACEHORSE IT FLEW OVER THE ICY STREETS. The reporter, riding on a small covered platform in front of a shiny black delivery wagon, wrote with all the passion of a convert: "There has always been at each decisive period in the world's history some voice, some note, that represented . . . the prevailing power. . . . And now finally, there was heard in the streets the murmur of the newest and most perfect of forces, the automobile, rushing along at the rate of 25 miles an hour."

Henry Ford, the forty-year-old mechanical superintendent of the Detroit Automobile Company, assured the reporter it would take no more than a few days, maybe a few hours, to learn how to drive the gasoline-powered wagon. Ford was an optimist. He promised that within the coming months he would build a dozen vehicles. Driving past the shop of a harness maker, Ford declared, "His trade is doomed."

At the same time, in an unprepossessing bicycle shop in Dayton, Ohio, a thirty-two-year-old self-taught engineer, Wilbur Wright, was reading everything he could find on the theory of aeronautics. "There was no flying art in the proper sense of the word, but only a flying problem," he explained. "Thousands of men had thought about flying machines and a few had even built machines which they called flying machines, but these were guilty of almost everything except flying. Thousands of pages had been written . . . but for the most part the ideas set forth . . . were mere speculations."

Wilbur had written Samuel Pierpont Langley, one of the country's most prestigious scientists and secretary of the Smithsonian Institution, asking for information on manned flight. Wright explained he was an aviation enthusiast—not a crank. Langley, one of the first scientists to believe that motorized flight was possible, had been pursuing the problem for years and had predicted "a great universal highway in the sky . . . soon to be opened."

In 1900, as Wilbur Wright began his initial experiments at Kitty Hawk, he promised his father he would take no dangerous chances. But he also confided in a friend that he feared his belief in flight "will soon cost me an increased amount of money, if not my life." A number of aeronautical pioneers had been killed trying to fly experimental aircraft.

In 1896, from atop a houseboat anchored in the middle of the Potomac, Langley had launched a twenty-six-pound aerodrome, powered by a small steam engine. The craft had flown over a half-mile, gliding to a landing on the river when the engine gave out. The experiment, photographed by his friend Alexander Graham Bell, so impressed the War Department that the government appropriated $50,000 for further research.

But in 1900, Langley was bogged down by a succession of mechanical problems, not the least of which was building an engine light enough to be carried by an air machine, yet powerful enough to support the weight of a man. Wilbur and his brother, Orville, would go quite a different route. In time the engine problem would be mastered. They would begin by studying the "problem of equilibrium."

Watching the flight of buzzards, Wilbur had come to understand that "when partly overturned by a gust of wind," the birds regained their balance "by a torsion of the tips of the wings. If the rear edge of the right wingtip is twisted upward and the left downward the bird becomes an animated windmill and instantly begins to turn." The Wrights would test Wilbur's theories of control in the air by building a glider large enough for one of them to fly.

Wilbur knew they were embarking on an outrageous undertaking for two fellows running a bicycle shop. He wrote a friend that he feared his obsession would soon cost him an increased amount of money, if not his life. Most Americans were skeptical about mucking around with the laws of gravity. An astronomer at the U.S. Naval Observatory, Simon Newcomb, wrote: "The example of the bird does

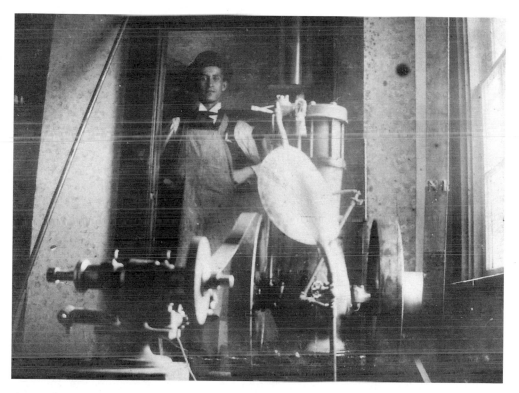

A rare family snapshot of Orville Wright in his bicycle shop in Dayton, Ohio. An excellent mechanic and inventive man, in 1895 he developed a calculating machine that could multiply as well as add. Once the two brothers began their collaboration on the airplane, they worked so closely there was no way to identify their individual contributions.

not prove that man can fly." But the Wrights paid Newcomb not the least attention. They would test their theories in the fall, after the bicycle business quieted down.

In February 1900, it was the railroads that were making news, pushing the limits of time and space. Early in the year, *The Washington Post* reported on a race between freight trains competing for a U.S. Postal contract. "Steam and steel fought steam and steel in the great fast mail contest." The trains were said to have reached eighty miles an hour. The story was probably exaggerated, but no matter. Whatever speed record was set today, it would be broken tommorrow.

The Baltimore & Ohio line was testing a train called "The Wind-Splitter" that on one downhill grade had reached over 102 miles an hour. But for the dreamers that was not enough. Publisher Frank Munsey declared: "Distances in this country are too great. Space must be annihilated." He wrote of trains designed to "diminish air resistance," bullet-nosed trains that could reach two hundred miles an hour. "We want to bring Chicago within five hours of New York, and San Francisco within fifteen." It would be, he said "the American way of doing things."

Munsey conjured a Chicago businessman leaving home at six in the morning, attending a luncheon meeting in New York at noon, and being back in his own bed in Chicago that same night. Within Munsey's own experience—he had been born midcentury—the railroads had so revolutionized American life that his flights of fancy were a logical progression. In 1900, people spoke of the time "before the coming of the train" or "after the coming of the train."

Everything had changed. It was not just the creation of Kansas City or San Francisco, or the thousands of towns that lay between; the railroad, in ways now hard to recall, had come to dictate where people lived and how they lived, where they worked and when they worked. Men who once measured time by the setting of the sun now reached for a pocketwatch. Until the coming of the railroad, "each locale set its own time by tested methods of solar readings," Alan Trachtenberg writes. "Bells and clocks struck at noon, when the sun stood directly overhead: never exactly the same moment from place-to-place or week-to-week."

But railroads could not run on varying times. "The situation became increasingly eccentric, to the point of danger and economic loss." So, without the help of God, Congress, or presidential fiat, the railroads had acted, placing the country under four standard time zones. *The Indianapolis Daily Sentinel* noted: "The sun is no longer to boss the job. People . . . must now eat, sleep, and work as well as travel by railroad time."

If one wanted a graphic illustration of the need for the railroads to run on standardized time, this photograph of the Grand Trunk Depot in Durand, Michigan, would serve the purpose. Whether this clutch of trains arrived simultaneously by design is not known, but in 1900 rail collisions were still all too frequent.

While the railroads had made Americans the most time-conscious people on earth—and the pocket watch had become the source of power for a million petty tyrants—the railroad had also unleashed a million fantasies, of worlds beyond the known. Before he went into the army, seventeen-year-old Carl Sandburg had abandoned his job on a dairy farm and, like thousands of other young men, took off to ride the rails, an uninvited guest of the rail systems.

"I would take my chances on breaking away from my hometown where I knew every street and people in every block and farmers on every edge of the town. . . . I would beat my way on the railroads and see what happened." In 1900, Americans who still measured distance by the endurance of their horse were reading about the newly opened Siberian Railroad, making its way from St. Petersburg to Irkutsk with a library and piano, a barber shop, a gymnasium, and an English-speaking staff. Americans were already planning to visit St. Petersburg in the summer. How many would go on to Irkutsk was an open question, but travel had become an American addiction.

In that blustery winter, farmers and businessmen with a bit of extra time were heading south. One railroad man said wryly, "It is against the policy of Americans to remain locked up by ice one-half of the year." Guidebooks were recommending "winter stations" in the Carolinas, Florida, and California for those "afflicted with consumption, gout, rheumatism, neurasthenia, or chronic bronchitis."

A touring Scotsman, the Reverend David Macrae, described how a few extra dollars secured richly furnished rolling parlors with cushioned sofas and chairs, gilded racks for parcels, and a conductor who "wakes you in the morning [with] breakfast and the papers." By 1900, there were even a few Pullman cars with bathtubs. Macrae, a romantic, saw the American rail system as the great equalizer, "one of the ways in which the people high and low are being educated for the new form of society to which the world is moving."

For decades now, the railroad had been the symbol of American power. We had not invented the steam engine. The English had. But it was said that if they had not, we would have had to. Everything about the country, from the sprawl of the continent to our widespread natural resources, demanded there be a rail system. But by 1900 the rail companies were also among the most hated and corrupt institutions in the country.

The historian Brooks Adams described how the railroads had taken control of the "public highways," and thus control over the life of the nation. A raise in rates, he pointed out, was often a form of taxation "on those individuals and localities that could least resist." During the depression in the mid-1890s, tens of thousands of small farmers and businessmen had been forced into bankruptcy when the railroads hiked their rates.

In Los Angeles now, the orange growers were collecting evidence that the Santa Fe and Southern Pacific lines were guilty of collusion and fraud. In the Midwest, manufacturers were protesting prohibitive rates, and members of the Anti-Trust League in Chicago were urging that the government take over the railroads. It was not about to happen. But throughout the year, the power of the railroads would be a central issue.

Armed mountaineers gathered in front of the State House in Frankfort, Kentucky, minutes after the shooting of Senator William Goebel. The fatal bullet was said to have been fired from a window on the third floor of the Executive Office building on the right.

II

By the end of January, the situation in Frankfort, Kentucky, was bordering on the absurd. Each day's report was more remarkable than the last. From mid-month there were predictions of insurrection—even civil war—coming out of this capital city. Two men were claiming to be governor of the state, and Frankfort had been turned into an armed camp. The Republican incumbent, William Taylor, had barricaded himself in the State House, protected by soldiers with fixed bayonets, and was refusing to give up his office. The Democratic contender, William Goebel, a former state senator, was hovering near death at the nearby Capitol Hotel, protected by rival forces who were equally intransigent.

During the election campaign Goebel had accused Governor Taylor of being a lackey of the Louisville & Nashville Railroad, the most powerful corporate interest in Kentucky, declaring that the issue of "whether the trusts or the people shall rule . . . whether the Railroad is the servant or the master of the people," transcended all others. It was commonly accepted that a man could not be elected dogcatcher without the sanction of the L & N. Goebel had cast himself as a David, up against a corporate giant.

It was a popular position, but over the course of the campaign, the Democrat had also managed to collect as many enemies as votes. He called one opponent "Gonorrhea John" and offended Confederate veterans by describing one of their own as "a drunkard with the cancerous face of a beefsteak." He outraged members of his own party by openly campaigning for black votes. August Belmont, owner of the L & N, later said that he had spent half a million dollars trying to defeat the man.

In truth, Goebel may have been defeated—no one would ever know. Everything about the election was suspect. There was fraud on both sides, stories of bribery, charges of intimidation, of the use of imported desperadoes and tissue ballots. Both men claimed victory and a legislative committee was charged with deciding between them. But with the Democrats in control of the Assembly, it was assumed that Taylor didn't have a chance.

At first the affair in Kentucky was seen as just one more example of corrupt local politics. But in January, the story gained national prominence when, just before the election committee was to announce its decision, a thousand "armed mountain men" arrived in town, stacking their weapons by the State House steps. The partisans made clear Taylor was their man. The local paper reported that "thoughtful men were alarmed by the possibility of bloodshed." When William Goebel arrived in the capital, accompanied by his aide, Jack P. "Dirk Knife" Chinn, everyone in town was expecting trouble. It was just a question as to how and when it would happen.

On Tuesday, January 30, 1900, in the midst of a severe cold spell, with the wind howling and the temperature well below freezing, Goebel was making his way across the capitol grounds, bundled in his great black chinchilla coat, when shots rang out from the east wing of the State House. As the senator fell gravely wounded to the ground, Chinn was reported to have said, "Goebel, they have killed you." The townsfolk responded as though rehearsed—schools immediately closed, businesses shut, women and children disappeared from the streets. Goebel was carried to the nearby Capitol Hotel where a physician stopped the bleeding, began a saline solution, and gave the wounded man opiates for his pain.

As Goebel drifted in and out of consciousness, wires went out for "the best surgeons in the state." The Republican contender remained locked inside his office, calling on the militia to quell "the insurrection." Crowds gathered in front of the State House and witnesses reported they had seen men with guns standing in the windows of the east wing just before the shooting. Fifty-one-year-old Holland Whittaker was grabbed and arrested as he emerged from the building. With the mob calling for a rope, marshals quickly shoved the suspect into a buggy bound for Louisville. In a saloon, when a black porter named I. Williams had the audacity to argue against mob violence, he was shot dead by a white patron.

All afternoon, trains filled with partisans from both sides poured into town. Frankfort took on the air of a Roman circus. Members of the bayonet-toting militia were seen rolling dice, playing cards, and getting drunk. The lobby of the hotel filled with curiosity seekers waiting for bulletins on Goebel's condition. Grave-looking physicians, friends, and family made their way to Goebel's room. The following morning, three ominous-looking Gatling guns stood on a knoll by the State House steps. Guards blocked the doorway, bayonets across their chests. Governor Taylor, locked in his office, was reported to be taking his meals at his desk.

When members of the Assembly arrived at the State House to vote on the election committee's findings, they were presented with an order from Taylor, instructing them to adjourn for a week. With reports that Goebel was sinking and might not last the day, the Democratic majority was frantic to declare their man governor before it was too late. And so began an absurdist contest between the legislators and the militia. An impromptu meeting in the streets was broken up by the militia; the legislators raced to city hall but were not allowed to enter the building; there were similar confrontations at the opera house and the courthouse.

A reporter for *The Courier-Journal* wrote that "the spectacle of nearly a hundred members of the Assembly running in a body through the streets, chased by companies of militia on the double quick is one seldom witnessed." Eventually the legislators made their way, one and two at a time, to the Capitol Hotel, where they met in secret session and signed a petition recommending that Goebel take the oath of office at once. Propped up in bed, able to raise his right hand, though with great difficulty, Goebel was sworn into office by the chief justice of the court of appeals. Later, some said that the justice had sworn in a dead man. Prominent citizens testified that Goebel was still very much alive.

Kentucky now had two governors, one barricaded in the State House surrounded by blue-coated shivering soldiers, the other clinging to life on the second

Members of the state militia, sympathetic to Governor Taylor, preparing a meal on the grounds of the State House at Frankfort. The militia, which functioned like Taylor's own private army, protected him while he remained barricaded inside his office.

floor of the Capitol Hotel. It was at this junction that Governor Taylor called for federal intervention. But there was nothing in this unhealthy situation that was to President McKinley's advantage. Even conservative newspapers had turned on the Republican governor. After a brief meeting with his cabinet, McKinley sent word that it was his wish that the issue be settled peacefully in the courts.

In Frankfort, while members of the militia were being drilled beneath Goebel's window, one man was heard to say it would be good for Kentucky if Goebel should die. The following day the governor obliged. As he closed his eyes he said, or at least was reported to have said, "Tell my friends to be brave and fearless and loyal to the great common people." Goebel proved to be better loved in death than he had ever been in life. At his funeral in Covington, ten thousand mourners paid their respects.

Goebel's office was filled by Lieutenant Governor Beckham, barely old enough to qualify for the job. His position was contested for months, but in time the United States Supreme Court would declare him to be the legal governor of Kentucky. In a swirl of speculation, William Taylor moved out of reach, across the state line. Sixteen men were eventually indicted for Goebel's assassination, including the Republican secretary of state and the original suspect, Holland Whittaker.

Only three were convicted and all three were eventually pardoned. The gunman was never found. And Governor Beckham had absolutely no interest in continuing Goebel's vendetta against the railroad.

Americans, who had started off the year more entertained than dismayed by the Goebel-Taylor affair, in the end were outraged. Government by bayonet was revolution, wherever it was practiced. As one paper noted, it took little imagination "to see what a few regiments of Federal soldiers might do in Washington under the order of a President who decided as Governor Taylor [had] 'to stick even if he precipitated a bloody war.' "

III

Fortunately, in February, Americans were no longer watching the heavens in search of omens. No good could have been predicted by the wild swings of weather. In Chicago, the temperature dropped from sixty-three degrees to three degrees in less than seventeen hours. In Washington, on February 8, there was springlike weather in the morning and by evening the city was caught in a blizzard. But whatever the weather, guests at the White House noticed that the president was in particularly fine spirits.

The Washington Bee reported that week that there was every reason to believe that McKinley had decided to run for reelection. Most political observers agreed. Mrs. McKinley appeared to be less frail, and nothing seemed to slow down her social life. Following the reception New Year's Day, the president and his wife had held a series of dinners for cabinet members, who in turn had held dinners for the McKinleys. There were other clues as well.

The president had just signed a contract to expand his house in Canton, Ohio. Americans were familiar with the McKinley home, with its trumpet vines and gingerbread trim. Throughout the presidential contest in 1896, for five months, McKinley had stayed in Canton with his wife and mother, posing for photographers in the rocker on the porch. He had not thought it seemly for a presidential candidate to campaign for his own election.

But almost every important Republican in the country had gone to Canton to pay his obeisance. Excursion trains had made Canton a tourist stop that summer, and every day but Sundays thousands of admirers and curiosity seekers had made their way to North Market Street. McKinley and his family, along with their more important guests, were often forced to seek refuge in the second-floor bedrooms. Over one Saturday McKinley made sixteen separate speeches to thirty thousand people.

In the midst of all the tumult, McKinley had remained surprisingly serene, looking, John Hay said, like "a genuine ecclesiastical face of the fifteenth century." But the strain on the old house had been almost too much. The lawn was destroyed, the fence ripped into fragments by souvenir hunters, the porch so weakened that the roof threatened to collapse. Now the house was being expanded to accommodate larger groups of people.

Additional rooms were being added, the president was to have a commodious new office, the old kitchen and dining room were being modernized, and the entrances to the drawing room and the reception area were being widened. All was to be finished by summer, before the start of the next presidential campaign. Reporters were now raising questions about McKinley's running mate. Vice President Garret A. Hobart had died the previous November. Rumors were circulating about Theodore Roosevelt, but the New York governor did not seem to be interested.

The New York Times, February 2, 1900
Gov. Roosevelt Will Refuse

NEW YORK—Under no circumstances will Gov. Roosevelt accept a nomination for Vice President on the Republican national ticket this year. This statement was made by some of his friends last night on hearing the persistent report that the Governor had agreed to be a candidate.

IV

In February, on the first anniversary of the war in the Philippines, news from Asia was dominating the newspapers. In Philadelphia, *The Evening Bulletin* reported that "colored" soldiers from the Forty-eighth Infantry, stopping off in Yokohama on their way to the Philippines, had given a concert for the diplomatic

A wounded soldier in the Philippines, being placed in an ambulance. Over four thousand American soldiers died in the Philippine islands during the course of the war; most were victim to disease.

corps that would be long remembered. The infantry band had opened with John Philip Sousa's "Stars and Stripes Forever," and then the glee club had sung a collection of "negro" melodies. Europeans in the audience who had never heard these songs before were enthusiastic in their calls for encores. But there was little else to cheer in the news from the East. The Twenty-fifth Infantry had been lured into a trap at Subic Bay. Five men were dead and a number were wounded. Insurgents were using flaming arrows to set towns and depots on fire. For every American who died, hundreds of Filipinos were killed, but the insurgents kept coming.

Americans knew little about the war—how it began, who the Filipinos were, or why they were fighting. Daily the papers referred to a welter of unfamiliar places—Luzon was said to be the size of New York State, and Mindanao was described as larger than Maine, but that clarified little. In January, *National Geographic* had published a primer on the islands by John Barrett, the former minister to Siam and an enthusiast for American expansion.

Barrett envisioned a great American city rising in Manila, the geographical center of the Far East. China, just six hundred miles away, he said, "affords America the most tempting field of trade expansion yet undeveloped in the world." He wrote of the English in Hong Kong who were making a fortune and the French who were doing well in the beautiful city of Saigon. Java, "the Garden of the East," was said to be blossoming under the Dutch.

And Barrett found that the Philippines themselves had much to offer: rice, hemp, coffee, spices. The forests were filled with the most valuable woods and minerals—perhaps even gold. He brushed off concerns about the climate. While letters from soldiers described miserable heat and a rainy season that seemed to go on forever, Barrett pointed out that "within near distance of Manila," Americans could seek relief in the cool of the mountains, which he thought could also "be utilized for hotels and barracks."

Most important from the diplomat's perspective, in a region of five hundred million people, America's influence and commercial position had changed radically in just two years. Before the war throughout Asia, America had been seen as a second-, even a third-rate power. Following the battle of Manila Bay, Barrett said "a tidal wave of prestige" had swept through the region and the United States had become "the first power of the Pacific."

In February 1900, as the arguments for retention of the Philippines grew more sophisticated, the opposition became more intense. In the Senate the debate was so bitter that it recalled the days just before the Civil War. When Richard F. Pettigrew, the senator from South Dakota, tried to read a statement from Emilio Aguinaldo, leader of the Filipino insurgents, into the congressional record, he was accused of treason.

Aguinaldo claimed that in return for his help in fighting the Spaniards, he had been promised that America would honor Filipino independence. The Republicans dismissed the claim "as a tissue of lies," and moved to stop Pettigrew from putting the statement into the record. Paraphrasing Patrick Henry, Pettigrew declared, "If telling the truth is treason, you can make the most of it." A senator from New Jersey called Pettigrew a traitor. Paling at the charges, Pettigrew closed the debate, saying, "I yield to no man in my devotion to the country or the flag . . . but I have my own opinion as to how its honor may be sustained."

In the House, John Fitzgerald was accused of having violated his mailing privileges by providing five hundred of his own franked envelopes to be used to send a pamphlet entitled "A Protest Against the President's War of Criminal Aggression" to members of the government. A spokesman for the U.S. Post Office declared that mailing documents for the purpose of giving aid and comfort to those in rebellion or insurrection against the authority of the United States was subject to a $10,000 fine or ten years' imprisonment.

The matter would die, but Fitzgerald had made his position clear.

V

In the last weeks of winter, a blizzard struck the middle states. The snowfall in Chicago was the heaviest ever recorded. Huge drifts brought the city to a standstill. Nearly five hundred men and as many teams were at work, but the streetcars were blocked and one hundred and fifty railroad cars of livestock were stranded on Madison Street. In Toledo, Ohio, coal was running low; the storm had shut down the oil fields and not a pump was running. But it would be the last heavy snow of the year.

Up in the Klondike in Dawson City, the more adventurous souls were packing dogsleds for the first leg of the journey a thousand miles north, to Nome, Alaska. American prospectors had been in the Yukon now for three bitter years. One hundred thousand men and women—professional miners, salesclerks, farmers and bankers, housewives and con men had been lured north by the promise of "a ton of gold"—gold for the taking. By 1900, Dawson City was filled with dispirited men and women who had survived the hazardous journey only to discover that the most productive claims were long gone.

There was gold, to be sure, but what remained was trapped beneath dried riverbeds, under feet of permafrost. Day laborers back home were making more money than the gold seekers. But when new fields of gold were discovered in Nome, on the coast of Alaska, thousands of prospectors—inspired by the promise of a second chance—were moving on. The first wave headed out in the midst of a spectacular spring thaw. A special correspondent for *The New York Times* reported that "the sun pours down on the snow in such fury that it is impossible to see without green glasses."

Blinded by snow and dreams of fortune, prospectors headed for the Yukon River as the ice began to break up. The travelers waited on the banks for every

When news reached America in 1897 that gold had been found in the Klondike, ten thousand people jammed the Mission Street dock in San Francisco to watch the steamer Excelsior *heading north with the first prospectors. Over a hundred thousand gold seekers followed. Most returned empty-handed. But in the spring of 1900, hope was rekindled by the news that gold had been found on the beaches of Nome, Alaska.*

possible conveyance to carry them downriver to the Bering Sea and the beaches of Nome. The first argonauts to strike it rich back in 1898 had returned to Seattle with sacks of gold, paid for their drinks, boots, and rail tickets with nuggets as large as a man's fist—and gold fever had swept the country. But the arithmetic of mining was now running against those still working claims in the old primitive way.

In Oakland, California, Jack London drew again on his own experience in the North to write about the impact of technology in the Klondike. The early prospectors had used tools that had changed little over a thousand years. But shovels and picks were now being replaced by modern machines that could tear up the tundra. Frontiersmen and amateurs were making way for well-financed speculators and businessmen, and London was making far more money writing about the North than he had ever seen in the gold fields.

He was converting his own memories of desire—of hardship and nature and the camaraderie of men locked together in a smoky cabin for a winter—into stories and books that were beginning to gain national attention. In February he was working on three or four magazine articles and every Wednesday was holding open house for an ever-growing circle of friends—writers, artists, and Socialists, who ate, drank, played cards, and argued about politics and one another's work.

London was also continuing to see Anna Strunsky. Somewhere in the second month of their relationship, she finally agreed to call him by his first name.

> Dear Anna—
> Now I feel comfortable. Nobody ever "Mr. London's" me, so every time I opened a letter of yours I felt a starched collar drawn round my neck. Pray permit me softer neck-gear for the remainder of our correspondence.

In between their meetings they wrote each other. Anna lent Jack a novel called *Gadfly* about the tyranny of the Catholic Church, which he said had left him weeping. In turn, he sent her romantic poetry and confessed he would like to write poems, but explained, "It doesn't pay, and I don't." Memories of an impoverished childhood lurked over his writing desk: "I had been in the cellar of society, and I did not like the place. . . . The pipes and drains were unsanitary, and the air was bad to breathe. . . . If I can procure fame that means more money. More money means more life to me."

The pursuit of money seemed to cloud his belief in Socialism. "I lose faith in any cooperative, commonwealth; cannot see how, after all, there will be incentives." He asked Anna if she shared his doubts. But as winter began to turn to spring, mostly he wrote to the striking dark-eyed girl like a young man in love:

> And need I say that your company has ever been a great delight to me? That I would not have sought it had I not desired it? That (like you have said of yourself) when you no longer interest me I shall no longer be with you? Need I say these things to prove my candor?

Other Stories of Interest

The New York Times, February 1, 1900
Famous Sporting Man Dead
LONDON—The Marquis of Queensberry is dead. He was the author of the well-known Queensberry boxing rules, under which all prize ring contests of importance are now conducted. . . . Lord Alfred Bruce Douglas, the third son of the Marquis, became notorious on account of a sensational case of some time back.*

*The scandal *The Times* refers to so archly was the relationship between Lord Douglas and the famed Irish writer Oscar Wilde. Queensberry, enraged, accused Wilde of homosexuality and the writer sued the Marquis for libel. Wilde was promptly charged with homosexual offenses, convicted, and sent to jail for two years. In February 1900, Wilde, impoverished and ill, was living in Paris.

The New York Times, February 4, 1900
What It Costs to Go to Yale
NEW HAVEN, CONNECTICUT—Some interesting figures have been gathered as to the average cost of a year at Yale . . . : Tuition, $155 per year; room rent, $200; board, $200; books, $35 to $45; subscriptions, society dues, etc., $100; clothing and incidentals, $150. This makes an average total of $850, which is however, more often exceeded than diminished.

The Washington Post,
February 8, 1900
LONDON—Sir Henry M. Stanley, the celebrated African explorer, was taken ill in the House of Commons last night and is in a somewhat serious condition.

The Washington Post,
February 13, 1900
Roosevelt Will Not Run, Definite Statement as to the Vice Presidential Nomination
ALBANY, NEW YORK—Gov. Roosevelt today gave out a statement . . . that he will not accept the honor under any circumstances. "In view of the continued statements in the press that I may be urged as a candidate for Vice President, it is proper for me to state definitely that under no circumstances could I, or would I, accept the nomination for the Vice Presidency."

William Jex, standing far right, supervises the family business in Spanish Fork, Utah. Like many in the region, this family was Mormon. The cockatoo was brought home by one of the sons, who had served a mission in Zealand.

The crew of a steam-driven threshing machine, near Climax, Minnesota. Equipment of this kind was out of reach for most small farmers. It was common to hire a team of men and equipment as needed. This crew included an operator, a fireman, and a tender to haul fuel and water. Note the screen over the smokestack to prevent ash and sparks from igniting dry straw.

CHAPTER FOUR

March

I

In early March, fifty miles north of Minneapolis, the fields were still eighteen inches deep in snow and planting would not begin till mid-April. But state forecasts predicted that Minnesota would harvest more grain in 1900 than all of Great Britain and Ireland together. *McClure's* was estimating that Great Britain would consume her entire wheat crop in about thirteen weeks and be forced to buy grain overseas. It was one of those statistics that made the heart quicken. Traveling on the sleek hard crust of ice, through patches of giant spruce with trunks five and six feet thick, Axel Jarlson, a twenty-two-year-old Swedish immigrant, was heading south over a trail he now knew well. For Axel, gold, if it was to be found, lay in the rich farmland of Minnesota.

When he arrived in 1899 he wrote back home to his parents in Sweden that "the soil was black loam on top of fine red sand and the corn seemed to spring up the day after it was planted." His oldest brother, Gustav, had followed an uncle to Minnesota, in 1891, and immediately began urging the rest of his family to join him. "All about me," he had written, "are Swedes who have taken farms and are getting rich." Three of Axel's brothers now owned their own farms and his sister Hilda, married to a man from home, was living in a fine brick house in Minneapolis, with two servants and a carriage.

Working for his brother Knut, Axel had saved enough money over the course of one year for the down payment on a farm of his own, ten miles away. He knew the configuration of the land by heart and could see the house he would build one day "on the side of a hill that sloped southward to a creek that emptied into a river a mile away." There was much about Minnesota that reminded him of home: the long dark nights, the long-lasting snow, the brilliant redemption of spring. But the rich and boundless land, which seemed almost for the taking, infused in Alex a sense of optimism he had never known.

As a boy he had been told that in America food was cheap and a man could earn ten times as much as he could in Sweden and he had seen for himself that those who worked hard seldom went hungry, as his own family had, not many years before. Living among farmers and small-town people who cherished their independence, Axel wrote, "Here there are no aristocrats to push a man down, and say he is not worthy because his father was poor. . . . In Sweden my father never had the vote because there is a property qualification that keeps out poor people. Here any man of good character can have a vote after he has been a short time in the country." Jarlson planned to become a citizen as soon as he passed the residency requirement.

He was setting out to tame his own land with minimum equipment—axes, spades, hoes, and one pickax. He had bought his farm for $150, with $50 down. In a few months he would buy a pair of oxen, with harness, for $63 more. In 1900 there were still tens of thousands of farmers who depended on their own muscles and tools that had changed little in a thousand years. They grew what they needed to care for their own and sold or traded for those necessaries—the horseshoes and nails, flour, salt, and sugar—that they could neither grow nor make themselves. Most farms were years away from electrification. Jarlson would start out with one oil lantern to light his makeshift cabin.

The first spring, when the ice and snow were gone and the sun began to warm, he planted twelve acres with hoe and spade, and then, with his friend Jake, an Indian from Canada, set out to build a proper house of logs with a birch bark roof. Within months he was able to grow his own provisions and soon would be able to sell some wheat, corn, and carrots. In time he might have the money to rent modern equipment from the owner of the general store. But for all of Jarlson's optimism and the optimism of his brothers, technology was pushing many a small farm out of the path of progress. Men who for generations considered self-sufficiency just this side of a biblical injunction had mortgaged their farms to buy sophisticated equipment and then fallen hostage to forces beyond their control.

Axel had arrived in the country at the tag end of an extraordinary revolution that, as historian Carl Degler wrote, "transformed raw nature at an unprecedented pace. It was as if the cover of half a continent was ripped off in those . . . years." Following the Civil War, manpower had been replaced by horsepower and horsepower by machines. Where a lone farmer took two and a half hours to reap, bound, and thresh one bushel of wheat, a combine performed those same tasks in four minutes. It was this marriage between the richest land and advanced technology that made America the envy of the world. But here, too, progress had its price.

In the 1890s thousands were victim to skyrocketing rail rates, plunging prices, and bank failures. Tens of thousands of small farms went under. By 1900, more and more land was concentrated in the hands of a few. In Minnesota, the Dakotas, and Kansas there were enormous spreads, seas of wheat on farms that sprawled over ten thousand acres and boasted as many as ten threshing machines, fifty reapers, and hundreds of horses. These huge mechanized businesses, with outbuildings connected by telephone, were run by men who, as a matter of course, read reports from the Chamber of Commerce and knew "the reigning prices for grain in Liverpool from day to day, almost as soon as the most sophisticated city trader."

From its earliest days, America had been a nation of farmers, but as farms were consolidated, the national balance began to tip. Older people, who believed that those who lived on the land beyond the contaminating cities were closer to God, watched the young leave home for alien places like Chicago or New York, women as well as men. Families that had stuck together for generations were splitting apart. The young promised to return; the old knew they never would.

A million different reasons were given for their leaving, but those lugging packets tied with twine and suitcases bought from a Sears & Roebuck catalog, those wearing their stiff new city shoes, were part of a move of rural people, almost seven million over the past twenty years, who left the countryside and headed off for city life.

II

When a Scottish journalist named William Archer arrived in New York harbor, he wrote of the great buildings at the lower end of the island looming out of the fog like "a deputation of giants." He had not been in America for twenty-two years and, like Jack London, was fascinated by the compression of time and space. "We are slow to realize," he wrote, "that time is the only true measure of space." Crossing the Atlantic—"the Straits of New York"—now took only six and a half days. The new steamers were "giant ferryboats plying with clockwork punctuality between the twin landing-stages of the English-speaking world. . . . It is surely no Jules Vernism, to look forward to the time when one may set foot on American soil within, say, sixty-five hours of leaving Liverpool."

After clearing customs, Archer, mindful of his budget, sent his baggage on ahead to the hotel and climbed aboard the platform of a horsecar on West Street. The car skirted the wharves, passing pockets of small, tired buildings, some of the oldest in the city, and wagons filled with immigrant families sitting atop their baggage, still marked with fresh steerage tags. In the week of March 6, 1900, twelve thousand steerage passengers were expected in the city.

For those arriving in New York for the first time, the noise, the dirt, the crowds were overwhelming. Nothing in the city ever seemed complete, streets were torn up, buildings torn down, the city was in a state of perpetual regeneration. The traffic jams in the financial district rivaled those anywhere in the world, although Archer insisted London traffic was as bad. And the noise—the clanging trolleys, the steel-clad hooves on cobble streets, the hammering of the ironworkers on new construction, the babble of voices in a dozen different tongues, the nervous, arrogant bell of the ambulance—melded into one great city sound wave, tearing at the nerves of some, exhilarating others.

As Archer rode north, he noted the roadway was ill-paved, that oily mud congealed on its surface, and that in the middle of the side streets one could see "relics of the blizzard, grubby glaciers slowly oozing away." But whatever charm was lacking—and the city had indeed placed its mean face to the riverfront—was more than compensated for by the tram conductor who, on hearing Archer's accent, greeted him with news that Rudyard Kipling, the beloved English poet

Lower New York City, as seen from across the Hudson River. When the Pulitzer Building (dome on far left) was completed in 1889, twenty-six stories high, it was the tallest building in the world. By 1900 the nearby Park Row Building, identified by its twin peaks, held the record with thirty-three stories. Visitors were stunned to discover that some buildings had express elevators that did not stop until they reached the fifteenth or even the twentieth floor.

who was living in Vermont and had been so very ill, was now pulling through. The conductor hoped Kipling would be named Poet Laureate, and Archer thought that "fate could not have devised a more ingenious way" of making him feel at home.

Entering the Waldorf-Astoria through a plate-glass turnstile, an invention designed to keep out drafts, the journalist was carried up to the thirteenth floor in a gorgeously upholstered elevator. This first elevator voyage was but a prelude to many others; over the next few days Archer would discover New Yorkers moved almost as much on the "perpendicular as on the horizontal plane." Before he left the city, he computed, he had traveled miles on miles, at right angles to the earth's surface.

"Americans," he wrote, "have practically added a new dimension to space. When they find themselves a little crowded, they simply tilt a street on end and call it a skyscraper. This hotel, for example, is nothing but a couple of populous streets soaring up into the air instead of crawling along the ground." He loved "these aerial suburbs, these mansions in the sky." Most major cities had high-rises by now, but New York had more of them, which only increased congestion even further. Three-and-a-half million people now lived in New York, spilling over into its outer boroughs.

Morning and night, tradesmen, secretaries, and factory workers were caught in a devilish rush of people all going in the same direction at the same time. In the evening, Grand Central terminal was said to look "as if a panic-stricken population were fleeing a doomed city." The incessant stream of elevated railways, belching smoke, and soot had made commuting possible but the city less pleasant. After years of political shenanigans, contracts had finally been signed to begin

Laying cable car tracks at Union Square, New York City, in the heart of the shopping district known as the Ladies' Mile. Tiffany's was close by. So was the city's most important toy dealer—F.A.O. Schwartz—if one could get there.

construction on the city's first subway, but it would be years before the underground line was finished. In the meantime the construction would just add to the chaos.

More and more the underpinnings of urban life—the gas mains, the sewers, the conduits for electric and telephone lines—were being pushed underground. Unexpected bursts of steam escaped from manholes as if some mythical animal were trapped in the caverns beneath the streets. Maintenance of all the modern paraphernalia was difficult and often dangerous. A veteran of the charge up San Juan Hill was badly burned when boiling paraffin exploded as he was laying cables on lower Broadway.

On Friday morning, March 2, two New York detectives, William Funston and Henry Foye, were working out a route for President and Mrs. McKinley, due to arrive in the city at the height of the afternoon rush. Funston and Foye, known for their impeccable manners and their tact, had been assigned to McKinley on two previous visits. When the presidential train arrived midafternoon in Jersey City, they were waiting on the platform with the president's brother Abner and niece Mabel.

The McKinleys were accompanied, as they almost always were, by their private physician, Dr. Rixey, the ever present Secretary Cortelyou, a stenographer, a military attaché, a valet and a maid, and on this occasion by Ida McKinley's niece, Mary Barber. With Mrs. McKinley in her invalid chair, the president briskly led the party down the platform, acknowledging salutations from bystanders with a tip of his hat.

Once all were settled into four closed carriages, their trunks secured aboard an open wagon, the entire caravan was driven directly onto the ferry to cross the Hudson River. Ida McKinley enjoyed these royal journeys—the mounted police who served as outriders, clearing passages through the crowds that gathered along the way; the flag-decked hotels; the presidential suite filled with all her favorite flowers. That evening, leaving her husband to tend to business, the first lady set out with family and friends for an evening at the theater.

There was a spectacular quality to New York at night, which alone was worth the journey: the brilliant illumination of the streets, the restaurants and stores, outlined now by incandescent lamps that turned the night sky into a purple haze. Archer described "huge electric trolleys sailing in an endless stream, profusely jewelled with electricity." On the cross streets he could see elevated trains, like "luminous winged serpents, skimming through the air."

In a restaurant, Archer found himself sitting at a table next to Thomas Edison.

"Reflections, Night, New York," photographed by Alfred Stieglitz.

He studied Edison's "furrowed, anxious, typically American and truly beautiful face," and found "a reminder that the over-strain had not been incurred for nothing." Electricity is the "true 'white magic' of the future," he concluded, "and here, with his pallid face and silver hair, sat the master magician—one of the great light-givers of the world."

On Saturday, March 3, the weather was chill and uncertain. After breakfast in a private dining suite, the president was able to spend a quiet morning at the hotel, smoking cigars, reading the papers, and greeting old friends. It was precisely the kind of morning McKinley most enjoyed. In the news that day was a report that the Nicaraguan government was ready to sell the rights to the United States to build a canal across the Isthmus. With Asian trade growing, eastern manufacturers and shipping magnates were pressuring for easier access to the Pacific.

There was a dispatch from South Africa, written by the young British journalist Winston Churchill, on the Boer War, the deadly confrontation between Great Britain and the Dutch settlers. Ten thousand British troops were already dead or wounded and Churchill was warning his readers back home "to nerve themselves" against even greater losses. The United States was taking a neutral stance on the war, but Irish and German Americans, with their loathing of the British, were supporting the Dutch. And then, of course, there was the daily ration of bad news from the Philippines. More fighting in Luzon.

Among McKinley's visitors was the lieutenant governor of New York, Timothy Woodruff, who was said to be angling for the vice-presidential nomination. Woodruff told reporters his call on the president was purely social, and there was nothing in McKinley's demeanor to suggest anything else. But if there was one subject on which the president refused to be engaged, in public or in private, it was on the selection of a running mate for the coming election. McKinley knew that a campaign was building for Theodore Roosevelt, but the president was uneasy with the hotheaded young New Yorker and a number of his top advisors thought TR suspect.

As governor of New York, Roosevelt had shown an irritating propensity for reform. At the beginning of the year he fired the well-connected superintendent of insurance because he was too connected to the industry he was supervising. Recently TR had questioned the "damnable alliance between business and politics"— not too loudly, of course, but loud enough to irritate New York's political bosses. Among younger Republicans the brilliant and vocal Roosevelt was a clear favorite. He would appeal to the western states, where he had spent a lot of time, but most important, he could pull New York into the Republican column.

TR was a brilliant and charming man. A highly publicized hero of the Cuban campaign during the Spanish-American War, he had led his Rough Riders through a brief but bloody engagement and returned home one of the most famous men in America. A naturalist and big-game hunter, he was a man who embraced life with such passion that a friend described him as a steam engine in trousers. By the age of forty-one he had probably written more books than McKinley had read. His friend and ally, the Kansas newspaperman William Allen White, recalled a dinner with Roosevelt sharing "seas of speculation . . . excursions of delight into books and men and manners, poetry and philosophy." An ambitious man, TR saw the vice presidency as a job leading nowhere and was vocal in his disinterest. McKinley wasn't certain he had any interest in Theodore Roosevelt, but true to his fashion was holding his tongue.

Two men could not have been more different. The president was an amiable nineteenth-century man, good-natured and cordial, conservative in dress and manner. He didn't much like taking chances and would do nothing to embarrass himself or the presidency. When photographers came around he carefully removed his cigar lest he corrupt the young. A modest hero in the Civil War, he had been decorated for driving a mule team during the height of the battle of Antietam, to bring hot food and coffee to the men under fire. He would be the last Civil War veteran to move into the White House, the last president to have been mustered out of the service on orders signed by A. Lincoln.

But McKinley was a tougher man than he seemed, and he kept his own counsel. He had sent American troops off to the Philippines without consulting Congress. He understood the evils of the enormous business combines—the trusts and monopolies—but he was not about to tamper with big business, at least not in an election year. And he would handle the vice-presidential contest in his own way.

In the evening, the president took his carriage to the Waldorf-Astoria for the Ohio Society banquet. The hotel, which was the largest and most luxurious in the world, had a subbasement that contained $300,000 worth of cigars and a superb collection of fine wine. As the president was led into the hall, four hundred men rose to greet him. The elegantly gowned women were remitted to flag-draped galleries overlooking the ballroom. A little after nine, as Mrs. McKinley made her entrance into the center box, the president impulsively rose from his seat and blew his wife a kiss. In an instant, every man in the hall was on his feet toasting the president's wife. *The World* (New York) reported that Ida McKinley "flushed with pleasure at the unlooked-for tribute."

Then, halfway through the dinner, Governor Roosevelt suddenly entered the hall accepting a salute of "three cheers for Teddy." The governor always had impeccable timing. As he made his way to his seat next to the president, reporters noted that McKinley, who was serenely enjoying his meal, was surrounded by candidates for the vice-presidential nomination. He was cordial to them all. When the president finally rose to speak, the diners waved their napkins and stamped their feet. There was great affection for McKinley that night, and he took the opportunity to meander a bit. Drawing a bundle of papers from inside his jacket, he laid the groundwork for his coming reelection campaign.

"Markets have been increased and mortgages reduced. Interest has fallen and wages have advanced. The public debt is decreasing, the country is well-to-do. Its people for the most part are happy and contented." Then he reached the most contentious issue he would deal with, the Philippine question. "We believe," he said, "that the century of free government which the American people have

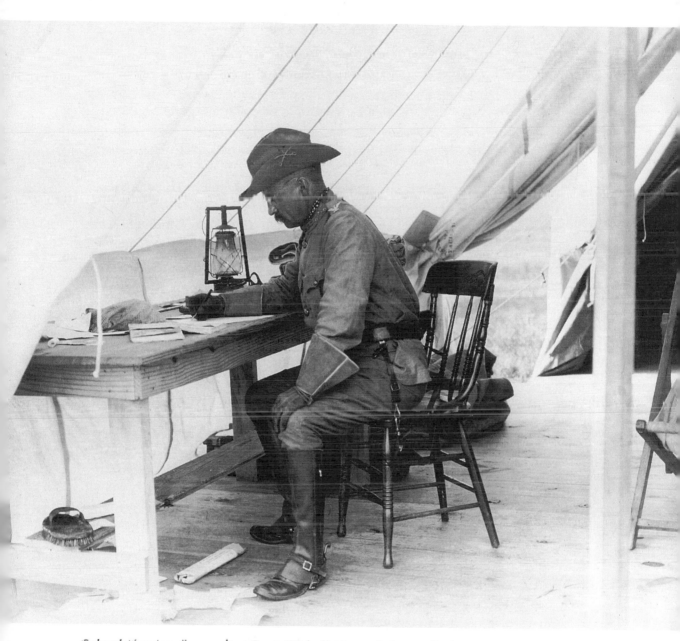

Colonel Theodore Roosevelt at Camp Wickoff, Montauk, Long Island, in 1899. An unlikely looking war hero, when TR led the Rough Riders up the hills of Santiago, Cuba, under continuous fire, bullets nicked his elbow, punctured his boot, and eighty-nine of his men were struck down by Spanish fire—but TR appeared invincible. The Spanish garrison fell and Roosevelt returned home one of the most famous men in America.

enjoyed . . . have fitted them for the great task of lifting up and assisting to better conditions and larger liberty those distant people who have . . . become our wards. . . . Nations do not grow in strength . . . by the doing of easy things. . . . The liberators will never become the oppressors. . . . It is not possible that 75 million American freemen are unable to establish liberty and justice and good government in our new possessions."

Theodore Roosevelt had not been scheduled to speak, but he could not resist. When he took to the podium reporters noted that the governor said little but was cheered almost as warmly as the president himself. It was after midnight when McKinley was tucked inside his carriage and, with Detective Funston up on the box, was driven back to his hotel. It had been a splendid evening.

III

As the McKinleys and their entourage made their way back to Washington, New Yorkers were occupied with the latest chapter in the obscenity case featuring Olga Nethersole, the glamorous star of *Sapho*. The provocative French play had been denounced from pulpits, condemned by women's clubs, branded as "fatally demoralizing to young men and women." The story had been dominating the popular press for weeks.

Newspapers in 1900 liked nothing better than finding stories about unspeakable conduct that could be run for days providing readers with an opportunity for both appropriate disapproval and high amusement. The *St. Louis Post-Dispatch* had a fine time reporting on the case of a brewer named Jennings, a married man with "a mustache like a walrus and watery eyes" who came home every night to his wife and five children and climbed into women's clothes. In court, Jennings's wife testified that for five years he had "dressed himself in women's fixings, corset and all. Sometimes he sleeps in the garments, only for bed he takes off his plumed bonnet and dons a monstrous wig." In a firm moral tone the paper reported that the judge sent Jennings away to "where he would have to dress like a man, for a while at least."

On the same day, the paper also carried a well-illustrated story about a couple accosted in a love nest, fitted out in Oriental splendor, with "geishas and kimonos and perfumed capsules." When the police arrived, the gentleman involved opened the door dressed solely in a loose-flowing Japanese silk robe while his lady friend lay trembling in bed wearing even less. It was the stuff on which a reader's imagination could feast for days.[*]

But the Nethersole case was more than just another story published to titillate readers. At a time when sexual explicitness in any public forum was forbidden by law, the case was raising some very basic questions about the extent to which writers and actors could explore the nature of women, and the right of women to be included in that debate. "The Sapho Affair," as it became known, set off a contro-versy across the country.

Nethersole, an English actress, was the director and star of *Sapho,* a four-act play about a seductive woman named Fanny. The caper had been adapted from a French novel by Alphonse Daudet. When the curtain came down on the most controversial scene, the star, wearing a "diaphanous gown open to the apex of the heart," was being carried in the arms of a leering admirer up a stairway to God knows where. In response to applause—and there always was applause—the curtain was raised, revealing the couple even farther up the stairs on their wayward journey.

That was quite enough to raise the wrath of the righteous. *The Evening Post* (New York) declared, "It is not necessary to soil the columns of this paper with a particular account of the reeking compost of filth and folly. It is enough to say that this heavy and foul rigmarole of lust, sap-headed sentiment, and putrid non-sense tells a vulgar, commonplace and tiresome story about a harlot and a fool."

Dr. Newell Dwight Hillis, a well-known pastor, weighed in with a confession that as a college boy he had read the novel in one evening and "spent the next two months burning mental brimstone, trying to fumigate my mind." He reminded his readers that "Athens put to death the people who made it their business to trade on the passions of men," and suggested that "a common whipping post might be very wholesome for New York today."(Hillis made some of the great quotes of the year. Commenting on the nation's prosperity, he described art, invention, liter-ature, learning, and government as "all captives marching in Christ's triumphant procession up the hill of fame.")

The vice squads in New York City were particularly busy in 1900, shutting down gambling dens and music hall shows, destroying licentious material of

---

[*]In Vienna, Austrian psychiatrist Sigmund Freud, already known for his studies on human sexuality, had just published *The Interpretation of Dreams.* Freud was proud of the book, but it would take another eight years to sell six hundred copies, and even longer—until 1913—before it was translated into English.

every kind. A photographer named Charles Schenk was pressing the patience of the pure, publishing some four hundred photographs of women with small breasts and large thighs, draped in spider-thread thin gauze. The moral crusaders were more concerned about the impact of sexual material on women than on the passions of men. Women were to be protected from contamination by those "lower forces of their nature," lurking just beneath the surface of even the most submissive. *The World* was outraged by the "*Sapho*-crazed" women, thronging the theater to see "Fanny Le Grand's Amours with Many Lovers."

When the paper launched its campaign to suppress *Sapho* there was every expectation of success. Plays, books, and photographs far less explicit had been banned that year with little opposition. In 1900, when Theodore Dreiser published *Sister Carrie,* a realistic novel about a young woman from the country who uses her sexual talents to climb out of poverty, the novel was declared immoral, and after selling four hundred and fifty-six copies, was quietly withdrawn by the publisher.

But the reaction to *Sapho* proved quite different. An inspector for the New York Police Department informed reporters that in the line of duty he had attended *Sapho* five or six times and "had not been able to discover wherein it was immoral." The candid inspector set off a firestorm. The portrayal of women as sexual creatures was considered salacious if not subversive, and furthermore just plain inaccurate—it was contradictory to all the teachings of the time. Ministers, physicians, the leading marriage manual—stated for a fact that "the great majority of women are largely devoid of sexual pleasure."

In a book called *What a Young Husband Ought to Know,* men were told that "the sexual impulse in the male . . . marches like a mighty conqueror, arousing and marshalling the mightiest human forces [leading to] the attainment of the world's greatest and grandest achievements in art, in letters, in inventions, in philosophy, in philanthropy, and in every effort that is to secure the universal blessing of mankind." They were also assured that with patience and self-control, they could lead their wives to accept sexual intercourse as a basic requirement on the road to motherhood. That unpleasant consequences might occur when men and women were imbued with such different visions of sex did not seem to be of much concern.

Former President Grover Cleveland had declared that "the relative positions assumed by men and women were assigned long ago by a higher intelligence," and most men tended to agree with Cleveland. They would continue the fight to

It was this scene in Sapho, of an unprotesting Olga Nethersole being carried upstairs to the hero's bedroom, that touched off a campaign to suppress the "obscene" and "prurient" play, said to be "a menace to the public morals." Audiences of "Sapho-crazed women" were described as wallowing in ignoble thoughts. Nethersole herself was accused of having "a weakness for warm plays."

keep women out of the voting booth, to hold on to their all-male enclaves and preserve the patriarchal society that seemed to suit them so well.

But in 1898, at a closed meeting on Sexual Hygiene at the Physicians Club in Chicago, a doctor testified that schooling women to believe that any "manifestation of sexual feeling was indecent, immoral, and silly" had produced "a race of sexless creatures, married nuns [whose] only pleasure in intercourse is the unselfish one of gratifying her husband." The physicians had determined that less than half of married women found any pleasure in sex and that few husbands knew the pleasure of mutual sexual union.

The minutes of the meeting were not published until 1902, and then for doctors only. Summing up their findings the physicians agreed that "from all over the land has gone up the cry for 'more light.' " The paper closed with the rhetorical question, "How many homes are rendered miserable, how many women driven to desperation . . . because the family doctor does not know how to give advice on sexual relations." The truth was that few male doctors had interest in encouraging women to emerge as sexual creatures. They had the language to be helpful, but not the desire.

Over the years there had been numbers of attempts to break women out of their psychic prison. In the 1870s, a free love movement attracted a curious collection of outspoken ministers, spiritualists, anarchists, and suffragists who encouraged women to take charge of their bodies and their lives. Victoria Woodhull, a beautiful and eccentric spiritualist, drew enormous audiences lecturing on the sexual emancipation of women. Woodhull assailed male hypocrisy, urged that sexual science be taught in schools, and went so far as to declare, "If I want sexual intercourse with one or one hundred men, I shall have it."

But by 1900 Woodhull, exhausted defending her radical role, had retreated to London, married an aristocratic English banker, and was trying to persuade the American press to destroy all her lectures on free love. Similarly, the lyrical Angela Tilton Heywood, who with her husband, Ezra, had extolled the joys of marital sex, had also been quieted. The Heywoods had once exuberantly accused *The Penis Trust* of creating a double standard that encouraged men to act as sexual bullies. They had suggested that "to bring sex-meeting into the domain of reason" might require the establishment of a "Fucking Trust."

But for his candor, Ezra Heywood had been hauled into court by the secretary of the Society for the Suppression of Vice, Anthony Comstock, and sent off to jail at the age of sixty-two. By the turn of the century, Comstock and his legion of vice hunters had far more power than those trying to rescue women from sexual limbo. A former dry goods salesman, Comstock had succeeded in pushing through a federal law banning obscene material from the mails and had been made a special postal agent with the power to enforce the statute.

Comstock had also been charged by the New York Police Department with monitoring and regulating the city's sexual behavior, and he approached that assignment with a singular passion. Over the years he arrested thousands for a variety of sins. He posed as a distraught husband to convict a well-known abortionist, boasted of confiscating over sixty thousand "rubber items" in just one year, and was credited with the destruction of one hundred and sixty tons of literature and pictures. George Bernard Shaw, the Irish playwright, mockingly called the American obsession with sexuality "Comstockery," and refused to visit the city for fear of being jailed.

By 1900 there was some question as to what Comstock's crusade was actually achieving. He had certainly made it dangerous if not impossible to publish information about contraception, and now the abortion rate was rising. He had destroyed, banned, and repressed sexual information with great efficiency but family life was not improving. Divorces were increasing and there seemed to be a widespread though ill-defined disaffection with marriage.

Clearly, all marital problems could not be laid at Comstock's door. What was coming into question was the inherently unequal nature of marriage. By law and social custom, women were being raised to be dependent—their emotions, their bodies, and their minds bound like a Chinese woman's feet. Subservience was the mark of a well-trained woman and marriage the primary means of livelihood for most. In one of the extraordinary paradoxes of the Victorian Age, girls were taught to be seductive but not sexual, prepared for the chase that led to marriage but not for marriage itself. Young women were too often moving from girlhood into marriage and overnight dependency on men they barely knew or didn't necessarily like—let alone love.

In 1900 Elizabeth Cady Stanton, the great aging battler for women's rights, was asked for a comment on the shocking assertion that "ninety percent of all marriages were failures." For Stanton the fundamentals were simple: "People marry for all sorts of reasons," she wrote, "except the true ones—love and affection and attraction and respect for each other." The marriage and "sex problem," she concluded, were the result of a masculine civilization and would not be solved as long as women were "suppressed and fettered."

In *Women and Economics*, published in 1898, Charlotte Perkins Gilman noted, "In no other animal species is the sex-relation for sale. . . . We justify and approve the economic dependence of women upon the sex-relation in marriage [and] condemn it unsparingly out of marriage." But Gilman took heart from the millions of independent young women now moving out of the home and into the workplace. Most went out to work because they had no choice, many worked until "they could be supported," but nonetheless, in 1900, 20 percent of American women had jobs and the numbers were growing.

The moves of women to break their dependence on men, to change the basic rules of engagement, to shift the balance within marriages, were cautious and uneasy but were surfacing in a thousand different ways. Eleanor Foster Comegys, a well-known southern club woman, expressed irritation with the condescending, pretty little lady talk so skillfully used to keep women in their place: "I want men to stop calling me a queen and treating me like an imbecile." At a national meeting of women suffragists, the Reverend Ida C. Hulton said, "Women today have the keys to the doors which have been barred against them and they will open them without asking consent." Those thronging to see *Sapho* wanted to make up their own minds as to whether the play was licentious or simply realistic.

Olga Netherole, the director and star of Sapho, *did not look like the leader of a sexual revolution.*

The moralists could rattle the obscenity code and threaten the defendants, but when Olga Nethersole was finally brought to trial, it was quite clear that attitudes had begun to change. In his charge to the jury, the judge infuriated the prosecution when he warned, "You are not the guardians of the morals of this community, or the participants in a crusade against vice. . . . You are to consider *not* whether the play would shock the modesty of an innocent young girl but whether it shocks the sensibilities of the people at large."

It took the jury less than fifteen

minutes to acquit Olga Nethersole, and even less time for the manager of Wallack's Theater to announce that after a four-week hiatus, the play would be reopening the following night. Three-sheet posters with striking purple backgrounds were splashed around the outside of the theater announcing that *Sapho* starring Olga Nethersole would return intact, including the controversial stairway sequence.

IV

In March, Jack London felt his life careening out of control. There were too many friends, too many speaking engagements, his writing machine was moving too fast, the ordinary domestic chores were cutting into overcrowded days. He was living with his mother and her adopted son and needed more space, more room for thinking. In the grip of his obsession to make more money he had just sold a story to *McClure's* magazine, another to the *Atlantic Monthly*, and a third to *Youth's Companion*. The variety of work was astonishing. In an essay on "The Impossibility of War" published that month, he was again exploring the impact of technology on modern life.

He described the new mechanisms of war—the modern rifle with "a range of two to three miles," melanite bombs that could "turn farmhouses, villages, and hamlets to dust, destroying everything that might be used as cover, obstacle, or refuge." He wrote about the impact of war on the civilian population, the enormous expense of maintaining large modern armies, and concluded that "from the technical standpoint the improvement in the mechanism of war has made war impossible. Economics not force of arms will decide; not battles, but famine." He was optimistic that the socialist-led antimilitary movement was growing.

Midmonth he was writing a story about a Turkish belly dancer he had known in Alaska, had just finished reading Leo Tolstoy's *The Death of Ivan Illych*, and written Anna that he was thinking of moving, but "O the turmoil and confusion and time lost during such an operation." In recent weeks he had made more money than he ever had in his life, but it was never enough. He wrote, "The habit of money spending ah God! I shall always be its victim. I received three hundred dollars last

Jack London and his wife, Bessie Maddern, in Santa Cruz, California, after their marriage.

Monday. I have now about four dollars in pocket. . . . How's that for about three days?"

London needed someone who could still the chaos—he wanted a wife, a non-demanding other-mother, a secretary-housekeeper always on call yet never intrusive—and that would not be Anna. Anna Strunsky was too young, too independent, and had too great a claim on his emotions to keep his days in line. He needed a partner, a companion—not a passion—and he knew the perfect candidate: Bessie Maddern, Fred Jacobs's fiancée, who had been freed from her vows by Jacobs's death. He wrote a friend about his plans:

Sunday evening I opened transactions for a wife; by Monday evening had the affair well under way; and next Saturday morning I shall marry—a Bessie Maddern. Also on said Saturday, as soon as the thing is over with we jump out on our wheels for a three days' trip, and then back to work. . . . Divers deep considerations have led me to do this thing; but I shall be steadied and can be able to devote more time to my work. . . . Besides, my heart is large and I shall be a cleaner, wholesomer man because of a restraint being laid upon me in place of being free to drift wheresoever I listed.

How London informed Anna of his coming marriage is unclear, but however that message was delivered, her response must have been carefully reassuring because the day before the wedding he wrote her this letter:

Dear Anna—
How glad your letter has made me. It was rather sudden. I always do things that way. . . .
Am going away for several days. Will write you more fully on my return. Are you in the mood in the near future to take advantage of that invitation to Mrs. Stein extended to you and I? For a thousand reasons I think myself justified in making this marriage. It will not, however, interfere much with my old life or my life as I had planned it for the future.

As the year unfolded, the mechanics of London's daily life did become smoother. He would drift less, but in the end would achieve less control over his emotional life than he desired.

Other Stories of Interest

The Cyclopedic Review, March 1900
"The Degenerates," a comedy in four acts by Sydney Grundy with Mrs. Langtry was given at the Garden theatre, , , , This play when presented in London was violently assailed by the critics as "degenerate" indeed, both dramatically and morally. In New York the judgement seems to have been that, though cynical, it reflects truthfully enough the life of "high society."

The World (New York), March 8, 1900
Bomb Thrown in Paris
PARIS—A bomb was thrown yesterday through a window of the Paris residence of M. Alfred Picard, Commissioner-General of the Paris Exposition. It did not explode. A lady who saw the men light the fuse and who gave the alarm was attacked and severely handled by them.

The Washington Post, March 10, 1900
Ameer of Afghanistan States His Position Towards Russia
LONDON—The Ameer of Afghanistan has authorized his agent to publish the following statement: "I have come to the conclusion that Russia feared Afghanistan, as a war with the Afghans would mean a general rising of all Islam, which would spread through Russian Asia. Russia has not troops enough to combat such a rising. Her hold on the Mussulman countries she has conquered is insecure. They hate her and with ten times her power Russia could not fight Afghanistan and India successfully.

"The Afghans prefer death to slavery."

The New York Times, March 12, 1900
Preaching by Telephone
ELKHART, INDIANA—The Rev. Dr. E. H. Gwynne of the First Presbyterian Church preached to a number of his flock by telephone this evening and every word was as distinctly heard as though the listeners were present in the church.

A delicately constructed transmitter was placed on the pulpit. . . . The use of the invention was for the benefit of Francis Hoover, a helpless victim to rheumatism.

A crew mounting the great star that crowned the Palace of Electricity at the Paris Exposition. Panels of flint glass, held in place by gilded tubes, reflected light from fifty-seven-hundred incandescent lamps and six powerful arc lights. The star, which could be seen from all over the city, became a symbol of the Exposition.

CHAPTER FIVE

March–April

I

Mid-March, as the first American tourists began arriving in Paris, the Universal Exposition was well behind schedule. The French blamed the weather; it had been raining for weeks. The Americans blamed the inefficiency of French workmen. Whatever the reasons, with the opening just a month away, the streets were filled with cranes and debris. *Scientific American* reported "gawkers wading through quagmires of sticky whitish mud." Decapitated stone heads lay in a shed waiting to adorn buildings that were long overdue. On street corners along the Seine, waffle makers and map sellers were already jockeying for positions.

An entirely new city was fantastically rising on both banks of the river. The American writer Henry Adams wrote a friend that the Exposition was "a huge architectural Inferno of unfinished domes, minarets, Greek temples, and iron frames." Workmen were wiring the decorative star atop the Palace of Electricity, while in the Luminous Palace the crystal stairs were being moved into place. The Exposition promised to be a magnificent tribute to the nineteenth century and the progress of the world. Every civilized country—and some nations not considered to have achieved that status—had been invited to participate.

Along the Quai d'Orsay on the Left Bank the United States pavilion with its great dome and oversized eagle towered above the other foreign palaces. Americans were presenting over six thousand exhibits—the most powerful steam engines, the most modern electrical switches, the newest linotype machines, and telephone switchboards. Businessmen from Kansas City, Chicago, and San Francisco were setting up displays to hawk everything from tourism to processed meats.

American goods were being uncrated all over the city—at the Publishers Building, the Agricultural Annex, and the Forestry Building. Out in the park of Vincennes, beyond the city limits, a vast American workshop was being set up to demonstrate American tools and American machinery. Europeans were not surprised that the United States was presenting more exhibits at the Exposition than any nation save France. The English writer W. T. Stead noted that "the Americanization of the world," was well under way.

Half the motors on British streetcars had been made in America. All the government telephones in London came from the Western Electric Company in Chicago.

"The race for commercial supremacy" (Harper's Weekly, *June 2, 1900).*

In Germany, the American typewriter was now supreme. Over seven hundred of the most powerful steam engines in the world were being shipped out of Philadelphia for Europe and Russia, Africa and Asia. In Paris, Europeans were using cameras and film from Eastman Kodak, eating ice cream at imported American soda fountains, and indulging in American musical comedies and American-style cocktails.

In a book called *The Invaders,* Fred MacKenzie wrote about a day in the life of a mythical Englishman who rose from a bed made with New England sheets, shaved with a Yankee safety razor, pulled on Boston boots over socks from South Carolina, slipped a Waltham or Waterbury watch into his pocket, ate a breakfast that included bread from prairie flour, tinned oysters from Baltimore, along with a little Kansas City bacon. In the office, MacKenzie's Englishman used a Nebraskan swivel chair and a Michigan rolltop desk and signed his mail with an American pen.

The emergence of the United States as the most powerful commercial force in the world had not only caught Americans by surprise but stunned the Europeans. That the upstart nation of America had reached commercial supremacy in such a brief spate of years was attributed to American technical ingenuity, efficiency, and manufacturing skills. England was hiring American managers to upgrade their production systems. Albert, the Prince of Belgium, after a tour of the States told an American friend, "Alas, you will eat us all up."

Opposition to America's invasion was building in Berlin. The Kaiser had failed to stop the wave of Germans emigrating to the States and chafed when they returned home on visits, bringing with them American ways and American political ideas. His increasing dependence on American food—Germany could no longer feed her people—was extremely worrisome. There was talk in Berlin of forming a European union to blockade American commerce. The secretary of the German Industrial Union declared the time had come "for some Bismarck to rise and throttle the American peril."

In March, Germany shipped the most powerful dynamo in the world to Paris, a gigantic steam-driven machine, capable of producing 3,000 horsepower. Most Americans were too exuberant and proud to worry about German machines from the Siemens Corporation or the Krupps works. But Henry Adams would visit the Hall of Dynamos with his friend Professor Samuel Langley and find in that great German dynamo a profoundly disturbing symbol of the future.

In an essay called *The Dynamo and the Virgin,* Adams explained that from Langley's perspective "the dynamo was but an ingenious channel for conveying somewhere the heat latent in a few tons of poor coal hidden in a dirty engine house carefully kept out of sight," but from Adams's perspective "the dynamo became a symbol of infinity." He was drawn back to the hall again and again. "The planet itself seemed less impressive, in its old-fashioned, deliberate, annual or daily revolution, than this huge wheel, revolving within arm's length at some vertiginous speed, and barely murmuring. . . . Before the end, one began to pray to it." He had come to believe that "man had translated himself into a new universe which had no common scale of measurement with the old."

Months later a writer in *The Washington Post,* speculating on the awesome forces of the future, had a similar epiphany. "There will be a universal cry for power. More power. We know already that power is latent in the sun's rays and is dispensed with wanton extravagance. . . . It is more than light, more than heat, more than electricity. It is waiting for the genius that will triumphantly seize it."

The article went on to say: "When all that is to be learned about electricity is in the human ken . . . its development in warfare might easily bring the world to a point where mankind would stand aghast at the wholesale destruction of human lives and thus compel universal peace."

II

Mid-March, in Washington, D.C., in her studio on V Street, surrounded by a garden barely coming into bloom, Frances Benjamin Johnston—her mother still called her Fannie—was working in her laboratory on a series of platinum prints for the Exposition. Johnston, one of the most successful photographers in the country, was a proper Victorian and member of the Daughters of the American Revolution. She traveled with her mother or Aunt Nin, moving in and out of diplomatic receptions with a grace born of generations of assurance.

But she was also a bohemian with a wicked sense of humor and a taste for bourbon. A small woman, with a nose that went in too many directions and an overprim mouth, she used her camera to reveal a playfulness her face denied.

In a self-portrait she posed with her skirts above her knees, a ciga-

Frances Benjamin Johnston, clowning in this self-portrait as a "new woman," with a cigarette in one hand, a beer stein in the other, and photographs of men said to be admirers carefully lined up on her mantel.

Aboard Admiral Dewey's flagship Olympia, *Frances Benjamin Johnston made a series of candid photographs of the crew. Johnston began her career as a photojournalist and had a talent for catching the informal moment.*

rette in one hand and a beer stein in the other. As the leader of a pack of artists and writers who called themselves "The Push," she documented their parties and informal teas and posed her friend, artist Mills Thompson, in white gauze with flower branches around his head. Sent to intercept Admiral George Dewey as he steamed home following his great victory at Manila Bay, Frances had photographed the admiral with all the dignity he expected and then went down to a lower deck where she photographed young sailors dancing together in each other's arms.

Johnston had a talent for putting celebrities at ease, catching presidents and their wives in unguarded moments. In the spring of 1900 she had more work than she could handle. Her friend Ida Tarbell, managing editor at *McClure's*, needed a photograph of the handsome and much admired Secretary of State John Hay, and Lord Pauncefote, the ambassador from Great Britain, wanted Johnston to photograph the wedding of his daughter. But the assignment dominating Frances's mind that spring was of a very different nature.

Since early December she had been commuting by coach and steamer down to Hampton, Virginia, setting up her cameras at an old and well-respected black college, Hampton Institute. She had been commissioned by Thomas J. Calloway, the special agent in charge of the "Negro Exhibit" in Paris, to illustrate progress in African-American life over the years since the Civil War.

By spring she had about one hundred and fifty photographs of young black Americans studying art and science and music and the cathedral towns of Europe. She was now collecting material for picture stories—an image of elderly folks in a run-down shack would be juxtaposed with a photograph of a Hampton graduate and his family in a well-appointed dining room. Barefoot children pumping water in an ill-kempt yard would be shown in contrast with a photograph of starched and prosperous youngsters.

The series was still incomplete when Calloway wrote from Paris to say he thought the photographs were the finest in the exhibit. Frances's studio photographs that spring were strong and stylish and the wedding pictures were lovely, but her work at Hampton was remarkable. She was producing a portrait of a time and of a people, young, dark-skinned Americans, clear-eyed and hopeful. Seen through the prism of that year the photographs would become a heartbreaking record of hope deferred.

And then Wednesday afternoons in her cluttered studio with its pale green walls and tigerskin rug, the collection of shawls and curios, and photographs said to be of her rejected suitors, Frances would continue to hold her weekly salons for artists and writers, journalists and diplomats. Ida Tarbell promised to drop by for a mint julep. Spring would pass quickly. Johnston was booked straight through— and then she, too, would be off to Paris.

III

By April, the daffodils were blooming in the park land facing the White House, and down by the water's edge there were thousands of iris. The rituals of spring had resumed—winter carriages and sleighs sent off to be refurbished, lap robes packed away. At the Andrew Joyce Carriage Company customers were picking up their victorias. New models of these small open carriages were selling for $8.50. Better to have the old ones repainted and reupholstered. At the Capitol, where the hard winter had taken a toll, carpenters were repairing the leaky roof over the press gallery, which had been so bothersome for months.

On every pleasant day Mlle Marguerite Cassini, the beautiful young "niece" of the Russian ambassador, could be seen driving her new steam phaeton. It was quite like Marguerite to own her own automachine. In the warming sun, Washington society was taking to the streets. At noon, Secretary of State John Hay could be seen hurrying across Lafayette Square to his mansion opposite the White House for a frugal lunch of buttermilk and hoecake. Hay, literate and charming, had recently bought a Botticelli and was said to lie awake nights fearing it might warp.

Nearly every afternoon, a squad of Supreme Court justices walked down the south side of Pennsylvania Avenue, blocking traffic. On occasion, Justice John Marshall Harlan, the most liberal member of the Court and the most athletic, appeared in full golf costume. For Harlan, golf was not a sport but an obsession. President McKinley, too, was taking his daily constitution. Shoulders back, head high, arms swinging at his side, journalist William Allen White said the president looked as though he "was destined for a statue in the park, and was practicing the pose for it."

From McKinley's perspective things were going pretty well, except for the damnable war. Four soldiers from Massachusetts had been captured by guerrillas and tortured to death, the anti-imperialists were in an uproar, and the newspapers never seemed to let up. But the president was hoping that with General Arthur MacArthur taking over the command, the war would quiet down before the fall elections.

As the weather softened, the papers reported that the popular young poet Paul Laurence Dunbar had returned to the capital from the mountains of Colorado. Dunbar was in rare spirits that spring. There was enough money, at least for the moment; his wife Alice and mother Matilda were at ease with each other; and his consumption seemed to be under control. He was coughing less and the hemorrhaging had stopped. The mountain air had proved better for his lungs than his own home remedy—a bedtime snack of raw onion with salt and a bottle of beer.

The Dunbars settled into their home on Spruce Street, in what was known as "the camp," a black settlement on the edge of Howard University. The pleasant house was now decorated with Navajo blankets and rug, and Pueblo pottery Paul had bought out west. A delicate man of enormous grace and charm, in 1900 he was one of the best known African Americans in the country and one of America's most popular poets. His seventh book had just been published, the eighth was under way, and Alice was handling more requests for reading engagements than Paul had breath to fill.

Dunbar was a curious literary figure with a devoted following on both sides of the color line. He wrote in what amounted to two distinct languages, black dialect and classic white English. When he was still a regional poet skirting the edge of both obscurity and hunger, living with his mother in Dayton, Ohio, many of his readers had no idea whether he was white or black.

A doctor had written to say, "I learned that in a biblical sense, God Almighty had placed the stamp of Cain upon you, or in other words, your skin is black. Enclosed a check for five dollars (send me the number of poems that this amount will buy)." In 1896, when he was invited by a young classics professor at Wilberforce University to "come over . . . and read to us," the professor, W.E.B. Du Bois, who was familiar with Paul's work, "was astonished to find that he was a Negro."

A few months later William Dean Howells, the most influential literary critic in the country, devoted an entire column in *Harper's Weekly* to Dunbar's writing. "The world is too old now," Howells wrote, "and I find myself too much of its mood, to care for the work of a poet because he is black, because his father and mother were slaves, because he was, before and after he began to write poems, an elevator-boy. These facts

Paul Laurence Dunbar in his home in Washington, D.C. On the walls of his study are posters for his lectures and portraits of fellow writers, along with drawings by E. W. Kemble, who had illustrated several of Dunbar's books and magazine articles.

would certainly attract me to him as a man, but when it came to literary art, I must judge it irrespective of these facts, and enjoy or endure it for what it was in itself.

"Still it will legitimately interest those who like to know . . . the sources, of things, to learn that the father and mother of the first poet of his race in our language were negroes without admixture of white blood. In more than one piece he has produced a work of art." The review appeared on the morning of Paul's twenty-fourth birthday. Within days he had signed with a New York publisher, Dodd, Mead, received a $400 advance, and was being handled by the lecture bureau that represented Mark Twain.

Dubbed by the press the Black Robert Burns, Dunbar was now an international celebrity, with admirers turning up uninvited at his door. It was said that he walked about at home with a black chicken on his shoulder, probably not true, and that when he had a few drinks he would break into a war dance, which was more likely. In the spring of 1900 Paul was at the top of his form—except for his health. Tuberculosis was a pernicious disease without any cure; his mother watched him like a hawk, arguing with Alice over his care. His coughing spells had returned and he was forced to cut back on the readings he had always found such fun.

He brought to those engagements a musical bluesy sensibility, interacting with the audience, calling on them to participate, to join him in the choruses of his better-known poems:

Life

A crust of bread and a corner to sleep in,
A minute to smile and an hour to weep in,
A pint of joy to a peck of trouble,
And never a laugh but the moans come
double;
And that is life!

. . . And never a laugh but the moans come double. . . . And that is life!

Dunbar's writing was easygoing but often had an edge that black audiences identified with. White audiences left his concerts feeling they had eavesdropped on a world they barely knew:

We wear the mask that grins and lies
It hides our cheeks and shades our eyes . . .

In an increasingly segregated country, Paul Laurence Dunbar was one of a small group of Americans moving back and forth across the color line. From his perspective it was a logical way to live. He had grown up moving between the world of his parents, both former slaves, and Dayton's almost all-white public schools. At home he had absorbed tales of plantation life, told and retold in black southern talk, and in school he had read Shelley and Keats, Tennyson and Poe, and learned to speak and write in traditional Western cadence. His best friend was an outgoing fellow named Orville Wright. The boys appeared together in their class photograph, and at graduation marched down the aisle to an anthem Dunbar had written.

Critics were forever trying to wedge Paul into some tidy cultural niche, but he would have none of it. He defined himself as a cultural hybrid—a black man, an American, and a writer. Others might be confused about his identity, but Dunbar was not. On a scrap of paper found after his death he had written: "It is one of the peculiar phases of Anglo-Saxon conceit to refuse to believe that every black man does not want to be white."

In Washington, the Dunbars lived primarily within a large and congenial black community. Looking at photo stories of the city that year, one would assume the capital was an all-white town, except of course for the inevitable doormen, coachmen, and the black woman with a basket on her head. But there were ninety thousand African Americans living in Washington by 1900, and a large and prosperous middle class.

Black men and women were working for all the government agencies; Paul had worked as an assistant in the Library of Congress when he first came to town. In an essay published in *Harper's Weekly* in January, he had written about the postwar generation of dark-skinned doctors and lawyers and members of the board of trade and government clerks, "smoking as good a cigar as an Eastern Congressman." There were good schools and social clubs, churches and Howard University, and a gossipy black paper called *The Washington Bee*.

But for black Americans the capital was also a city of unmet promises, of dismal back alleys tourists never saw, jammed with the poor, the failed, and the damaged—southern rural people ill-fit for city life. The crime rate was up, the jails overfilled. And racial snubs, rudeness, and condescension were as much a part of the black experience here as anywhere else. Dunbar didn't mention it—he didn't have to, it was such a part of daily life. "Taking it all in all," he wrote, "Negro life in Washington is a promise rather than a fulfillment."

Those Americans, like Paul's parents, who had emerged from slavery with such a profound sense of hope, found themselves and their children trapped in a hostile and ever-narrowing world. In the thirty-five years since emancipation there had been progress to be sure, 60 percent of black children were now in school, 20 percent of black Americans owned their own homes, and there were five thousand businessmen, grocers, barbers, plumbers, and real estate men.

Dunbar's old friend W.E.B. Du Bois, now a professor of sociology at Atlanta University, was producing the first extended analysis of African-American life, and his findings were not reassuring. Of the nine million black people in the country, Du Bois wrote, most were "still serfs bound to the soil or house servants." Moving up the American ladder was far more difficult than black Americans had hoped. Novelist Sutton E. Griggs wrote of the torment and frustrations of a southern black man who "would have made an excellent salesman, clerk, cashier, telegraph operator, conductor—but the color of his skin shut the doors so tight that he could not even peep in."

In the South, where 90 percent of black Americans still lived, not only were most white-collar jobs off limits, but an entire legal system was being constructed to isolate black

Alice Ruth Moore, a young writer and poet from New Orleans, was twenty when her first book was published, in 1895. Her work caught Dunbar's attention and he wrote her a fan letter. The couple married in 1898. Alice Dunbar's writing was deliberately "raceless." She objected to those who insisted on wedging "the Negro problem" into their stories and argued with her husband over his use of dialect.

Americans from the mainstream of public life. Trains, trolleys, hotels, schools were being segregated by a growing and intricate body of law. Casual contact between the races was in some ways more limited than it had been in the days of slavery. Possibilities for advancement were being cut off in every direction.

In Mississippi, the state legislature was proposing to divide school funds in proportion to the real estate taxes paid in the white and black districts, all but guaranteeing that black school systems would remain penniless. T. Thomas Fortune, the black newspaper publisher in New York City, argued it would be "vastly cheaper to build schoolhouses than jails." Du Bois wrote: "Race antagonism can only be stopped by intelligence. It is dangerous to wait, it is foolish to hesitate. Let the nation immediately give generous aid to southern common school education."

But Du Bois was not hopeful. The most sensible suggestions were rejected with such contempt, and even hatred, that retaining one's equilibrium was proving difficult. After receiving a Harvard Ph.D., Du Bois had hoped to carve out a quiet academic life for himself and for his wife, Nina, but was now at the center of a

profound American controversy: how to move a nation hip-deep in racism to fulfill its most basic promise—justice for all. He was being urged to join Booker T. Washington, the most powerful black leader in the country, at Tuskegee Institute but was uncertain about the effectiveness of Booker T.'s philosophy.

Washington was urging his followers to pull themselves up by their bootstraps and practice patience. He would not publicly press for voting rights or social equality. He put his faith in vocational training, convinced that in the long run only economic success would lead to acceptance. The Reverend J. A. Jones, in Chattanooga, Tennessee, concurred: "When the Negro opens a first-class drugstore just across the street from the white man's . . . and every other form of business, prejudice will take wings." In time the marketplace would resolve the race problem. But everything in Du Bois's own experience argued against such reasoning.

Just the year before he'd been witness to a ghastly incident. A mob of two thousand people had assembled in Atlanta for the lynching of Sam Hose, accused of killing his employer in an argument over money. After Hose was tortured and burned at the stake, newspapers reported men, women, and children fighting over pieces of his charred flesh. Du Bois had seen Sam Hose's blackened knucklebones on display in the local drugstore. Historian David Levering Lewis writes, "Numbed by the horror Du Bois turned away from his work. From that moment forward he recognized that 'one could not be a calm, cool and detached [social] scientist while Negroes were lynched, murdered and starved."

In the spring of 1900, Du Bois was torn. He could leave Atlanta with all its ugliness and tension for a well-paying position at Tuskegee Institute, or stay in the city and ally himself with the more radical forces fighting for black rights. In an article in the *Atlantic Monthly* a few years back, he had asked, "What, after all, am I? Am I an American or am I a Negro? Can I be both? Or is it my duty to cease to be a Negro as soon as possible and be an American? If I strive as a Negro, am I not perpetuating the very cleft that threatens and separates black and white in America?" As the cleft widened, conciliation did not seem possible.

The capricious nature of racism was exhausting. It was not only those searing and horrific events—and there were more of those than many psyches could stand—but it was managing the most ordinary everyday encounters, to measure one's every gesture by another man's sensibility: to smile or not to smile, to make eye contact, to step aside or walk apace or modulate one's voice. Du Bois wrote with weariness, "In a world where it means so much to take a man by the hand and sit beside him, to look frankly into his eyes . . . in a world where a social cigar or a cup of tea together means more than legislative halls and magazine articles and speeches—one can imagine the consequences of the almost utter absences of such amenities between estranged races."

In 1900 those who daily banged up against the race wall were learning to walk the walk and wear the smile and mask their eyes. They bought Ozonized Ox Marrow, the Magnetic Comb to straighten their "Knotty, Nappy, Kinky Hair," and Imperial Whitener to bleach their skin—*every bottle guaranteed*. But there was not an ounce of compromise in Will Du Bois. He carried his independence in the set of his shoulders and the arc of his cane. He would reject Booker T.'s offer.

Like Frances Benjamin Johnston, Du Bois had also been asked by Thomas Calloway to contribute material to the Negro Exhibit in Paris. Calloway was an old college friend from Fisk; together they had waited table and sung in a glee club at a summer resort on Lake Minnetonka, Minnesota. Now, at Calloway's request, Du Bois had embarked on assembling a "brief but comprehensive history of the Negro people," pulling together a collection of books by black writers and military histories on black soldiers going back to the Revolutionary War.

In February, he had agreed to attend a meeting in Savannah, Georgia, on Exposition business. He boarded a night train in Atlanta, wearing his standard conservative three-piece suit. A small and quiet man with an elegant manner, he requested a berth in a sleeping car but was forced instead to spend the night sitting in the filthy, crowded, soot-covered "colored" car in back of the engine. Du Bois argued with the conductor, a train man, and a porter that the Jim Crow laws did not apply to interstate trains. The legal niceties of his argument were not heard. Later, he would file a formal protest but that, too, would come to naught.

He arrived in Savannah the following morning tired and grimy and raging at the railroad, and then proceeded to work on an exhibit heralding the progress of black citizens in America.

IV

That the opening of the Paris Universal Exposition went off on schedule was nothing short of a miracle. Overnight, three regiments of French infantry and eleven companies of engineers had worked alongside electricians, carpenters, and gardeners to transform the Champs de Mars from a wasteland of mud and rubbish into lawns and carefully sculpted flower beds. The streets remained blocked by debris, and traffic arrangements were so inadequate that hundreds of vehicles were simply abandoned while guests made their way to the ceremonies on foot. Few seemed to care—the weather had turned unusually warm and pleasant.

When the president of France, accompanied by his entourage, arrived at the great Salles des Fêtes, an honor guard was waiting at attention, horse plumes streaming from their shining helmets. The papers noted that most Parisians had stayed home, but diplomats and tourists—250,000 in all—lined the Seine. Not since Victoria's jubilee or the Czar's coronation had there been such an elaborate assemblage. Hungarian magnates arrived in magnificent velvet *dolmans* wearing fur toques topped by waving aigrettes. There were Arab sheiks in robes, and Cossacks with bandoliers across their chests, and more American flags flying in the city than those of any other country.

The minister of commerce, M. Millerand, overwhelmed by the occasion, described "the victorious march of the human soul." He spoke of humanity leaping "towards that luminous and serene region where, one day, will be realized the ideal . . . of the power of justice and good." The next day the Berlin paper *Deutsche Tageszeitung* dismissed Millerand's empty words. The newspaper saw no hope that the twentieth century would be any more peaceful than the nineteenth, "for international competition is growing more and more keen and is drowning every other consideration."

But cranky comments about the future did not deter enthusiastic Americans. Seventy-five thousand people, including Frances Benjamin Johnston and her mother, Professor W.E.B. Du Bois, and John Philip Sousa, would be heading for Paris.

Crowds jam the United States Pavilion for a John Philip Sousa concert at the opening of the Paris Exposition. The building offered a wide variety of amenities for the American businessman. In addition to typewriters, stenographers, telegraph and postal stations, and all the ice water an American could wish for, every afternoon between four and six, one could get the latest stock quotations.

Other Stories of Interest

The New York Times, April 5, 1900
Assassin Fires at Prince of Wales

BRUSSELS, April 4—Just as the Prince of Wales' train, bearing him to Copenhagen for the purpose of attending the celebration of King Christian's birthday, was putting out of the Northern Station, a sixteen-year-old tinsmith named Sipido sprang upon the footboard of the carriage and fired two shots through the window at the Prince. Neither shot took effect.

Sipido was immediately arrested, and when examined by the railroad officials . . . his pockets were found to be full of Anarchistic literature. He subsequently said he wanted to kill the Prince of Wales, "because he caused thousands of men to be slaughtered in South Africa."

In London, one high official remarked: "That settles the question of the Prince of Wales' visit to the Paris Exposition."

The Washington Post, April 5, 1900
Irish Glad to See Her, The Queen Drives Through a Gauntlet of Enthusiasm

DUBLIN, April 4—Queen Victoria's reception in Dublin today was devoid of the slightest jarring note. It is understood that the Queen expressed herself as wonderfully pleased. . . . Dublin went wild with delight. . . . Not one black flag or disloyal motto marked the line of march and the popular enthusiasm buried all political feeling.

On the city side of the gate were the lord mayor and council in their scarlet robes, the mace bearer, in blue and silver, and several hundred of the best-known Irish. . . . The Royal Inniskilling Fusiliers lined the road as a guard of honor.

Shortly before the coming of the Queen, the pursuivant-at-arms, wearing a gorgeous cape of royal heraldry, galloped up to the lord mayor and asked permission for the entrance of the Queen.

Then from the ramparts of the gate came a fanfare of trumpets. The Queen was in sight. Out upon a scarlet cloth, laid Raleigh-like upon the muddy road, stepped the lord mayor and the corporation, their robes glowing in the bright sunshine. . . .

Finally amid an almost perfect silence save for cries of "God Save the Queen," came the Queen herself. . . . Bands broke loose, men cheered and sang bareheaded, and the women waved their handkerchiefs and struggled to get a better view, many of them weeping.

Princess Christian took a prominent part in the ceremony, helping the Queen to take the sword, keys, and casket containing the address, for despite her ability to go through these functions, it was evident that this tiny old lady of eighty was really very frail and weak.

The Chicago Daily Tribune,
April 12, 1900
First Automobile Race

NEW YORK—The first automobile race ever run in America was contested today on the Merrick road from Springfield to Babylon, twenty-five miles out and back. The race was under the auspices of the Automobile Club of America. . . .

Nine machines . . . started, and all but two finished. The wind was with the contestants on the outward trip and dead against them on the return. The first seventeen miles was good going, but there came a stretch of seven miles of sandy road into Babylon, which had to be passed over twice. This gave many of the contestants a lot of trouble.

A. L. Riker won the contest, going fifty miles in 2:03:30. . . . The electric machine proved better than the others, as it made about as good time against the strong breeze as with it. . . . Riker was accompanied by Mr. A. H. Whitney. At the finish both gentlemen displayed every evidence of having gone through a terribly trying experience, the eyeballs being bloodshot. Both were terribly nervous from the strain.

Theodore Roosevelt playing with his children on the lawn at Sagamore Hill, Long Island. A firm believer in the strenuous life, TR encouraged his son Ted to box, believing the boy could be as "virtuous as he wished if only he was prepared to fight."

CHAPTER SIX

April

I

In April, in the great rambling governor's mansion on Eagle Street in Albany, New York, Theodore Roosevelt was delighting in the role of "vice-mother." He wrote a friend that he was playing bear with five-year-old Archie, was reading Hereward the Wake to the four older children, "while Quentin the two-year-old rides piggyback and has me sing 'Trippe-Troppa-Tronjes'—the only Dutch I know, and that by inheritance, not acquisition." His wife, Edith, had gone off to Cuba on a vacation with her sister; she wanted to see for herself the scenes of her husband's wartime triumphs.

The children, ostensibly left in the care of several nurses, had shanghaied their father, who was always good for a game of blindman's bluff or hide-and-seek. Particularly if he could be "It." "You must always remember," said a British ambassador, "that [Roosevelt] is about six." The governor had made some changes in the stuffy old Executive Mansion. The third-floor billiard room was now a gymnasium, and space in the cellar had been set aside for the family animals. The Roosevelt children kept rabbits, squirrels, a raccoon, an opossum, and twenty-one guinea pigs, including one called Father O'Grady, who TR said had belied his name by producing a large family.

For the governor, it would have been a lovely spring if not for the continuing unpleasantness with Senator Thomas C. Platt, the powerful boss of New York's Republican party. On April 10, *The New York Times* reported that Platt was trying to stop Roosevelt from running for another term as governor of New York by maneuvering him into the vice presidency. Platt wanted no more of TR. Roosevelt had been threatening to upend the exquisite relationship between the Republican party and New York's business interests. He had proposed a tax on corporations that were doing business with the state; had raised expectations among local labor leaders by supporting the eight-hour workday for state employees; and had directly challenged the Republican leader by speaking out on the need to control the trusts.

Platt had warned TR of the solemn right for "a man to run his own business in his own way, with due respect of course to the Ten Commandments and the Penal Code." TR had taken only modest heed. In a speech before the New York legislature he had started off well enough: "The machinery of modern business is so vast, and complicated, that caution must be exercised in introducing radical changes." But then he went on to add that "very many of the antitrust laws which have made their appearance on the statute books in recent years have been almost or absolutely ineffective. . . . To say that the present system of haphazard license and lack of supervision and regulation is the best possible, is absurd. . . . The man who by swindling or wrongdoing acquires great wealth for himself at the expense of his fellow, stands as low morally as any predatory medieval nobleman. . . . Any law which will enable the community to punish him either by taking away his great wealth or by imprisonment should be welcome."

Early in the year Platt had let word to party leaders that in the end TR would inevitably have to accept the vice presidency. Now he went further, declaring that "the governor will not be renominated for his present office." Privately he said he wanted the bastard out of the state. Roosevelt had never expected Platt to take such an arbitrary position. At best, the vice presidency was a boring job, frustrating and expensive. It called for endless entertaining, and with the children growing up and heading off to private schools, the Roosevelts were worried about money. At worst the office was a dead end, a graveyard for those with presidential ambitions.

TR hoped to run for reelection in the fall of 1900, and then as governor of New York continue to build momentum for the future. The summer before,

William Allen White had written: "There is no man in America today whose personality is rooted deeper in the hearts of the people than Theodore Roosevelt. . . . He is more than a presidential possibility in 1904, he is a presidential probability. . . . He is the coming American of the twentieth century." But now, Platt was trying to block him from the gubernatorial job and no one knew whether McKinley would even accept Roosevelt as a running mate.

In 1901, TR could find himself without a job.

11

In New York City's Central Park that April, while small boys continued sailing their miniature yachts and well-watched schoolgirls were sketching at the Lily Pond, everyone was a bit cautious. Foul-mouthed ruffians on rollerskates had been gathering on the bridges over the bridle path, throwing stones at riders and racing down embankments to frighten the horses. Several people had been hurt, and there were no police in sight. The Grey Coats, the old park police, adept at handling runaways, who knew most of the regular riders by sight and many by name, had been replaced by men who knew nothing about horses and spent their days lazing on benches off the beaten path.

For an ambitious policeman, being assigned to the park was like being sent to Siberia. The best a man could hope for was a hand-knit cap in winter or an envelope at Christmas passed on by someone's coachman. And many a policeman these days was making good money protecting illegal gambling dens throughout the city. Never had there been closer collaboration between the police and the gambling syndicate. *The New York Times* estimated that over three million dollars a year was being passed illicitly from the gamblers to the police and other city officials. An efficient shadow commission made up of two state senators, a man from the city, and the head of the poolroom syndicate met weekly in an apartment on West 47th Street to process new "applications."

To open a gambling parlor of any size, proprietors were required to apply in person at their local precinct. The $300 initiation fee—paid directly to the captain—was returnable in the unlikely event the application was denied. Monthly charges could run as high as a thousand dollars, but owners were guaranteed all the cooperation they could wish for. In March, when a well-known establishment on 13th Street moved from one block to another, attendants were seen carrying dismantled roulette wheels and green-baize-covered poker tables openly through the streets.

Anthony Comstock was being driven to distraction. Every time he organized a raid, the word was mysteriously passed on before the vice squad could arrive. He accused the police of tipping off the parlors, but a friendly magistrate dismissed the charges. A few years earlier when Theodore Roosevelt had been a police commissioner the gambling trust had found the atmosphere a bit more dicey. TR had been irritatingly incorruptible. Now, as governor, he kept talking about the need for reform in the city, but the gamblers could not be touched by the governor, the mayor, or even Comstock. Their future lay squarely with Richard Croker, the white-bearded pasha of Tammany Hall.

Little went on in New York without Croker's permission: every city contract, every nomination from alderman to mayor was said to be controlled by the Tammany chieftain. Not a bridge or street or sewer could be repaired, not a brick laid or a street lamp replaced without his permission. In the financial capital of America, Tammany Hall and Croker were accepted as the cost for doing business. Corruption was as much a part of city life as the rain of cinders from the elevated trains.

Croker lived and held court at the posh Democratic Club on Fifth Avenue, where, in well-appointed rooms with fat leather furniture he had selected himself, he met with magistrates, contractors, lawyers, and police captains. As he explained to a reporter one day: "There's a mayor and a council and judges—a hundred men to deal with . . . and you can't do business with a lot of officials, who check and cross one another and who come and go. . . . A business man wants to do business with one man."

The rise of Richard Croker from a penniless immigrant to party leader with kingly powers was the story of nineteenth-century urban politics. There had been bosses before him in this and other cities, and he was following a well-established path. He had arrived in New York midcentury from County Cork, a strong young man, a blacksmith by trade but without contacts or family. At the local Democratic clubhouse he had found camaraderie and education in what was to become his life's calling. White wrote that Tammany had taught him "to be kind to those in trouble, to look after the sick in the tenements, to see that the widows had food and fuel and that the men had jobs."

There was a well-developed system to convert "favors" to the poor—hand-outs, jobs, money, legal help—into the largest number of votes. Croker had learned to bring out the required number of votes: "Precinct captains may go far if necessary—may, in an emergency tip-toe right up to the door of the penitentiary and trust to the efforts of the organization to pull them back by the coattails." By 1900, as White pointed out, the kingdom of Richard Croker was "the kingdom of loot." When pressed by a reporter, he denied receiving even a dollar from the landlord of a poolroom or a house of ill fame, and it was likely true. But if he didn't personally benefit from illicit dealings, his party did.

In his youth Croker had been taught that "vice was a source of revenue, revenue was the sinew in the arm of political victory, and political victory was the chief end of man." That was the catechism he embraced when he was young and honored to this day, but now he was considering placing caution ahead of money. Circumstance had made Croker a key player in the coming presidential election. New York with its huge bundle of electoral votes was a swing state; it could go either way. If Richard Croker could bring out a large enough Democratic major-ity in the city, the party might carry the state—and with the state, go on to carry the nation. It was within the realm of the possible that in November Croker could emerge from the election as the architect of a Democratic victory and then, who knows, perhaps go on to become the ambassador to the Court of St. James.

With *The New York Times* hammering away at the "City's Record of Shame," and the possibility that the gambling scandal might widen and implicate them all, Richard Croker elected to play it safe. Word was passed to the chief of the pool-room syndicate, and within hours every gambling house in New York City folded. Gamblers of all description, from the poorly clad writers of policy slips to the bejeweled owners of grand establishments, were out of business, sacrificed on the altar of Richard Croker's greater ambitions.

III

New York was always a walking city, and with the coming of nice weather the streets were endlessly entertaining. In the financial district the peddlers were out in force—the suspender man with his basket of braces, the oyster hawkers, the women grinding fresh horseradish to order, selling pickled peppers and onions, the herb man and pretzel man, and the ice-cream vendor with his frozen concoction of doubtful composition. Young men from Wall Street with more money than they knew what to do with were buying all the latest mechanical monsters—squeaking frogs and coiling snakes and perambulating spiders.

Bloomingdale's at 59th Street and Third Avenue was featuring "Ladies' Bicycle and Bowling Skirts"—easily four inches off the ground—and in the store's fancy food department there were asparagus from California. Surely New York was the land of desire, the consumer paradise of the Western Hemisphere. There was meat from the Plains, oranges from Florida, grapes from California, dates from Syria, caviar from Russia, and, for Easter, barrels full of lilies just arrived from Bermuda.

On Fifth Avenue, men and women of what was called the leisure class were studying the shops and studying each other. The success of a walk could be measured by the briefest encounter, a meeting of eyes, the slightest bow of the head. Eighteen-year-old Stella Simm went home from her walk and wrote in a small gray-green linen diary that on the way to the dressmaker she "saw Algy and he saw me." That was all and that was enough. The meeting was accidental and it was not. Both Stella and Algy were steered by some inner compass to elect the same streets, attend the same theaters. They would meet again, of that there was no doubt.

The contact, fragile as it was, reflected traditions handed down over generations. Stella understood, as every well-bred, flirty eighteen-year-old woman knew, that even the most modest eye contact had to be confined to fellows from the right set. Given her background, the odds were good that Algy, too, came from a German-Jewish family. In the flickering of their eyes was a recognition that they both accepted the same rules of conduct that Stella would pass on to her own daughter, and then her daughter's daughters.

Among the privileged of New York, those who took for granted the existence of the coachmen, the chambermaids, the cook, the nurse, the woman who came in to wash your hair, the seamstress who appeared to keep your clothes in order also took for granted their membership in the particular social circle in which they had been born, and in all probability in which they would die. That it all began with race, religion, and ethnic background was also taken for granted.

What gave Stella an edge, beyond her good humor and flaming red hair, or that she had learned French and German and fine embroidery, played the piano, and was a member of the Barnard basketball team without attending Barnard, was that her parents had been born in America. Her grandfather, to be sure, identified himself as an Israelite, but he had also been a pioneer, a founder of Des Moines, Iowa, and was now a man of culture and means. However, that did not buy the family passage from one social world to another. Only the richest made their own rules, and for all of William Kraus's well-being, he had made his money in trade.

Anglo-Saxons seldom mixed with Catholics or Jews. August Belmont was born a Jew and became an Episcopalian, but he was also one of the richest men in the country. For the most part it was each to his own. Old money looked down on new, the Roosevelts condescended to the Vanderbilts, the very rich kept apart from the just rich, the upper-middle class and the professional class held off the middle-middle and lower-middle classes. The working class was distinguished from the poor and from those wretches who thrashed at the bottom of the social heap. But the social lines were refined even further. When a woman in Stella's family proposed to marry a Jew of Russian descent, her mother declared, "We don't bow to those people," and threatened not to attend the wedding.

Class had its ways—its dress and posture, pitch of voice, and passwords. In Stella's family one did not eat garlic or use one's hands in speaking or allow one's voice to rise, as the "others" did. Each group had its own signs of distinction. The hieroglyphics of class could be deciphered by the freshness of a hem, the clasp on a bag, the quality of a button on a woman's boot. Among those born with "standing," a mysterious condition, there was a sense that privilege and superiority were tightly bound.

In 1899, an angry young economist, Thorstein Veblen, published a controversial and cantankerous book called *The Theory of the Leisure Class*. Veblen wrote: "Much of the charm that invests the patent-leather shoe, the stainless linen, the lustrous cylindrical hat, and the walking stick . . . comes of their pointedly suggesting that the wearer cannot when so attired bear a hand in any employment that is directly and immediately of any human use. Elegant dress serves its purpose of elegance not only that it is expensive, but also because it is the insignia of leisure." It was Veblen who coined the term "conspicuous consumption."

Stella had a distant relative who had owned three ermine coats before she was eighteen, but in 1900 that was penny-ante excess. In April, William K. Vanderbilt, to assuage his wife's sudden yearning for jewels, was reported to have ordered a huge diamond rose with a yellow diamond center, similar to one she had seen worn by an Austrian duchess in Nice. The brooch was said to cost more than any ornament ordered by a husband for his wife, with the possible exception of the gold armband the German Kaiser had given to his empress, which contained 253 diamonds.

Great and ostentatious wealth was a relatively new phenomenon in America. At midcentury there had only been nineteen millionaires in the entire country, and they tended to live relatively reserved lives. But during the Civil War and in the years that followed the club of millionaires greatly expanded, and by the 1890s there were more than four thousand. Elaborate palaces were built along Fifth Avenue, rivaling the great homes of Europe. There were French châteaux, Italian villas and Renaissance palazzos, and architectural concoctions that defied definition.

The drawing room in Edward Lauterbach's residence at 2 East 78th Street was a proper setting for an ambitious lawyer living not too far from Billionaires' Row. Because heating was no longer a problem in 1900, public rooms were grouped so that when the drapes in the wide doorways were pulled back, the eye could behold two or three rooms at a glance.

In New York, on an evening when the front doors of one of the great mansions were flung wide and thick crimson carpets were stretched across the sidewalk, passersby caught sight of flunkies dressed in court costume and of halls grander than any in a museum. A French writer of the time noted, "On the floors of halls there are too many precious Persian and Oriental rugs." In the salons "too many tapestries, too many paintings. . . . The guest chambers have too many bibelots, too much rare furniture, and on the lunch table there are too many flowers, too many plants, too much crystal, too much silver."

There was endless fascination with those who had too much. The women's magazines featured articles about the armies of servants required to run a great house, and the guidebooks needed to lead the uninitiated into the arcane world of ladies' maids and chambermaids, parlormaids and valets, butlers and footmen, chefs and second cooks, and waitresses, scullery maids, and nannies to replace the nannies on their days off. It was said there was nothing worse than not knowing who to ask to wash the dog or dress one's hair or clean the jewelry. Women who had married into wealth without the proper training ran the risk of being snubbed by their own servants.

Those born to money understood the requirements of a palatial home; they knew the need to keep a supply of suits of livery in varied sizes for the extra hands hired to assist at large parties. They had learned along with their alphabets how to distinguish between an oyster fork, a fish fork, a luncheon fork, a dinner fork, a serving fork, or a fork used to skewer pickles. They knew how to modulate the voice when issuing an order, how to plan a dinner for two hundred, how to make small talk without ever raising a disagreeable subject.

A few years back, Ward McAllister, the social arbiter for New York society, had declared that being a millionaire had become a distinct profession. Mrs. Oliver Hazard Perry Belmont said she knew "of no art or trade that women are working in today as taxing on mental resources as being a leader of society." By the late 1890s the grotesque competition of the rich no longer seemed quite so entertaining. In 1897, with the country still trapped in the depression, Mrs. Bradley Martin spent $370,000 on a costume ball at the Waldorf, inspired by a similar event held at the court of Versailles during the reign of Louis XV.

Mrs. Martin explained that she hoped the ball would stimulate business and create employment. She greeted her guests draped in rubies and diamonds, and while ministers railed and anarchists threatened, the guests danced "'til dawn, in a delirium of wealth and an idyll of luxury."

Newspaper readers the next morning were fascinated by details of the gala—

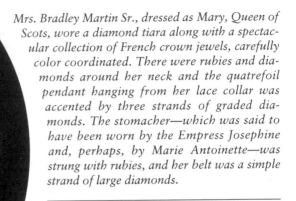

Mrs. Bradley Martin Sr., dressed as Mary, Queen of Scots, wore a diamond tiara along with a spectacular collection of French crown jewels, carefully color coordinated. There were rubies and diamonds around her neck and the quatrefoil pendant hanging from her lace collar was accented by three strands of graded diamonds. The stomacher—which was said to have been worn by the Empress Josephine and, perhaps, by Marie Antoinette—was strung with rubies, and her belt was a simple strand of large diamonds.

August Belmont had come attired as a knight in gold inlaid armor; Mrs. Astor's tiara was valued at $200,000; a staff of seven hundred attended the guests. But in the weeks that followed, the critics never let up. The city doubled the tax assessment on the Martins' home and Oscar Hammerstein staged a burlesque of the "Bradley-Radley Ball." The couple settled their taxes and left New York, seeking refuge in their homes in London and Scotland.

Far more interesting than the socialites with their grand excesses were the new millionaires, those men who had constructed elaborate and sophisticated industrial empires out of nothing but their own interior forces and unbridled ambition. Both Andrew Carnegie and John D. Rockefeller were in the news that April; both had acquired not just fortunes but a magnitude of power and influence beyond anything the country had ever known. Carnegie, the steel magnate, was Horatio Alger writ large, the poor immigrant boy who had become the richest man in the country through his own quick wit and diligence. Rockefeller, from a less romantic but modest background, had built one of the most powerful business combines in the world.

These were not the discoverers, not the men who found the great repositories of iron and coal and oil, but they were the ones who knew instinctively how to transform messy raw materials into goods that would become essential to American life. They had both begun at a time when the government was encouraging empire builders, when there were no legal limitations on the size of an enterprise, no income tax, when labor unions were weak or nonexistent and neither was encumbered by concerns for those who might be caught in the cross fire of their ambitions. In months Andrew Carnegie would become the richest man in the world. Rockefeller would be right behind him.

Carnegie was the largest manufacturer of steel in the country. He controlled every step of the transformation of rich red iron ore into steel rails and beams and plates and girders. He could not walk down a street in New York, or in any other major city for that matter, without seeing products of his own commission. Carnegie steel had been used in the Brooklyn Bridge and the girders for the el trains, provided the basic skeleton for the skyscrapers and the tracks for the trains arriving at Grand Central.

But at sixty-five, Andrew Carnegie was being pressured by his associates to slow down, sell the business, and allow them all to enjoy their gains. And indeed there was much besides business demanding his attention. He had been campaigning hard against U.S. involvement in the Philippines, writing magazine essays and angry letters to the president and his old friend John Hay. And then there was his family. Three years earlier he had been blessed with his first child, a daughter named Margaret whom he adored. He wanted to spend more time with her and with his beloved wife, Louise, and more time at Skibo, his castle in Scotland. He had begun to follow through on his promise to give away his fortune. His philanthropy was more than a rich man's public relations gesture. He had said many times, "The man who dies rich dies disgraced," and Carnegie would die in a state of grace.

But there was yet one more business matter to settle before retirement was possible. Out on the horizon

In his younger days Andrew Carnegie had sworn to devote his life to benevolent purposes. In 1868 he had written: "To continue much longer . . . with most of my thoughts wholly upon the way to make money in the shortest time, must degrade me beyond hope."

loomed J. P. Morgan, the financier with the small eyes and improbable nose who had suddenly become a serious competitor in the steel business. There was not room in the industry for them both. Carnegie and Morgan did not much like each other. Morgan, born to privilege, had built his empire leveraging his father's connections and money. As the two moved toward confrontation, Carnegie wrote his closest associate, Charles Schwab, "A struggle is inevitable, and it is a question of the survival of the fittest."

John D. Rockefeller, chairman of Standard Oil, also seemed to be coming to the end of his active business life, but it was hard to tell. Where Carnegie was open and ebullient, Rockefeller was muted and secretive. He was a man of such rectitude he went swimming with his hat on. April 13, when he announced the engagement of his daughter Alta to a forty-year-old attorney from Chicago, *The New York Times* noted that neither Miss Rockefeller "nor members of her family has ever figured in fashionable society, caring more for domestic life."

The Times reported Rockefeller was greatly expanding his estate, about thirty miles north of the city in Westchester County. Rockefeller loathed ostentation and was known for his frugality, but he was now buying up farms, laying out a four-hundred-and-fifty-acre private park, which in time would grow to five thousand acres, with a private game preserve, an eighteen-hole golf course, and seventy miles of winding drives that led out to plazas overlooking the Hudson. There were vine-covered walks, miniature lakes, and "other charming retreats." But for all its charm, the Pocantico estate was also a fortress.

While Carnegie had certainly overstepped the bounds of business ethics, he was now seen as a benign and amiable fellow, who was giving away his millions. Rockefeller, who had given away just as much money—and by the end of his life would give away far more—was simply disliked. It was as much as anything a matter of style. Carnegie was rounded and outgoing, had a sense of humor and a softly graying beard, while Rockefeller was too thin, too cold-eyed, and remote. In 1900 *The Times* was estimating his fortune at one hundred million dollars, but Rockefeller's income was derived from a corporate web so circuitous and dense that what he owned and controlled, where his interests began or ended, was all but impossible to decipher. He ruled not a company in the old-fashioned sense of the word, but an interlocking trust of forty corporations tied together by a common board of trustees and one central office over which he reigned supreme.

At the time the Standard Oil trust was created there had never been anything like it. It was one of the great organizing achievements of the century and perfectly legal.

Monopolies were against the law, but Standard was not a monopoly; it was, on paper at least, a combination of companies with a common understanding. One state legislature after the next tried to limit Standard's power, but each attempt only pushed the company's attorneys to greater creativity. As laws were written, loopholes were found and sidestepped.

By 1900 Standard had inspired ice trusts and beef trusts, sugar trusts and rail trusts, combinations of corporations all with the power to fix prices, destroy competition, and hold down wages. There had been repeated attempts to curb the trusts, but the alliance between business and government, particularly between the corporate giants and the Senate, had overwhelmed every attempt at reform. When John D. Rockefeller went into the oil business he was twenty-six, the quintessential bookkeeper, frugal and orderly to the point of obsession in a business that was mucky, messy, and chaotic. The oil fields were filled with small companies and aggressive men competing with one another who had neither the instincts nor the vision to create an industry virtually from scratch that Rockefeller did. It was the perfect marriage, an obsessive man in a field crying for order.

By the end of the 1870s, Standard controlled 90 percent of the nation's refining capacity. The company produced high-quality kerosene, the fuel Americans had come to depend on to light their homes. Standard brand fuel neither flickered nor exploded, their deliveryman was as dependable as the milkman, leaving five-gallon containers of kerosene at the kitchen door and at a reasonable price. Rockefeller, like Carnegie, had succeeded in gaining control over an entire industry, from the oil in the ground to the production of lamp wicks. Later he explained that his rivals "had not the means to build pipe lines, tank wagons . . . they couldn't manufacture their own acid, bungs, lamps, do their own cooperage."

He had bought, bribed, and bamboozled control of virtually an entire industry, had used threats and strong-arm tactics to buy out rivals, and crushed those who refused to knuckle under—including his brother Frank, who had foolishly tried to go into the business for himself. In the oil fields, mothers began to warn their children to be good or Rockefeller would get them. From John D.'s perspective, he had only done what any good businessman should have done, gained control over the market, stabilized prices, developed the most efficient way of producing an essential product. If his way of doing business was controversial, he didn't seem to care. In January, testifying before a government commission, he had said that the object of his company had always been the same: "to extend our business by furnishing the best and cheapest products."

But in March, with breathtaking arrogance, Standard Oil declared an extra $17 million dividend, and at the same time raised the cost of kerosene. Kerosene lamps were still lighting all but the most affluent homes in America. In Congress, John Fitzgerald accused Standard of imposing a tax on the middle and poorer classes. "Never in the history of the world," he said, "have corporations and monopolies been allowed to exist and thrive and extort money from the people as they are doing now right under our very noses." Fitzgerald demanded the government respond: "To say that Congress is unable and has not the power to restrict these combinations, is to insult the intelligence of the American people."

While some Republican leaders agreed, in an election year criticism was muted. For the record, Senator Mark Hanna and the powerful senator from Ohio, Joseph P. Foraker, would write a statement of concern for the Republican platform. What was not known at the time was that Foraker enjoyed a close and profitable relationship with Rockefeller's chief associate, John D. Archbold.

February 16, 1900

My Dear Senator:
Here is still another very objectionable bill. It is so outrageous as to be ridiculous, but it needs to be looked after and I hope there will be no difficulty killing it.

Very sincerely yours, *John D. Archbold*

March 26, 1900

Dear Senator:
In accordance with our understanding I now beg to enclose you a certificate of deposit to your favor for $15,000. Kindly acknowledge receipt, and oblige.

Very sincerely yours, *John D. Archbold*

April 17, 1900

My Dear Senator:
I enclose you a certificate of deposit to your favor for $15,000. . . . I need scarcely again express our great gratification over the favorable outcome of affairs. . . .

Very sincerely yours, *John D. Archbold*

In the House of Representatives, John Fitzgerald demanded that the attorney general investigate Standard Oil for the violation of antitrust regulations. He was probably not surprised when the government took no action.

Other Stories of Interest

The Chicago Daily Tribune, April 7, 1900
Apaches on the Warpath
TUCSON, ARIZONA—The Apaches apparently are on the warpath. A detachment of cavalry from Fort Grant is in pursuit, and a young ranchwoman is leading a body of cowboys. One white man had already been shot, and there is an unconfirmed report that others have been killed.

The Chicago Daily Tribune, April 10, 1900
Gen. Funston Under Charges
MANILA—Brigadier General Frederick Funston is under investigation for the execution of two Filipinos and a court martial may result.

The story is that the Filipinos captured three scouts and were preparing to kill them when one escaped and found General Funston with a scouting party near.

This man guided the Americans to the rescue of his companions. Several of the Filipinos were shot and General Funston captured two of them, took them to the village square and hanged them without a trial as a warning.

The Chicago Daily Tribune, April 10, 1900
Lodge Defends Foreign Policy
CHICAGO—Enthusiasm for the foreign policy of the administration as annunciated by Senator Henry Cabot Lodge was cheered [at a Hamilton Club banquet].

"We are not going to retreat under fire. It must be plain to the American citizen that the insurrection in the Philippines is nearly at an end. But I will tell you it will go smouldering along until William McKinley is reelected President. . . . When the proper time comes we will lead them along the path to good government."

The Chicago Daily Tribune, April 11, 1900
Bill to Preserve Buffalo
WASHINGTON, D.C., April 10—For the purpose of preventing the complete extinction of the American buffalo the Senate passed a bill setting apart a preserve in New Mexico . . . for one hundred full-blooded animals.

In its report the committee says: ". . . there are at present 400 living bisons in the whole world. . . . There are still perhaps twenty in the Yellowstone National Park and a few scattered 'wood buffalo' west of Hudson's Bay, which embrace all that are left of countless millions of a generation ago."

The Chicago Daily Tribune, April 12, 1900
Automobile Kills a Man
CHICAGO—Since the accident to Richard W. Kenney, who was killed last night by an automobile, there is talk of a city ordinance being introduced to compel the horseless vehicles to carry fenders. Already a firm using them for delivery carts has begun equipping its wagons with man-catchers.

The New York Times, April 18, 1900
Mr. Carnegie Gives $3,600,000
PITTSBURGH—Andrew Carnegie has promised the Trustees of the Carnegie Library and Institute to become responsible for $3,600,000, for the proposed extension and enlargement of the already fine building at the entrance of the Schenley Park. . . .

When completed the structure will be one of the largest in the world and in architectural beauty will have few if any equals. In appearance it will resemble the new Congressional Library at Washington, which is claimed to be . . . the most beautiful building architecturally in America.

In 1900, the old world and the new were growing ever closer. This Italian family, on their way to Ellis Island, would have been able to buy steerage tickets from Naples for only $15.

CHAPTER SEVEN

April

I

———

"America fever" swept through the small Jewish town of Vaslui, Romania, in the spring of 1900. A townsman named Couza had returned home from vacation with a trunkful of presents from the States, a pen that did not need an inkwell, a neat little razor in a leather case, and Yiddish newspapers that listed the limitless opportunities for earning money in New York. Marcus Ravage, a sixteen-year-old boy living with his parents, later wrote of that moment when America "flashed upon our consciousness." The people of Vaslui were suddenly stirred by a grand ambition, and within months, "Vaslui had the appearance of a town struck by war or revolution. . . . The streets witnessed a continual procession of trays and carts bulging with . . . feather-bedding, because rumor had it that the commodity was unobtainable in America."

The Romanian authorities had "stood by idly while the caravans kept moving on," Marcus wrote, "apparently only too happy to be rid of an element of its population for which it had always entertained a quite frank antipathy. . . . Ordinarily the getting of a passport had been a matter of endless trouble and very considerable expense. But in this Messianic year of 1900 the bars were unaccountably let down, and every person not of military age who made application for a passport was cheerfully sped on his way."

In New York, Commissioner Fitchie of the city's Immigration Bureau was bracing for the arrival of half a million newcomers. He told a reporter, "Unfortunately for the United States most of these immigrants are not so desirable as those of ten years ago." The bureau had been warned that tens of thousands of Jews from the Hebrew centers in Europe were on their way, along with dark-skinned Catholics from southern Italy.

At a Methodist meeting in Brooklyn, a woman minister described New York as a heathen city. The story was carried in papers across the country. Only nine-tenths of one percent of those living on the Lower East Side were members of a Protestant Church, an extreme example to be sure, but there were now far more Catholics than members of any single Protestant denomination, and probably a million Jews. Americans of Anglo-Saxon Protestant stock were once again raising the specter of watering down American stock, weakening the Republic.

In 1900 there were moves to tighten the immigration laws to stop the tide of undesirables, but, as Kate Holladay Claghorn wrote in *The Atlantic Monthly,* ethnic distaste was often overridden by a desire for cheap labor: "Here is a half-worked country in need of a larger labor force [and] across the sea is a labor force in need of employment. It will be as impossible to keep these apart, under modern conditions of intercommunication, as to shut out a rising tide with a board fence; the water will force its way in, either over, or under or through the cracks."

In Vaslui, Marcus, considering "the prohibitions and repressions" of Jewish life in Romania, urged his father to allow him to join those young men who had already set off for the land of promise. "My parents had ambitions for me which their clinging, hopeless poverty made impossible of attainment. Supposing I wanted to study law, then 'aliens' were not eligible to the bar. The ministry? Romania forbade the establishment of rabbinical seminaries. Well, I could go into medicine, if only the Government allowed [my father] to earn the means of seeing me through."

Special taxes and new laws and endless restrictions had cut off possibilities and destroyed any chance of living an interesting and comfortable life. And "there was the dreadful horror of the recruiting officer constantly lurking in our path like a serpent." Ravage's brother Paul had been captured by the "scarlet monster," and packed off "to learn senseless tricks with his feet and a gun, to spend days and whole weeks in prison cells, as if he were a criminal . . . and

The extraordinary mix of people living on New York's Lower East Side astonished new arrivals. In 1900, an English writer named Israel Zangwill romantically described America as a "melting pot." In fact there was little melting at the turn of the century, particularly among Jews from eastern Europe and immigrants from southern Italy.

to live in constant terror of war and the manoeuvre for the rest of his life."

And so his father sold the family cow and his mother knit him socks and began to weep. She made her son flannelette underwear, mended his shirts, and "just before train time . . . put the gold-clasped prayer-book into my grip which father had given her on their betrothal." With two gold napoleons sewn into the lining of his waistcoat, Ravage embraced his mother for the last time. "There was despair in her way of clinging to me which I could not understand. I understand it now. I never saw her again."

As he headed west across the Danube, the boy saw "the gate of the great world opening up before me, with its long roads radiating in all directions. In a very few days I should be out of Rumania. And then in two weeks more, New York would no longer be a vision but an inspiring reality."

In Albany, New York, Theodore Roosevelt settled down to write a note to his old friend Jacob—Jake—Riis, thanking him for his offer to send the Roosevelt children a cote full of pigeons. TR said they "would be overjoyed at such a regal gift," but he would have to wait to see how his wife felt about the matter and she was still in Cuba. Riis and TR had met ten years earlier, just after the publication of Riis's revolutionary book, *How the Other Half Lives*. The Danish-born reporter had used his considerable talents as a writer and photographer to bring attention to the horror of life in New York slums, to force middle-class Americans to see that which they had chosen to ignore.

He had produced a book designed to assault the eye and nag the conscience—stark portraits, many taken at night by magnesium flash, of men, women, and children staring into the camera, wrapped in rags in windowless rooms with battered peeling walls and leaking pipes; of rank alleys with filthy rat-infested water closets; of seven, eight, ten people crammed into the confusions of one dark loathsome space. Riis described the slums as "hot-beds of epidemics . . . nurseries of pauperism and crime that . . . above all, touch the family life with deadly moral contagion."

Shortly after the book was published, Riis received a scrawled note from TR: "I have read your book, and I have come to help." During the days when Roosevelt served as city police commissioner, Riis had taken TR into buildings the Tenement Commission had described as "veritable slaughter houses," where young children were dying at the rate of one of every five. Tuberculosis, the plague of the poor, ruled entire buildings, even blocks of buildings. TR went into dark, disease-ridden rooms that in time would claim one tenant after the next.

Before his stint with the city was over, Roosevelt had come to see Riis as "the most useful citizen in America," and Riis had acquired enormous respect and affection for the reform-minded police commisioner. One day in 1895, he arrived unexpectedly in TR's office at police headquarters with another reporter—Lincoln Steffens—to ask the thirty-seven-year-old Roosevelt if he would consider becoming a candidate for president in the coming election. TR lept to his feet in a rage.

"Don't you dare ask me that," he commanded. "Don't you put such ideas into my head. No friend of mine would say a thing like that. Never, never, must either of you remind a man on a political job that he may be President. It almost always kills him politically. He loses his nerve; he can't do his work; he gives up the very traits that are making him a possibility." The subject was closed; the friendship continued.

By 1900, Riis's ten-year campaign had rid the city of some of the most offensive conditions. Cellars could no longer be used as living quarters; stables could not be kept on the same lot with a tenement house; cholera, smallpox, and yellow fever had been all but banished. But tuberculosis remained unchecked, and hundreds of thousands of people still lived under dreadful conditions. Water closets still lined the rank narrow alleys that lay behind the slums. Landlords continued to encourage overcrowding by charging exorbitant rents and the situation was only going to get worse.

With almost half a million immigrants expected in New York that year, Roosevelt appointed a Tenement Commission to pick up where the last one had left off, six years before. Riis hoped the commissioners would impose a small tax on tenement owners—just two or three dollars a building would provide the city with the $100,000 needed to hire additional sanitary police. Riis was moving into dangerous territory and he knew it. "The delicate task is to propose . . . [a tax] that will do the least violence to the Anglo-Saxon reverence for property," he wrote, "and so provoke the least opposition while accomplishing the most good."

———————

When Marcus Ravage finally arrived on Rivington Street at the edge of the ghetto, he had an insane feeling that "this was not America"—the stench of the slops in the streets, the narrow alleys that never saw the sun, "upset all my calculations, reversed all my values and set my head swimming." At Ellis Island he had been "jostled and dragged and shoved and shouted at," but American officials were no different than those bullying bureaucrats he had encountered all across Europe. It was not until he had reached the East Side that he lost his bearings, overwhelmed by "the dreadful level of life" to which his countrymen had sunk.

"This was the boasted American freedom and opportunity—the freedom for respectable citizens to sell cabbages from hideous carts, the opportunity to live in those monstrous, dirty caves that shut out sunshine." Beyond Grand Street he found the Romanian section of the ghetto, and men he had known back home, "clad in an absurd medley of Rumanian sheep-pelts and American red sweaters. . . . Here was Jonah Gershon, who had been the chairman of the hospital committee in Vaslui and a prominent grain-merchant . . . dispensing soda-water and selling lollypops on the corner of Essex Street. This was Shloma Lobel, a descendant of rabbis and himself a learned scholar. In America he had attained to a basket of shoe-strings and matches and candles."

To Ravage, America seemed a diabolic country, as narrow and confining as the land he had just left, but without the Old World's comforting traditions. He found his fellow countrymen "cut adrift from their ancient moorings, floundering in a moral void. Good manners and good conduct, reverence and religion, had all gone by the board, and the reason was that these things were not American. A grossness of behavior, a loudness of speech, a certain repellent 'American' smartness of intercourse, were thought necessary, if one did not want to be taken for a greenhorn or a boor."

In time Ravage would develop a deep love for America, but the transformation from immigrant to citizen was a far more difficult and dangerous journey than he had envisioned when he set out from Vaslui. In his early weeks in New York, he read the want ads and tried to find a job as an errand boy or a butcher's assistant, but he had neither the language nor the shoes—the "alien's shoes are his Judas," he wrote. "In order to have a job one must have American clothes, and the only way to get American clothes was to find a job."

II

Reading the newspapers in the spring of 1900, one might have assumed America was in the midst of revolution. All over the country workers had gone out on strike—bricklayers and granite cutters, cigar makers and stonemasons, the men producing piano plates, mill hands, and hod carriers, track men, and factory hands—all were demanding better working conditions, shorter hours, and higher pay. In Cincinnati, the ironworkers were out. In Kansas City, it was the tinners and sheet-metal workers. In Akron, six hundred boilermakers and molders had shut down a plant filling orders for the Russian navy.

In factories and mills, men, women, and, too often, children were still working ten- and sometimes twelve-hour days, six days a week—when they could find a job. In 1900, six and a half million people would be idle, many for months at a time. The workplaces themselves were often foul and dangerous—one worked to survive, but many did not survive their work. Machines mangled bodies; coal, cotton, and tobacco dust clogged the lungs. Among railroad workers that year, twenty-five hundred men were killed and almost forty thousand injured.

The grievances of American workers were not new, but in 1900 hundreds and thousands of men and women were trying again to change the course of their lives. In the coalfields of Pennsylvania, where the lot of the anthracite miners had been compared unfavorably with that of medieval serfs, handsome Johnny Mitchell was about to lead the United Mine Workers into a historic confrontation.

Twenty-nine-year-old Mitchell wore a jeweled ring, a Prince Albert suit, and was said to have the face of a priest. But he was more effective than he looked. Orphaned at six, he had gone into the mines at twelve and could remember taking comfort from the rats nosing round his food bucket. If they had air enough to breath, so did he. At thirteen, he had helped drag bloated bodies from a flooded mine in Braceville, Illinois. He had seen it all—the boys even younger than he, some no more than eight—staggering home at close of day, scarcely able to walk. Dust covered dead-eyed children of the damned. When he was young, Mitchell had worked in tunnels with ceilings so low that over time his shoulders had been rounded, his body stunted.

"My shoulders are only square," he wrote, "when I have my Tailor made coat on." By 1900 he had more than one tailor-made suit, a private office, a secretary, and a handsome salary. He had worked his way up out of the mines as a union organizer and by 1899 was president of the UMW. Early in 1900 he moved into a region where a union organizer was about as welcome as a smallpox epidemic: the anthracite fields in northeast Pennsylvania. While Mitchell and the UMW had made important strides organizing miners in the soft coal regions, no one had made headway among the 150,000 hard coal miners.

Everything was stacked against the union. Writer Donald L. Miller says, "The American Constitution wasn't a fact of life, in the coal towns of Pennsylvania." Miners had no control over their own lives; the company owned the homes they lived in, the stores where they were forced to buy tools and provisions; law and order was preserved by the company militia; in some places the company controlled the water supply and even the selection of ministers and priests. Anyone suspected of union agitation could be evicted on twenty-four-hour notice.

Mine managers had skillfully pitted English-speaking miners—the Irish, Welsh, and Scottish—against the Slavs, the Hungarians, and Germans, making collective action all but impossible. To make matters worse, J. P. Morgan's huge railroad cartel controlled almost the entire region. By early 1900, Mitchell had signed up nine thousand new members. Among the more aggressive there was talk of a strike, but Mitchell was uncertain the UMW was strong enough to take on one of the most powerful capitalists in the world. He promised to call a union convention in August. He would judge their collective strength at that time.

Unions were still weak and fractured. The American Federation of Labor, led by Samuel Gompers, had only half a million members, and the International Ladies Garment Workers Union had yet to hold its first meeting—it was scheduled for the summer. Most labor actions that spring were local affairs without union support, and doomed from the start. In April, an incident in a small New York town called Croton Landing, some miles north of the Rockefeller estate, began and ended much like other walkouts that year.

A handful of Italian blacksmiths working on the Croton Dam were demanding their wages be raised and their hours cut. New York State employees were now guaranteed a minimum of $1.50 for an eight-hour day, and the blacksmiths who were getting only $1.35 for a ten-hour day were asking for the same. But the company was intransigent, and within days, six hundred men, most of them Italian, had laid down their tools and all work on the dam was brought to a halt. Because Croton was part of the New York City Waterworks, the walkout was covered by every newspaper in the Northeast, and without much sympathy. Italians were a

suspect people—not only were they dark skinned, clannish, and Catholic, it was also widely assumed that many were Socialists, anarchists, or all-around trouble-makers.

But the men at Croton Dam, like so many foreign-born workers, were living at the very margins of life. Even on $1.50 a day, a man could scarcely maintain himself, let alone properly feed his family. In 1900, a sociologist named Robert Hunter, working on the first extensive study on poverty in America, found that millions of workers were paid so little they were unable to eat enough even "to maintain a state of physical efficiency." It was a brilliant and brutal phrase to describe the precise balance required to keep the body of a laboring man in order, just enough calories to keep him at his appointed labors. Hunter estimated that in a country in which wealth was seen as a sign of God's approval, over ten million people in America were "underfed, underclothed and poorly housed," and he suspected those figures fell far short of the truth.

Some years before, Walt Whitman had written a chilling projection about America's growing underclass: "If the United States, like the countries of the Old World, are also to grow vast crops of poor, desperate, dissatisfied, nomadic, miserably-waged populations, such as we see looming upon us of late years . . . then our republican experiment, not withstanding all its surface successes, is at heart an unhealthy failure."

While the walkout had been peaceful, on the thirteenth day, with frustrations growing, rumors spread that the strikers were preparing to blow up the reservoir and flood the valley. A state negotiator, ordered to the site by Governor Roosevelt, declared the rumors nonsense, but no one could be sure. At the insistence of the contractors one hundred men from around the area were rounded up, sworn in as deputy sheriffs, given arms, and sent up to the dam. Local papers described the deputies as thugs, and were likely right. Ruffians and former convicts were often employed as company police.

The workers were enraged. They massed on the bridge leading to the dam and, as the deputies approached, stopped them with a hail of stones. A sympathetic deputy made his way into the enclave and was told by the strikers that they did not want to defy the law, but could no longer accept starvation wages. The Italian consul released word that if the contractors would raise the base pay to $1.50 a day the men would relent on the issue of the hours, but the contractors would not budge. In Albany rumors of violence had not subsided. Roosevelt was repeatedly told that the New York City water system was in jeopardy and that the sheriff of Westchester County was calling for the militia.

On Easter Sunday, Little Italy was quiet for the moment. The small, makeshift chapel in the middle of the village was crowded with strikers and their families sharing benches with some of the sheriffs. The priest that morning counseled moderation, and Angelo Rotella led a small orchestra—two mandolins, two guitars, and a reed organ—in a program of Easter music. But the sweetness of the day was marred when word reached Rotella that Governor Roosevelt had finally ordered two New York City infantry companies and three hundred and fifty cavalrymen to Croton Landing. Rotella was visibly depressed. In too many strikes, the arrival of the militia signaled the beginning of violence.

In New York City that evening, crowds began to gather outside the armory as the troops assembled. Blacksmiths were readying the horses as quickly as possible. Some were seasoned animals that had seen service during the Spanish-American War. Others were said to be in poor repair. Replacements were sought from nearby stables. Monday morning, April 16, with sabres clanking and battle flags flying, and small boys cheering them on their way, the cavalry headed out of town. Troop C was led by the company mascot, a fierce bull terrier named Spider. An ammunition wagon and two large carts carrying tents and cooking equipment made up the rear. The press reported that the veterans of the Puerto Rican campaign seemed pleased by the promise of active duty.

The commander had been informed that two-thirds of the strikers were armed and bloodshed was expected, and the newspapers reported that the strikers in Croton Landing gave every appearance of preparing for war. It was in fact a desperate sham. A few men had pistols, but most had armed themselves with sticks of wood. In the saddest gesture of all, a large iron water pipe had been hauled to the edge of the hill that appeared from the valley below to be a six-inch naval gun.

The first troops arrived by train just before nightfall, dressed for trouble in their heavy service outfits. Among them was Robert Douglass, a tall twenty-eight-year-old sergeant, born in Scotland, known within the regiment as an outstanding basketball player. Each man carried three days' rations and twenty rounds of munitions. It was a soft spring evening, and as the men pitched their tents on the edge of the wood nearest the village they began to relax. In spite of all the rumors there had been no signs of trouble. Italian children had drifted into camp.

At about 8:15 P.M., as the moon was beginning to rise, Douglass led a squad of twenty men to relieve the sentinels along the guard line. At the ninth station, in a curious quiet, Douglass suddenly issued a horrifying cry and fell to the ground. No one remembered hearing a shot. One moment the sergeant was in charge, the next he was bleeding to death on the new spring grass. Some of the men thought he had been killed by an air gun. His squad mates, calling for revenge, had to be restrained from moving in that night to "clean out" the Italian village on the hill.

Troubled strike leaders denied any involvement with the shooting. Some insisted the contractors had killed Douglass to make the Italians appear even "blacker." Throughout the night, shots were heard as jumpy sentries fired at shadows. Tuesday a cold rain drenched the encampment. The death of Sergeant Douglass had left the troops edgy; guards were posted on all the roads. No one was allowed to enter or leave the enclaves. The strike leaders were questioned at length, but the search for the assassin proved fruitless.

Reinforcements arrived later in the day, along with a large press contingent. One officer told reporters, "There are enough soldiers here now to make a lunch out of all of the Italians within two miles of the dam." The governor, outraged by the death of Sergeant Douglass, sent word to the commander of the militia to see there was no further violence. Tension increased, but the day passed without incident. Early Wednesday morning, military officers went into the village to inform the strikers that anyone willing to go back to work would be fully protected, but when the work whistle blew, only a few men responded. None were Italian.

Then, on Thursday, the Seventh Regiment quietly moved in to break the strike. Neither the press nor the strikers were prepared for what was to follow. A cordon of troops with fixed bayonets, backed by the cavalry, were positioned along a six-mile perimeter. In the Italian enclave,

The National Guard encampment at Croton Dam. The use of state militia to intimidate workers and end strikes was common practice in 1900. At Croton, the well-armed troops had so little to do that on their first Sunday, wives and sweethearts of the men came up the Hudson for a visit and the camp was turned into a huge picnic ground.

the entire area was closed off, and as troops took command of the streets an order was given and the search for a secret cache of arms got under way. As sullen-faced women watched from their windows, every home was entered, every piece of furniture searched, bedding upended. In yards where the ground had been newly turned for small kitchen gardens, bayonets flashed in the warm spring sun as soldiers probed pigsties and woodpiles. An older officer said there had been nothing like it since the days of the Civil War.

In the end there was no cache of weapons. Only three guns were found, including a pistol taken from a hack driver who had the misfortune of having made his way to the town in the midst of the excitement. With their families watching, the strike leaders were arrested and led off in handcuffs. Eighteen men were charged with inciting to riot, among them Angelo Rotella, his brother, and their father. Eight other men, identified by the sheriff as having been present at the early demonstrations, were seized without the benefit of warrants.

Once the strike leaders had been driven out of town, the contractors announced that work would resume the following week. If necessary, replacement workers would be imported from New York City. Before the day was over, as groups of exhausted strikers gathered on street corners, four men, all strangers, arrived in the village. Moving from one group to the next they urged the men not to return to work until they had won their demands. Later it was learned that the strangers were arrested as they left the enclave, charged with being labor agitators.

In New York City that evening, down in Greenwich Village, leading Italian-American businessmen assembled at a hotel on Bleecker Street, hoping to find a solution for the crisis at Croton Landing. They had barely settled down when a band of Italian anarchists burst into the room shouting, "Death to the Italian consul. Death to the American soldiers. Dynamite, dynamite." *The Times* reported the meeting broke up "in the utmost disorder."

On Monday morning, April 23, when the work whistle blew, numbers of men, driven by fear and hunger, particularly those with families, were heading back to the dam. Later that day, as the most militant of the Italians prepared to leave Croton Landing forever, fifty Hungarians were making their way up the hill to take their place.

Other Stories of Interest

The Chicago Daily Tribune, April 8, 1900
New Baseball Faces

Less than two weeks intervene before the introduction of American league baseball in Chicago. It will be interesting to see what degree of interest the big minor league will arouse in Chicago compared with the attention that has always been given to the National league.*

*The newly formed American league also had teams in Kansas City, Minneapolis, Milwaukee, Chicago, Detroit, Indianapolis, Cleveland, and Buffalo—all good baseball towns.

The Chicago Daily Tribune, April 15, 1900
Charles Comiskey yesterday received a signed contract from "Dummy" Hoy. . . . Comiskey is much pleased. This player, he declares, is one of the best all around men in the business. He is a good batter and fielder and a gentleman on the field.*

*Outfielder William Ellsworth Hoy was known as "Dummy" because he was a deaf mute.

The Chicago Sunday Tribune,
April 22, 1900
Brewers Win Opening Game

On a brand-new baseball grounds yesterday a new Chicago baseball club opened a new baseball season. The associations to which the rival ball nines belong is new to Chicago, the grandstand is new . . . and many of the players were so new that as they walked out one by one . . . the bleachers on the east side would pathetically echo "Who's de guy?"

Just one good old touch that made the fans feel at home . . . was the score. It was 4 to 5 with Chicago possessing the smaller number.

In spite of a cold, sad sort of day . . . over five thousand people saw the first game in Chicago of the American League. [The game] was played at its new grounds at 39th Street and Wentworth Avenue. Here is where the old Wanderers used to play cricket and where college teams have played football, and where of late years small boys have played rounders and disconsolate-looking goats have grazed from the thin herbiage and gaudily colored wrappers from ex-tomato cans.

Yesterday all was changed. A brand-new grandstand, as yet innocent of paint, stood in the southwest corner of the grounds. Two painters were just starting work on the fence . . . while twisting their heads around to see whether "Dummy" Hoy would make third or die on second.

The Chicago Daily Tribune, April 23, 1900
Twelve Thousand People
Over-Tax Comiskey's Stands

April 22—Chicago fans got pretty well acquainted with Comiskey's White Stockings yesterday afternoon, accepted them as their own, yelled like mad all through the game, and rebuked the umpire when they thought he should have given the home team a home run instead of a foul.

The American Leaguers were almost swamped with unexpected popularity. . . . There were not enough tickets to go around and not enough seats. . . . Small boys being relegated to the roof of the grandstand, fans formed an unbroken border half a dozen deep clear around the field, taking possession of the outer pasture and encroaching on the infield. Ground rules had to be made to fit the occasion, and a hit into the crowd was accepted as being good for only two bases.

The diamond was in much better condition than on Saturday, although it is far from being in shape yet. . . . The heavy going naturally interfered with the fielding, as some of the long hits into the crowd might have been good for two bases . . . but Chicago got one more two-bagger than the Brewers.

Even the smallest town boasted a variety of musical groups, but few carried their pianos with them. This ensemble was photographed in Clay Center, Kansas.

CHAPTER EIGHT

May

I

The city of Chicago had waited almost a year for the privilege of honoring Admiral George Dewey on May 1, 1900. But as the day approached, a curious ambivalence had taken hold of those in charge of the event. Hundreds of thousands of visitors were expected in the city from all over the Midwest, and Dewey Day was to be celebrated in much of the country. But the admiral had come perilously close to scuttling his own celebration. No one yet acknowledged that Dewey was something of a fantasy hero; only the most outspoken cynic dared suggest that the battle that had accorded him such fame and glory was really not much of a battle at all.

In 1898, at the outset of the Spanish-American War, he had steamed into Manila harbor where the aging Spanish fleet—seven armorless ships—was huddled in the shallows waiting for destruction. On the bridge in his summer whites, he delivered his now immortal order, "You may fire when ready, Gridley." A few hours of cannon fire later and the entire Spanish flotilla was destroyed without the loss of one American sailor. The press described the engagement as a glorious victory, and Dewey became the symbol of America triumphant.

For the first time since the Civil War, America had a national military hero, free of allegiance to either the North or South. Dewey mania swept the country: towns and babies were named after the admiral; there was chewing gum called Dewey's Chewies and a laxative named The Salt of Salts. On his return to the States, when his ship steamed into New York Harbor, three million people greeted him in a frenzy of patriotic fervor. A few days later, in Washington, D.C., Dewey was floated down Pennsylvania Avenue on the prow of a cardboard replica of his ship, presented with a gold-handled sword by the president, and provided a fine new home by his admirers. The admiral had quite reasonably assumed that the country was his for the taking.

Dewey, a vain and egotistical little man, had suddenly in March 1900, to the bafflement of the press, announced that he was a presidential candidate. Nothing was known about the admiral's political views; even his party affiliation was a mystery. When he was first asked if he was a Republican or Democrat, he answered simply, "I am a sailor." In March, he explained he was inviting a nomination from either party; it mattered little which.

No one knew where Dewey stood on any given subject—including, apparently, the admiral himself. He admitted that he had never voted in his life, but by way of reassurance told reporters that after long and serious consideration he had come to the conclusion that the office of the president was not a very difficult one to fill. When he finally declared himself to be a Democrat, and was asked about his plans in the event that

George Dewey, Admiral of the Navy, was a graduate of Annapolis. An executive officer of a side-wheeler during the Civil War, Dewey fought in the Battle of New Orleans and then ran his ship aground. The admiral's high regard for himself was never matched by those who knew him well.

Bryan won the nomination, Admiral Dewey replied, "I won't answer that question," and went off to a concert on the arm of his young wife.

With reporters nagging him, he turned irascible and in the daily press began to appear as a rather silly old man. One headline declared, "Dewey's Bomb a Blank Shot"; another called him "the spoiled favorite of fortune"; a third pointed out that "a great sailor should have a better chart in a strange sea." In Chicago, the organizers of Dewey Day were thrown into confusion. If the admiral was preparing to turn their patriotic celebration into a political rally, no supporter of President McKinley or William Jennings Bryan could afford to be associated with the event.

Briefly there was talk of cancellation, but the celebration had taken on a life of its own. Funds had been raised, special trains had been charted, hotel rooms booked, and caterers hired for the private receptions. There was no turning back. And so on the morning of May 1, the admiral and his wife arrived as planned in a flag-bedecked and mildly bewildered city. The reception committee was somewhat reserved, but the press reported that the schedule was so tight it would not be possible for Dewey to deliver any platform speeches.

But Americans do not give up their heroes easily. Six hundred thousand people turned out, at one point spontaneously breaking into a full rendition of "See the Conquering Hero," and the admiral was accorded all the pomp and admiration that he so desired. What he probably never understood as the bands played and the crowds roared was that the people in their wisdom had lifted him up and out of the political arena, putting him back on the pedestal where he belonged.

II

In Springville, Utah, on Dewey Day, the lilacs were out and George Edward Anderson was planting strawberries outside his photo gallery before packing his camera gear to head for the mine town of Scofield. Anderson would remember the morning as particularly bright and clear. For over a decade he had been recording the hardscrabble life in the Pleasant Valley coalfields. He knew that the miners were planning a dance that night in the newly completed Odd Fellows

Hall and that the children of the drum corps would be joining in the celebration.

A number of Springville men were now working in the mines—the Miller boys, and John Davis and his two oldest sons; Mrs. Davis and their eight younger children had remained in Springville where life was a bit easier. Anderson also knew Barney Dougall, who was starting work that day. There was not much news in eastern Utah on May 1; the local paper carried a sarcastic item or two about Admiral Dewey's political career, but more space was given to an item about J. W. Dilley, the Scofield school superintendent and town reporter who had been suffering from a severe case of tonsilitis and was heading back to work.

After the long, cold winter, the trees in Scofield had just begun to soften—what few trees there were. On the barren hillsides, eight thousand feet above sea level, were tufts of coarse grass; the land was too high and far too mean for flowers. There were small signs of spring—laundry on the lines and freshly painted trim on the houses. The mines were working flat out, two shifts a day, and a fair number of men had been able to move their families out of the old log cabins into neat new cottages. The single men in town were staying at the boarding house, including the farmers from Springville who had come to work the winter and then had elected to stay on. There was more money to be made in the mines than on the beet farms. The U.S. Navy contract was in place and production was being raised two thousand tons a day.

The men headed out that morning as they always did, in the dark pants, dark shoes, dark shirts that were meant to ward off dust but never did. Nothing could. The soft coal soot sifted into every pore of their clothing and skin. Cleanliness was a virtue impossible to achieve. With their oil lamps clamped on their caps and their double lunch pails—water in the top, food in the bottom—the men crammed into coaches that carried them the two miles up the canyon to the complex known as Winter Quarters.

The men, the horses with their special harnesses and trappings, the miners, the drivers, the stokers, the young boys who worked in the tunnels, the farmers from Springville, Barney Dougall with his surveying gear—made their way past the equipment shacks, past the weighing shed and the unruly stacks of timbers sprawled beside the rail tracks. The entrances into the mines, Number One and Number Four, were narrow, and it took time to thread their way down the shafts that led to their work sites. Underground, the two mines were linked by a complex series of tunnels, closed off by heavy doors that controlled ventilation.

At twenty minutes past ten o'clock that morning, the countryside was shaken by the explosion. There was no warning, there never was. At first some believed the blast had been set off in honor of Dewey Day, but then J. W. Dilley saw the women with blanched faces racing toward the mouth of Number Four. It was the moment they had all rehearsed in the silence of their minds and had prayed never to know. An explosion and fire inside a mine. There had never been any illusions among the men or their families; the youngest knew that mining was a deadly business—collapses, explosions, fires that could burn for years were not uncommon. A rich vein in one mine in the region had caught fire back in 1883, and seventeen years later it was believed that the fire had finally been smothered, but no one knew for certain.

The first witnesses to arrive following the blast found clouds of dust pouring from the mouth of Number Four, the entry blocked by timbers and a dead horse, but no driver. Someone looking down the gulch spotted the man, still alive, blown eight hundred and twenty feet away. Men who had been working around the entries were stunned and bleeding, cut down by flying debris. Suddenly, from out

The rescue team at Scofield wearing the most modern apparatus: closed-system helmets made in Germany. Oxygen was carried in glass bottles strapped to their backs.

of the entrance of Number One raced six fine white horses, cavorting down the hill to their stables, as if off for a feed. No one knew where the animals had been stationed.

The first relief party, the few able-bodied men left in town, led by mine supervisor T. J. Parmley, could not approach the entrance of Number Four—the heat was too intense. His brother was inside. They started down the entry of Number One but were driven back by the terrible "after-damp," the deadly gas unleashed by the explosion. One good breath and a man was rendered unconscious. As Number Four began to cool, the dead horse and timbers were dragged away. Close to the entrance rescuers found William Boweter, hardly conscious, sitting among the bodies of the dead, and Harry Betterson, who was so badly burned he was mistaken for John Kirton. Betterson died later in the day. The mine passages were blocked and progress was slow.

The horror of the disaster is etched on the faces of Sam Wycherly and Ephraim Rowe, who were working together in Number One mine. Most of the men in the mine were killed by the "after-damp." Wycherly and Rowe were both overcome and rescued just in time.

Mine superintendent T. J. Parmley (wearing the tall hat) led one of the first rescue parties. Many were searching for family members or friends. Parmley's brother was among those killed. One rescuer wrote: "[We] made up our minds not to give way to our feelings. . . . It was either that or drop by the side of my chum, take hold of his cold hand and cry."

Calls for help went out to nearby mines. Within hours, officials were besieged with inquiries from all over the state, but information was meager. Early dispatches reflected the hope that most of those in Number One would be found alive on the lower levels where the air had not been poisoned. And there were survivors. Ephraim Rowe, a driver from Spanish Fork, had been working on the sixth rise in Number One. Rowe had never heard a sound. The first thing he knew his horse fell over and he was carried by a powerful gust of wind. He crawled in the dark over a thousand feet on his hands and knees. It was the last he remembered. His uncle found him unconscious near the main entrance. Rowe remained comatose for almost thirty hours.

Mining was very much a family affair. Fathers worked with sons, brothers with brothers. William Clark died trying to rescue his father and brother. Fifteen-year-old Tom Pugh covered his nostrils with his hat and made his way from the fifth raise, about a mile and a half from the entrance, in an attempt to save his father, but he was too late. One of the six Evans boys had made it out alive, but it would be hours before he knew the fate of the others. J. W. Dilley described finding John James "clasped in the embrace of his son George, as though to shield him from the death he knew that was approaching."

At Number One, many in the rescue party were overcome. Dilley would be carried out unconscious several times over the course of two days. As the hours passed, the magnitude of the disaster was becoming apparent. The after-damp had claimed its victims so swiftly, men were found with tools still in their grasp; one had a pipe in his hand. Many who had tried to outrace the damp were lying in clusters, often on their backs. By early afternoon, the bodies were arriving at the surface by the carload; Clarence Nix, the clerk at the company store, identified the victims. Among the first was T. J. Parmley's brother.

Women and children waited at the entry; many were weeping, others ashen and too quiet. No one was certain how many men had gone to work that day, but it was well over two hundred. At Mr. Edward's boarding house, transformed into a makeshift morgue, volunteers with large sponges washed the dead, throwing their foul clothes on a pile outside the door. George Anderson photographed the bodies laid out in the meeting house; among them were men he had known all his life.

Early evening, the chief storekeeper was dispatched to Salt Lake City to buy coffins and sets of clothing for the victims, but all the coffins in the city were not enough. A carload more was ordered from Denver, along with a barrel or more of embalming fluid. In the mines, rescuers continued shoring up rooms deep underground to reach bodies still trapped beneath the pillars and debris. Twenty-eight-year-old Mayor H. H. Earl thought it advisable to close all the saloons for one week.

The following morning, Wednesday, May 2, Gomer Thomas, the state inspector who had been in Scofield less than two months earlier, arrived at the scene. Thomas suspected that a careless shot of dynamite had ignited the coal dust. Some blamed the Finlanders for taking chances—trying to increase their loads by using too much shot. But later all the dynamite was accounted for. In time, Thomas would conclude that a keg of black powder had been accidentally set off in a large room in the upper reaches of Number Four. Flaming dust carried by the blast had shot down the rooms and entries in Number Four, igniting kegs of powder far from the original explosion.

In Salt Lake City, children ran from house to house gathering flowers to send to the bereaved. *The Herald* reported that a carload of lilacs and cut flowers was

The family of Levi Jones.

being shipped to the mining camp. "The consignment went down with the regular train occupying the whole of the baggage compartment." In Scofield, on Thursday morning, a long line of wagons filled with coffins and women in their weeds and small children dressed in black pulled up to the flower train. Each coffin was carefully buried under a blanket of blossoms. A spokesman for the Finns arrived to ask that some flowers be reserved until their wagon train could make its way down the canyon. He was assured there were flowers enough for all.

That afternoon out at the cemetery, pale-faced, hollow-eyed women waited for their turn to bury their dead. Forty men from Provo had arrived to help dig the graves. Apostle Teasdale blessed the sites of those who were members of the Latter-day Saints. As rescuers continued to search for bodies behind rock falls, reporters found children wandering the town, frightened and hungry, their mothers lost in such a state of shock the children had gone virtually without food since the day of the explosion.

Every family in Scofield was grieving. Three coffins marked the home of the Evans brothers, professional musicians from Wales: one lay on the porch, two by the gate. Among the hundred and fifty men waiting to be buried were five members of the Levi Jones family. Zeph Thomas was burying two brothers and two nephews. The Finlanders had lost sixty-one men in all. Abram and Kate Luoma, who had arrived in America earlier in the year, buried five of their six sons, a son-in-law, and three grandsons. They had lost all but one of their family.

Friday, a flag-draped funeral train left Scofield with the bodies of fifty-one miners who had come from out of town. At American Fork three Padfields were returned to their family. At Ogden, the bodies of the Hunter family, ten in all, were taken off the train: fathers—John, David, William, and Adam Hunter; sons—John, Robert, and James A. Hunter, and their Strang in-laws, Frank Sr. and Frank Jr. At Springville, the bodies of John Davis and his two sons were lifted off the train and carried home to Mrs. Davis and her eight younger children. The Dougall family retrieved Barney's coffin covered with flowers that his mother had sent down to Scofield.

Abram Luoma and his wife, Kate, pose with the widows and children of their five sons, son-in-law, and three grandsons who perished in the Scofield disaster. A few months after this photograph was taken, Abram and Kate Luoma packed up and returned to Finland. Descendants of the family still live in the area.

Over two hundred miners were killed. Bodies were discovered for weeks after the explosion; some were never recovered at all. It was the worst coal mine disaster in the country to date. One hundred and seven women lost their husbands and two hundred and sixty-eight children were left without their fathers. President McKinley telegraphed an expression of sorrow offering "deep sympathy to wives, children, and friends," but condolences from a decent man two thousand miles away were of little use to the people around Pleasant Valley. Relief wagons began touring the region with butter, eggs and meat, and sacks of flour for women paralyzed by grief.

With the exception of $3,000 from "an anonymous Eastern industrialist," the relief effort was pretty much a regional affair. The coal company donated $20,000 and forgave all debts at the company store. In the end, most of the $117,000 raised was in small amounts. There were donations from the Odd Fellows of $50 and $60, and $25 from the Jewish Relief Society. *The Salt Lake Herald* reported a game of baseball between the Elks and the Brokers netted "the very neat sum of $177.50."

The money was to be distributed in the following fashion:

To each widow over the age of fifty years, $720;

> . . . each widow under the age of fifty, $576;
> . . . each boy under fourteen and each girl under fifteen, $108;
> . . . each full orphan, $432;
> . . . each full dependent parent, $720;
> . . . aged fathers and mothers fully dependent, $1,080 for the two;
> . . . aged fathers and mothers with partial means of support, $900.

Days after the explosion, the Pleasant Valley Coal Company announced that to keep from losing the navy contract there would be as little delay as possible in reopening the mines. Repairing Number Four would take months, but Number One had suffered no structural damage. At first the survivors swore they would never go underground again. Some packed up and left, but over the weeks, most changed their minds. The company had no trouble replacing those who had been killed. Within days of the explosion applications had arrived from miners all over the country.

Scofield was still deep in mourning when Number One mine reopened on May 28. A watchman was needed at each shift to keep curiosity seekers away; the mines had become a tourist attraction. The entries had all been retimbered, and the company announced the works had been thoroughly "sprinkled" to keep down the dust, assuring that "there will be no chances taken hereafter and this mine cannot help but be one of the safest in the country." But among those going back to work, threading their way through the narrow entries, suspicions lingered.

Other Stories of Interest

The Daily Picayune (New Orleans), May 1, 1900
Railroad News, An Illinois Central Engineer Killed

As a result of a rear-end collision on the Illinois Central, Engineer Casey Jones, of the southbound Chicago mail train was killed and a negro fireman badly hurt.

The accident occurred just before daylight, and it is said to have been due altogether to a misunderstanding of signals due to the dense fog. On account of the recent tie-up of the Illinois Central there has accumulated all along the line a considerable number of cars. . . . Freight trains have kept things moving so rapidly that passenger trains have had a hard time getting past meeting points. The collision was [with] a south-bound freight.

The signals given by the brakeman of the freight train were not seen on account of the fog, or were misunderstood, and Engineer Jones, in obeying what he thought was a move ahead signal, did not discover that his track was still blockaded by the rear of the freight until his train had gained too great an impetus to be brought to a standstill.

The Boston Globe, May 4, 1900
Standard Oil Raises Wages, Strike Would Hurt McKinley's Chances Is Reason Alleged for 10 Percent Increase

NEW YORK—Twenty five thousand men employed by the Standard Oil all over the country have had their wages raised 10 percent. This means an additional outlay of $1,500,000. One of the leading officers said to a reporter:

"The unrest of labor led to the advance at this time, although the Standard Oil company pays the highest price for labor as it is. However it is recognized that times have improved and labor evidently feels that it should share in the good times. This company recognizes that fact and raises wages 10 percent or reduces the working hours from ten to nine, which had the same result."

It appeared, however, from words dropped here and there by Standard Oil officials, that a strike at this time would hurt McKinley's chances of reelection, and in order to head off trouble and keep the men in line, it was decided to give the increase in wages.

Stella Simm clowning with friends aboard the Cunard ship, the Lucania, *on her way to Europe.*

Tourists often posed on the balcony of the Treasury building in Washington, D.C., with the sweep of Pennsylvania Avenue and the Capitol behind them. Washington was considered the cleanest city in the nation. No factory smoke marred the facades of the white sandstone buildings. No skyscrapers competed with the Washington Monument. And most electric-light wires, telegraph, and telephone lines were now in conduits underground.

CHAPTER NINE

June

I

In Washington the first week of June, all who could were fleeing before the hellish heat of summer. The diplomats and lobbyists were long gone, the national press corps was thinning out, and Congress was set to adjourn when, on Tuesday, June 5, partisan wrangling turned so nasty that work on the hill ground to a halt. With an eye on fall elections, outnumbered Democrats and Independents, frustrated all session, went on the attack. Senator Pettigrew accused Republican leaders of setting aside an antitrust bill in the hope of soliciting campaign contributions from big business.

As the exchange escalated, Pettigrew accused Mark Hanna, chairman of the Republican party, of bribing his way into the Senate. Outraged, Hanna questioned Pettigrew's sanity. *The Washington Post* reported that for an hour "the air in the Senate crackled as if an electric storm had been raging." In the House, Democrats accused the Republicans of being complicitous with the armor-plate trust, which was supplying steel plates for warships at exorbitant prices. For two days the debates were so bitter, *The Post* reported that "passion and personal rancor . . . brought [members] to the brink of actual riot."

On Wednesday afternoon President McKinley arrived on the Hill hoping his presence would settle things down, but to no avail. He wandered the halls, talked to old friends, signed a few bills, and went home for dinner. Finally, on Thursday, out of either exhaustion or eagerness to leave, members in both chambers went back to work finishing up the appropriation bills needed to keep the government going another year. But the theatrics were far from over. As the last bill was dispatched for the president's signature, John Fitzgerald and a handful of colleagues made their way to the Speaker's rostrum and without any prelude began singing a medley of patriotic airs: "Columbia the gem of the ocean . . . Three cheers for the red, white and blue."

As members on both sides of the aisle joined in this curious expression of fellowship, tourists in the halls raced back to the galleries and congressmen in cloakrooms abandoned their cigars to return to the chamber. After a rousing version of "Dixie," which brought the Democratic congressmen to their feet, the popular Fitzgerald, in a strong, clear tenor, launched into the national anthem and everyone, from the Speaker of the House to children in the galleries, added their voices, women waving handkerchiefs, men clapping in time. *The Post* reported that the gentleman from Boston had led "a magnificent soul-inspiring spectacle that made the pulses leap and the blood tingle."

Reporters celebrated their emancipation with a fine rendition of the doxology, and Speaker Henderson, after a graceful farewell, declared the first session of the Fifty-Sixth Congress over. As members raced for their trains, a gray-haired man in the gallery raised his hat and delivered a message to the retreating crowd: "from the Great White Throne—Jesus is Coming Soon." Peace settled over the House and the old man was led away.

———✦———

At the Washington Monument, long lines of tourists waited in the sun for the elevator ride to the top of what the guidebooks described as the tallest stone structure in the world. The ride was seven minutes long—a terrifying prospect for the claustrophobic—but visitors were assured the cab was brightly lit by an electric light and would stop for those who wished to get out along the way. On the platform at the pinnacle, the tourists felt cut loose from the world. Few had ever been at such a height before.

The capital was now precisely one hundred years old and many knew in outline, if not in detail, how the magnificent white sandstone buildings had been willed into being in the middle of a forest just a century before. Washington and

Jefferson had been ridiculed for commissioning ornate palaces in the woods when the nation's survival was not at all that certain. A French writer of the time remarked, "You may wager a thousand to one that the town will not be built." In 1800 when the government moved down from Philadelphia and President John Adams and his wife headed for the Executive Mansion, Pennsylvania Avenue was still a morass of mud, lined with alder bushes and shrub oak. Only one wing of the Capitol had been erected, and the president's house, one mile distant, was not yet finished.

In 1800, three thousand people lived in Washington City. By 1900 there were three hundred thousand. Guidebooks and magazines celebrating the city's centennial delighted in publishing comparative figures. In 1800, only "one packet-sloop" had been needed to carry the nation's archives and furniture to the banks of the Potomac. The entire cost of the move came to about $48,000. In 1900, the Postal Department was spending more than twice as much on string. It was in these details that Americans were coming to understand just how large and complex their country had become.

The Bureau of Engraving and Printing was now a great money factory, producing a million dollars' worth of bills a day. In a hot and steaming print room three hundred printers with ink to their elbows—each with a woman assistant—were turning out dollars like "corn from a sheller." Four billion stamps were being printed, pressed, perforated, and counted every year. At the Census Bureau, in an oversized room with an enormous vaulted skylight, an army of young women were

By 1900 the government was manufacturing over four billion postage stamps a year at the Bureau of Engraving. The women worked in teams of two, carefully lining up sheets of stamps under a thin black thread to feed into the new perforating machines. A third of all federal employees were women. Because of their "passive natures," women were considered best suited for jobs like this one.

collating information on complex new machines that would create a giant statistical mosaic.

Since the beginning of the year, fifty-two thousand enumerators had been collecting data, house to house, farm to farm, one workplace to the next, from the most northern reaches on the coast of Maine to the smallest crossroads in Southern California. By summer, the raw data was arriving at the Bureau by the ton. A thousand clerks were translating this handwritten material onto individual punch cards, which in turn were being fed one by one into electrical tabulating machines. A relatively new invention, the Hollerith machines, using sophisticated circuitry, scanned each card, collating random facts into useful statistical portraits.

Described as smart machines, the tabulators rejected any card that was incomplete, improperly punched, or contained doubtful facts—a female blacksmith or a male dressmaker. The director of the Census, William Merriam, was a bureaucrat in love: "Such a machine," he said, "has the advantage that it will not make mistakes because it is tired or does not feel well, or because the weather is warm." Working on a very short deadline, Merriam was offering a $15-a-month increase to every processor able to handle six hundred cards a day, but during the worst of summer, when an unrelenting sun beat down on the glass roof, twenty women a day fainted at their tables.

Even before the census was complete, newspapers began running columns of comparative statistics, some based on fact, others on whimsy. It was said there were now more telephones than bathtubs; whether this was true, no one seemed to care—the fascination with statistics had bred an appetite for more. How many bolts would an architect need to build a steel skyscraper fourteen stories tall? How many people would inhabit the United States in the year 2000? *Popular Science* predicted that within one hundred years the population of the United States would reach three hundred and fifty-eight million people, and within a thousand years there would be forty-one billion in the country.

The essay concluded "that life in the future must be subject to constantly increasing stress."

II

At the White House, with the Republican convention only days away, reporters were hoping to be briefed on the vice-presidential question. Senator Platt's campaign was gaining support, more and more delegates seemed to be leaning toward Governor Roosevelt, but McKinley steadily refused to comment on the matter. The press was told the president was neutral but didn't believe it. Reporters liked McKinley and knew he was a man of strong opinions, but he was not granting interviews these days and speaking to him directly was out of bounds. Journalists might silently watch his comings and goings but would learn little. The president was unfailingly polite and totally unrevealing.

Roosevelt was far less formal with the press. He confided in reporters, was often playful, and what he did not say directly could sometimes be gleaned from his manner. All year they had been recording his denials while registering his ambivalence. TR's emotions were never far from the surface, but now he, too, seemed withdrawn. On June 12, he wrote a friend: "I am doing my best to prevent the corporations and the Machine making [me] the . . . candidate in order to get rid of me here as Governor." But his situation was more compromised than this note reflected. While Tom Platt was trying to push him out of the state and into the vice presidency, Mark Hanna, the most powerful man in the Republican party, was doing everything he could to block Roosevelt's nomination.

Hanna told party leaders that TR was "unsafe and erratic." But Hanna, too, had been unable to convince the president to take a stand. In the midst of all the political maneuvering McKinley remained cheerfully noncommittal.

In the all but empty corridors on Capitol Hill a reporter for *The Washington Post* spotted technicians lugging a curious assemblage of equipment from one office to the next. Behind closed doors in ornate committee rooms, the most effective orators in the Republican party were being coached on how to use a recording device in a professional manner. The graphophone had been around for some twenty years but had never been used for political purposes. In private rehearsals

Graphophones were still expensive in 1900; prices ranged from $5 to $150. But purchasers were promised the machine was worth the price: "The Graphophone is the greatest entertainment of the age. It not only produces all that is best in music, song or story, but you can talk to it yourself and it will repeat all that you say."

snatches of Kipling poems and lines from set speeches were being painfully recorded on wax cylinders and then played back through a big brass funnel.

The Post reporter followed Representative Mercer from Nebraska in his "stint with the graphophone man." Mercer was placed in front of a trumpet-shaped tube of pasteboard that protruded from a boxlike contrivance. He was urged not to shout, which was counterintuitive to a man who had been taught to deliver every speech in full voice, but once he got the hang of it and listened to the playback, Mercer was well pleased.

Political speeches could now be sent into those areas beyond the major rail lines that Republicans considered the "benighted regions of doubt." Democrats in every crossroads and corner grocery would be wooed with Sousa martial music, ragtime songs, and speeches lauding the inspiring deeds of William McKinley. No American citizen in the future would be beyond the sound of a political message.

III

On Saturday, June 16, three days before the Republican convention, TR strode into Philadelphia continuing to insist that he had no interest in the vice presidency, but on the streets there was a brisk trade in McKinley-Roosevelt badges. On Monday *The Washington Post* reported that the lasso was around Roosevelt's neck and he was perceptibly weakening. On Tuesday TR declared once again that his "best usefulness to the party [was] in New York State." But behind the scenes the battle of the bosses continued. Senator Platt drumming up support for TR; Hanna working just as diligently to block the nomination.

With McKinley's nomination a foregone conclusion, opening day of the convention was lusterless. Delegates drifted from one hotel room to the next discussing the stalemate between Platt and Hanna. In the all but deserted convention hall "fans moved ceaselessly to and fro like a cloud of alarmed gulls beating the hot and humid air." A small flurry attended the introduction of the ten surviving members of the first Republican convention in 1854, but out in the streets ticket speculators were hurting and spectator seats were selling for an "unpatriotic low" price.

The second day found the convention in a "blight of listlessness." The most exciting moment of the day was when an elevator fell seven stories injuring five delegates and the elevator boy. Platt and Hanna continued their maneuvering; the nomination for vice president was still in doubt. TR was said to be in "a mental condition that beggars description." He had been told by Hanna that if he remained in the field he must regard himself as an enemy of the president. In the hall, delegates listening to an endless reading of the party platform, awash in boredom and frustration, were uncertain whether they would be released to nominate TR as they now wished or be forced to support one of half a dozen uninspired choices.

By Wednesday afternoon it was clear that Mark Hanna was losing the public relations battle; the convention was slipping out of his control. He had hoped until the last for a presidential reprieve, a declaration of support for anyone but Roosevelt; instead he had just received instructions that "the President did not want his friends to dictate to the convention." Hanna moved to put an end to the

This cartoon appeared in Harper's Weekly *(June 30, 1900) immediately after Roosevelt's nomination for the vice presidency, with a caption that read, "What could the poor boy do?"*

torment. He called reporters to his suite and read a prepared announcement: "Given the strong and earnest sentiment for Governor Roosevelt," he said, it was his judgment that TR should be nominated unanimously. The news of Hanna's capitulation was like an infusion of oxygen in the airless hotel. Groups of men were seen cheering in the lobby. Shortly after, TR left the hotel to join his wife who was staying in a private home. The governor had no comment.

The following morning twenty thousand people pressed their way into a hall that had been designed to accommodate no more than fifteen thousand. Among the spectators was Edith Roosevelt, "pale as paper." After the assembly sang "The Union Forever" and McKinley's name was placed before the delegates, Roosevelt moved to the podium to second McKinley's nomination and the convention went wild. A correspondent for *Harper's Weekly* wrote that TR's "speech was in effect his own nomination. He was all that the idolizing thousands wanted . . . direct, dashing, fearless, possibly a little careless and everything he was, the people liked him for."

When TR's name was finally put before the convention, one reporter said the governor looked like a man "who did not know whether he stood on the edge of a precipice or on the high road to glory." Roosevelt received every vote in the hall but his own. It was done at last. Tom Platt, exhausted and feeling his age, headed home for New York.

At the White House that day, as the chief telegrapher monitored messages from the wire room in Philadelphia, workmen were erecting a striped awning for an evening reception in honor of the American Institute of Homeopathy. Palms from the greenhouse were being carried into the reception rooms. Upstairs in his office the president was making a point of going about his business as usual. Periodically Secretary Cortelyou slipped in with handwritten bulletins from the convention. At 12:14, when his renomination was confirmed, the president lay aside his work and walked down the hall to see his wife.

That evening, as the homeopaths mixed with McKinley friends from Ohio and delegates who had just arrived by train from Philadelphia, Senator Mark Hanna, genuinely troubled by TR's nomination, wrote the president a note: "Your duty to the Country, is to live for four [more] years."

IV

In Galesburg, Illinois, Carl Sandburg was brooding about TR now that "Boss Platt had got him shelved into a job he didn't want." Sandburg noted that "no vice president except Martin Van Buren had ever been elected President of the United States." With his studies over for the summer, Sandburg was setting out on his bicycle to tour the farm country of Bureau County, Illinois, with a collection of Underwood & Underwood stereographic slides.

Over that hot summer Sandburg would meander through Wataga, Oneida, Galva, and Kewanee, selling stereo views farm to farm. The images of those towns, the people, and the landscape would emerge and reemerge in Sandburg's books and poetry. Fifty years later he would remember how in the village of Neponset in the best hotel in town he had found a room with a wide bed with slats, a washstand, and a "yellow china chamber pot" for three dollars a week. Meals were an extra twenty-five cents each.

The people Sandburg met that summer for the most part lived and worked close to home, courted and flirted and visited with neighbors within an easy carriage ride away. But the isolation that had long held farmers remote from the rest of the country had slowly been eroding. Newspapers and periodicals were now delivered to newly improvised mailboxes. Rural Free Delivery was a wondrous service. Farmers and their families were as curious about the world beyond their own as any city folk. Captured in Sandburg's plush-lined leatherette carrying case was an assortment of three-dimensional images, views of the beautiful Amalfi coast, of Jerusalem and the Holy Land, of exotic people in Africa and Asia.

His own family had owned a stereoscope and Carl understood the magic of sitting in a parlor in the middle of the prairie studying images of places thousands of miles away. In 1900, collecting "views" was a wildly popular hobby. Under-wood & Underwood were producing three hundred thousand cards a year. Almost every parlor seemed to have a stereoscope and a basketful of stereo views. Sandburg had become a canny salesman; if a farmer grumbled over a stereo of McKinley it was quickly replaced by a view of Bryan. Sandburg himself was not enthusiastic about either candidate that year.

He sold views of the rich and famous, of the overdressed and underclad, of snowtopped mountain ranges and giant sequoias, and carefully staged scenes of American soldiers on the firing line in the Philippines. Carl would do well that summer; photography of every kind had become something of a national craze. He would not only make enough to pay all his expenses but return home with a one-hundred-dollar profit.

For decades now every town of any size had a photo studio, and out in the country traveling cameramen, a patient breed, had long been luring entire families to sit for group portraits. Posing had required an unnatural stillness, producing stiff and ungiving photographs of frozen children, sober-eyed lovers, and tight-lipped old folk hiding their lack of teeth. But newer cameras with faster film were catching people smiling and playful, recording candid images of daily life.

In 1900 with the arrival of the new Kodak, the easy-to-use Brownie camera that cost just a dollar, the inventor George Eastman was urging Americans to make "mementoes of the future" and they happily complied. Young soldiers heading overseas were packing cameras in their duffels. Amateurs were recording family courtships and honeymoons, graduations and reunions, collecting all in ornate family albums. The great moments of life no longer needed to be left to the unreliable vagaries of the mind.

Sandburg recalled that in his home, "On the center table next to the Bible was a big book with red-plush covers and fancy nickelwork on the front cover, our Photograph Album. Our fingers locked and unlocked its metal clasps. We could see how Papa and Mama looked about the time they got married. When visitors came they looked through the Album and we told them who was who. You couldn't eat the Album nor wear it. You couldn't say it was useful, and you

William Krueger, the white-bearded patriarch, posed for this photograph with his children, grandchildren, and great-grandchildren on the family dairy farm in Watertown, Wisconsin. Krueger had left Pomerania (Germany) in 1851. His oldest son, August, and his wife, the sober-looking Mary, are holding their twin grandchildren, Edgar and Jennie. The father of the twins, Alex Krueger, was the family photographer. Their mother, Flora, and her sister-in-law, Minnie, probably made their dresses from the same bolt of cloth.

couldn't get along without it. The Album was something extra. It was one of the things we had in mind when we said, 'We're not rich—but we're not poor.' "

———·•·———

In farm country that summer—even though June was a particularly busy time of year—somehow in those dawn-to-dusk days there was also time for "leisure," a new word in the American vocabulary. Years before, President James Garfield divided the struggle of the human race into two chapters. First, the fight to acquire leisure and then the struggle to know what to do with it once you got it. By 1900, that no longer seemed a problem. To be sure, for many folks in the Midwest, time off meant time for self-improvement. There were lectures, and study groups, and Bible classes, and the stereopticon was often used to teach lessons in morality, to uplift and ennoble, and to expand the mind. Sandburg himself had been moved by a Jacob Riis lecture, with stereo views of the squalid life of New York tenements.

But there were also baseball games and traveling vaudeville shows and circuses and concerts and musicals of every kind. The popular actor James O'Neill, who had built an entire career playing the Count of Monte Cristo, was on tour yet again, dragging along his recalcitrant twelve-year-old son Eugene. Most entertainment still tended to be homegrown. Every lodge, social society, and church group had its singers and musicians, at least one banjo player or someone able to pick a guitar. More people, particularly young women, were studying piano. Once a mark of the very rich, pianos now were commonplace in middle-class life.

That summer, sentimental ballads—"She was Only a Girl in a Gilded Cage" and "Daisy, Daisy, Give Me Your Answer True"—were played more often than they deserved. Popular songs were safe and tidy and utterly predictable. And then there was the music of John Phillip Sousa, the greatest romantic of them all. Sousa's music was everything Americans wanted: optimistic; expansive, patriotic marches that made the spirit soar. A Sousa concert remained among the very few certainties in life. This was God's in His Heaven and all's right with the world kind of music.

But a new form of American music, less certain, less predictable, and considerably more edgy was gaining attention in a social club on the shady side of Sedalia, a small Missouri rail town. On East Main Street, surrounded by honky-tonks, saloons, and brothels, above the Blotcher Seed Company, customers from all over the state were crowding into Tony Williams's Maple Leaf Club. At an upright piano in one corner near the bar, an unusually gifted musician named Scott Joplin was beginning to make a name for himself with his "raggedy" compositions.

Joplin had not invented ragtime—no one knew who had—but by the late 1890s he had begun to make the form his own. At its most basic, ragtime was an exuberant mix of traditional black melodies, of slave songs and work songs, of hollers and blues with syncopated African rhythms all filtered through European forms. For generations black and white Americans had borrowed freely from each other's culture. Stephen Foster had used "coon" songs, Sousa had picked up syncopation, but neither composer strayed far from the cultural mainstream.

Ragtime however was more black than white, freer, easier. One couldn't listen to ragtime and eat white bread or deny the music's African heritage. The coloration of ragtime led one critic to declare that it would "stifle the nostrils of decency." Composer Edward MacDowell dismissed the form as "nigger whorehouse music." But a few years earlier, when the great Bohemian composer Antonín Dvořák had toured the United States, he came to the conclusion that the future music of America "must be founded upon what are called the negro melodies . . . these beautiful and varied themes are the product of the soil. They are American."

Critic E. R. Kroeger was outraged: "Is it true that we must accept the music of another race as being that which is American? Have not the white Americans sufficient individuality to develop a characteristic style of composition?" But whether the critics liked it or not American music was no longer all black or all white. Scott Joplin, much like Paul Laurence Dunbar, had absorbed a very American mix of cultures. As a child, growing up along the border between Texas and Arkansas, he had learned European dance music from his father, an accomplished violinist and former slave, and plantation songs and spirituals from his mother, who played the banjo and sang in church choirs.

Joplin studied the rudiments of harmony and composition with a neighbor music teacher who has variously been described as a German, a Mexican, and an African American. By the time he wandered off in his teens, making his way as an itinerant musician, he was composing music that drew on the landscape of his life, the sounds from the past, many people's past, woven into a sound that was new and, like Joplin himself, distinctly American.

In the mid-1890s he settled in Sedalia and began studying composition at the George R. Smith College for Negroes, teaching private students and composing music for the Queen City Concert Band. While the town boasted numbers of musicians, the census taker in 1900 noted that thirty-two-year-old Joplin was the only one able to claim music as his full-time profession. There are any number of versions of how Joplin came to publish "The Maple Leaf Rag" in 1899. Some said that John Stark, the town's piano seller and a lackluster music publisher, happened into the Maple Leaf Club and persuaded Joplin to write down his composition.

Others claimed Joplin had turned up at Stark's Music shop and talked Stark into publishing his song. However it all began, each man completely changed the life of the other. The song started selling slowly. It was not easy to play, was marked from the start as "Negro" music, and was said to have come from a red-light district at that. But by 1900, orders were pouring in from F. W. Woolworth's 5-and-10-cent stores, an institution about as close to middle America as apple pie and the flag. Stark sold 75,000 copies that year and *The Sedalia Democrat* began referring to Joplin as "that well known musician."

The song would sell over a million copies, Stark would become rich, and Joplin would be recognized as one of America's first great composers. But not during his lifetime.

V

In mid-June, in San Francisco, a Federal quarantine was imposed on the city; no one was allowed to leave without a certificate from the U.S. health officer. For months there had been reports that the bubonic plague was taking hold in the city's densely crowded Chinatown. The stories were confused and often contradictory, but the plague was as terrifying in 1900 as it had been in biblical days. Almost always fatal, and with no known cure, victims suffered agonizing deaths—severe headaches, vomiting, and high fevers ending with a paralysis of the respiratory system.

The disease was associated with filth and famine; outbreaks were regularly reported in India and China, but not in civilized countries like the United States. At the beginning of the year, when three cases were identified in Honolulu, the gateway to California, Americans were alarmed. The Hawaiian Islands were still at some distance, but the plague was known to follow the paths of commerce, and San Francisco with its continuous Asian traffic was clearly under threat. Recent studies suggested that the plague bacillus was carried by fleas from infected rats and virtually every ocean-going ship was said to be infested.

At the time of the outbreak the U.S. health official in Honolulu issued a reassuring statement that his staff had all the chemicals and apparatus needed for "proper destruction of the microbes." A lengthy report in San Francisco's *The Examiner* detailed how officials sterilized a steamship with formaldehyde gas before the vessel was allowed to leave port. In spite of these precautions, in early March, the body of an older man named Wong Chut King was found in the basement of the Globe Hotel in San Francisco's Chinatown, and local officials were suspicious. Tissue samples were collected and sent to Angel's Island for analysis.

The mayor's office acknowledged the need to take precautionary measures but at the same time hoped to downplay the story. Even one case of plague would have dreadful commercial consequences. The federal health officer, Dr. J. J. Kinyoun, however, unwilling to take chances, ordered an immediate quarantine imposed on the quarter. Accompanied by reporters, work parties were sent in to purify the area: cellars were drenched with lyme, refuse burned, buildings whitewashed, disinfectant scattered in gutters, and the exits of sewers were screened with woven wire to prevent any rats from escaping.

Five days later, Dr. Kinyoun reported that two guinea pigs and one rat, inoculated with bacilli from the deceased Mr. Wong, had died from the bubonic plague. But in the days that followed, with no new cases reported, the city began to relax. On the twentieth day, Mayor Phelan wired fellow mayors around the country that, because of San Francisco's rapid response, the threat had passed. However, Phelan was premature. That very day, there were three more suspicious deaths.

In the weeks that followed everyone who died in Chinatown was immediately suspect. Cases were reported, denied, and then confirmed; quarantines were imposed, and when the disease seemed to subside, were lifted again. Throughout the spring there were rumors of missing corpses, of stolen tissue samples, of inaccurate lab work and suppressed information. By the end of May the crisis was undeniable. June 1, Dr. Kinyoun reported ten authenticated cases of the plague, all in the Chinese quarter. Seventy-five inspectors and fifty policemen were sent into the enclave to search every building, every subterranean passage and cellar, to root out every ailing resident.

The Chinese, known to be more fearful of autopsies than of death, refused to cooperate. One aged man, known to be ill, disappeared with the aid of friends, never to be seen again. Residents were begging to be vaccinated, but there was not enough serum in the city for them all. Fumigating stations were erected on the edge of the quarter so that Caucasians working inside the area could be cleansed before going back out into the city. Twenty thousand people were now sealed inside the enclave. The mayor announced that Chinatown was "absolutely shut away from the rest of the world."

No one was allowed to go out to work or market. Streetcars were barred, letter carriers, too. A double cordon of guards, sixty men, were stationed along a twenty-block perimeter. Ropes signaled the unwary that they were approaching the quarantine zone. Within days, food supplies were running low. Good Samaritans were found sneaking into the quarter to relieve the indigent. There were queries now from Secretary of State John Hay and from foreign governments, and the State of Texas imposed a commercial quarantine. So did Vancouver, B.C. Terrified merchants raised $30,000 to aid the health board in its work.

The quarantine began to take on a punitive air, as though the Chinese themselves were somehow responsible for the disease. Fear fed on fear. The Chinese, believing city officials were planning to poison their water supply, placed guards around the water tanks. When a white sanitation worker new to the quarter wandered near a tank he almost lost his life. At one point there was talk of forcing the entire population into detention on Mission Rock, a small isolated island in the bay. Chinatown was to be destroyed, the infested enclave burned to the ground.

The battleground now shifted to the courts. Chinese leaders argued that while white San Franciscans were free to pass in and out of the quarter if they chose, Chinese residents were virtually under house arrest. With ten thousand people facing destitution, the federal court lifted the restrictions. Dr. Kinyoun countered by placing the entire city under quarantine. Anyone wishing to leave San Francisco had to apply for a health certificate. No one could board a ship or train without an official document. Enraged businessmen appealed to Washington. Kinyoun's decision was rescinded a week later, with little explanation.

Toward the end of the month, with no new cases reported, the governor of California declared that in his opinion the plague had probably never existed at all. But the following year, a federal panel found that at least thirty-two people in San Francisco had died of the plague, and there had probably been cases that went unreported.

———— ·-· ————

Across the bay in Oakland, the city's problems seemed remote. Jack London, with "a glorious dose of sunburn," wrote a friend that he was exercising every day with Indian clubs and was swimming and diving and cycling three or four times a week, "ripping and tearing through the streets and roads, over railroad tracks and bridges, threading crowds, avoiding collisions at twenty miles or more an hour wondering all the time when you're going to smash up. . . . It is Voltaire, I believe who said: 'The body of an athlete and the soul of a sage.' "

His collection of stories about Alaska, *Son of the Wolf,* was published now and getting good reviews. And as he had promised, in spite of his marriage his friendship with Anna Strunsky continued:

Dear Anna—

Comrades! And surely it seems so. For all the petty surface turmoil which marked our coming to know each other, really deep down, there was no confusion at all. Did you notice it? To me, while I said "You do not understand," I none the less felt the happiness of satisfaction . . . that there was no inner conflict; that we were attuned, somehow . . . when we rushed into each other's lives—we, the real we, were undisturbed. Comrades! Ay, world without end! . . .

And when are you coming over?

Jack

Other Stories of Interest

The Examiner (San Francisco), June 2, 1900
Scourge May Be Cured
by Roentgen Ray, Physicians
Discuss Cure Discovery

The efficacy of the X-ray in the treatment of tuberculosis of the lungs (consumption) . . . was the subject of conversation and informal argument among medical men yesterday.

All agreed that any plausible method offering a cure for tubercular diseases, that are the cause of death of 12 per cent of the human family, should be treated fully. It was also generally admitted that while certain forms of cancerous ulcerations had been cured by the application of X-ray, the discovery of Roentgen is yet in its infancy; its power yet in an evolutionary stage.

Dr. George H. Martin: I use the X-ray for the treatment of lupus. . . . I also use it in the diagnosis of bone infections. . . . All those who use the rays know that ten or fifteen minute exposures to them once a day, or in some instances every other day, will create an inflammation that resembles a burn but is not a burn. It destroys the tissues and requires months to heal. . . .

From what we know of the treatment and cure of cancerous growths on the surface by the X-ray it is plausible that it will kill tubercular bacilli . . . but I cannot see how it can be applied satisfactorily without injury to the other parts of the body exposed.

Dr. Frederick G. Canney: I tried the X-ray in a case of cancer of the stomach. It afforded relief but not a cure.

Dr. Nelson Chamberlain: I have only used the X-ray treatment a few times. . . . It will be a great thing for humanity if it is concluded that X-ray will cure both the germs of cancer and consumption.

The Washington Post, June 6, 1900
Wants Dreyfus' Rank Restored

Representative Levy of New York yesterday introduced to the House a resolution . . . requesting that the Secretary of State be directed to "appeal to the fairness, justice and chivalry of France, to . . . restore to his full rank in the army Captain Alfred Dreyfus, whose legion of friends and sympathizers in the United States, as well as in the civilized world, believe in his innocence."

The Washington Post, June 11, 1900
NEW YORK, June 10—The Protective Association of Professional Ball Players is the name of the organization effected in this city today at a meeting of delegates from the eight National League teams. The question of ball players forming an organization for their mutual benefit has been agitated for some time.

The farming out of players against their will and other practices that are considered grievances by the players led up to today's meeting.

The Washington Post, June 17, 1900
The Chat of Paris

Monday evening the Salle des Agriculture was the scene of a brilliant gathering. . . . Pablo Casals, the distinguished Spanish cellist, played several selections. . . . M. Casals will undoubtedly be heard in America next year.

The Kansas City Star, July 3, 1900
ST. PETERSBURG—The official Messenger today publishes an imperial ukase providing in large measure for the abolition of banishment to Siberia.

Everyone of note who arrived in San Francisco was taken to Cliff House on the bluff at Point Lobos. This magnificent eight-story Victorian hodgepodge, with restaurants and bars and an observation tower, once had stalls enough to accommodate 1200 teams of horses. The precarious structure was held in place by iron rods cemented to the rocks. While the restaurants were expensive, for a dime one could sit out on the balcony, enjoy refreshments, and watch sea lions playing on the rocks below.

Bathing off Rutgers Slip in the East River, in New York City, was neither clean nor safe. The river, actually a saltwater estuary, was subject to strong tidal pulls and dangerous currents, but it was a popular escape for overheated youngsters every summer.

CHAPTER TEN

July–August

I

In Washington, by July the overbaked trees were turning brown, the grass had died, and with the temperature reaching over one hundred an eerie stillness had settled over the city. The government bureaus were closing early and all who could, the old and the young, hid inside shade-drawn homes. Trolley conductors stopped their cars at every water fountain, and ambulance horses were dropping in the streets. In Baltimore, the death rate among children had increased alarmingly. In New York, at Bellevue Hospital, white-jacketed surgeons plunged semiconscious patients into great vats of cracked ice. Across the eastern half of the country there was no relief from the unrelenting sun.

Those who put their trust in science and technology to modify the forces of nature were heartened by news of experiments in Europe. In Italy and France, vineyard owners were said to have diverted hailstorms by firing giant cannons at developing cloud formations. The U.S. consul in Lyons reported that the bombardment of the heavens was almost always successful. A rain machine was surely the logical next step. Writer Ambrose Bierce, less sanguine about man's ability to monkey around with nature, suggested two possible explanations for the European experiments—the scientific and the rational.

"According to the former," Bierce wrote, "the ascending gasses of the burnt gunpowder drive the hailstorms upward. The other (and more beautiful) theory is that the good Lord accepts the bombardment as an intimation that persons who live in glass-houses must not throw hailstorms. The new policy of military acts of Providence will be watched with interest and hope, but there is still some reason to believe in the superior efficacy of prayer." As the drought spread throughout the South and Midwest, most considered prayer the only solution.

Engineers in Washington were asking permission to run pipes beneath the pavement to distribute cold air from a central refrigerating plant direct to business buildings and homes in the city. Congress had yet to respond. Almost twenty years earlier, during another deadly summer, when President James Garfield lay dying from an assassin's bullet, the navy jury-rigged a machine that lowered the temperature in Garfield's bedroom by twenty degrees. A fan was placed next to an enormous tank of shaved ice and salt and the cooled air was pumped through a duct into the sickroom. Over the fifty-eight days that the president clung to life, half a million pounds of ice were consumed.

In July *The Boston Globe* ran an illustrated feature on the heroic life of a local iceman named Charlie White. Every morning before dawn, White, with the help of an assistant, hoisted by hand large blocks of ice—sixty-five hundred pounds in all—onto his wagon. Over the course of his eighteen-hour day White would return to the ice house for two more loads. Everywhere he stopped children swarmed his wagon hoping for handouts, but White was held to strict accounting, he could give away shavings, but that was it. In many cities, the price of ice that summer doubled. The ice trust became the most hated business conglomerate in America.

The first week in July, west of Kansas City, for a matter of hours the weather turned violent. A small tornado whipped through the area, tearing at roofs, demolishing small homes; then lightning set fields of wheat afire and the torrential rains that followed destroyed acres of grain. But in Kansas City itself, as the first delegates arrived for the Democratic national convention, the sun was unrelenting and the only discernible shift in the climate that week would be political.

Early Sunday morning, as the Democrats were settling into breakfast with three-inch chops and sirloin steaks, crowds of people, first hundreds, then thousands, were making their way through the city, pushing past the ubiquitous photographs of William Jennings Bryan that had been placed in office windows, past the gloriously decorated office buildings wrapped in tricolor bunting. Ignoring the heat, they raced down the steep hills to Union Depot for an impromptu trainside reception for Theodore Roosevelt.

With his impeccable timing, TR had selected the eve of the Democratic convention for his first appearance as the Republican candidate for vice president. As his train was being slowly pushed inside the shed, Roosevelt was stunned by the size of the crowd that swarmed out on the tracks to greet him. As he waved his oversized campaign hat, the crowd roared and began moving forward toward the oncoming car. The reception committee and the mayor were glowing with pleasure when suddenly it was evident to all that the train and the crowd were on a collision course. TR began to scream "Out of the way! Out of the way for Heaven's sake or you'll be run over!" but his voice could not be heard above the cheers.

As the crowd kept pressing forward, the reporter for *The Kansas City Star* noted, "They were lost to all sense of danger as they were pushed, pulled, dragged, lifted up, twisted around, their clothing torn . . . their faces streaming with perspiration, their eyes fixed on Roosevelt." And then at the last possible moment, with the train whistle screeching, they surged back before the oncoming car. No one lost his footing and disaster was averted. The mayor, trying to recover his composure, began a set speech, but the crowd had no need for his intrusion, brushing his words away they were moving again, arms upraised, cheering for Teddy.

Beneath the corrugated iron roof the heat had been building for days, clothing was bedraggled, collars wilted, hatbands soaked, but no one backed off. TR, red-faced, with perspiration clouding his glasses, bent low over the railing, trying to reach every outstretched hand. The mayor shouted for order, but there could be no order. To avoid being crushed, exhausted men were trying to climb aboard the train platform; some were clinging to the edge of the roof, knocking each other from the railings and the bumpers. After some minutes, Roosevelt shouted, "No more handshaking, no more handshaking, you must push back . . . you are killing people here!"

An old man responded, "But I'm the father of Sherod Coleman." TR reached for his hand and grasped it warmly. "I hadn't a better man in my regiment," he said. "Are you tired?" shouted another. "Tired not a bit," was the reply. "You've got to kill me with a club . . . but I am afraid for the lives of these folk," and with uncustomary caution, TR gave the signal for retreat. As the train pulled out of the shed, slowly at first, the crowd began to follow. TR waved his hat until the last man dropped from view.

The following day, on the front page of *The Star,* under a headline that read, "Wild to See Roosevelt," TR was described as calling on "heaven and earth to witness that the present trip had nothing to do with politics." But no matter his protestations, the once reluctant candidate had fired the first shot in the presidential campaign before the Democrats had even finished breakfast.

Convention week, Kansas City had never looked better. The hollyhocks were in full and startling bloom, as were masses of purple clematis, and ingenious machines were sprinkling the streets to keep down the dust sweeping in from the plains. In spite of the heat, eastern reporters were clearly taken with the town. Those who had been in Philadelphia a few weeks back found Kansas City far more entertaining. Columns were written about the "wide-open" western town where you could buy a drink on Sunday, gamble whenever you wished, and Sunday afternoon have a choice of either attending church or an unexpurgated version of *Sapho.*

Early morning on the Fourth of July, Richard Croker's men from Tammany Hall were taken on an unusual private junket. Whether the excursion was inspired by an excess of civic pride or some more malevolent ambition was never established, but hours before the convention

Theodore Roosevelt making a "cart-tail" speech from the rear platform of his private car, in Manhattan, Kansas, at the start of the 1900 campaign. These extemporaneous talks proved exhausting. Within weeks an additional speaker was added to the train to spell the governor, but it did little good. Everyone wanted to see TR.

officially opened, the New York delegation was taken on a tour of an abattoir, where "seven hundred cattle were dispatched for their benefit." Predictably, a slaughterhouse on a hot summer morning is not easy going. After watching "one particular heifer in its rapid transit from life into sirloins," some of the men from Tammany "beat a hasty retreat."

The opening of the convention was one long Fourth of July celebration, raucous and predictable. The nomination of William Jennings Bryan was a foregone conclusion. In 1896, during the depression, he had become the voice of the discontented—the small farmer and businessman, the hundreds of thousands of good Americans who through no fault of their own could not find a job. He argued for cheaper money, for the coinage of free silver and the end of the gold standard. At the Democratic convention, speaking directly to the powerful banking houses in the East, he had delivered one of the great lines in American political history: "You shall not press down upon the brow of labor a crown of thorns. You shall not crucify mankind upon a cross of gold."

If there had been an election then and there, Bryan would have been swept into the White House. He understood as well as any man what was wrong with America, but that was not sufficient. Bryan came on like an avenging angel; McKinley was avuncular and reassuring and won the election by half a million votes. On July 5, 1900, at his home in Lincoln, Nebraska, reclining on a lounge in the family parlor, Bryan was notified that he had once again been selected as his party's nominee. He would not abandon his fight for cheaper money or for an end to the trusts but, as expected, he would focus on the Philippine issue, charging the president with waging a war of "criminal aggression."

The same day in Washington, D.C., an "alienist," a physician dedicated to

William Jennings Bryan had a quick wit and a sharp tongue. Attacking the takeover of the Philippines, he said: "If we steal a man's purse we are thieves. If we steal twelve hundred islands we are patriots. If you steal a man's money you will be sent to the penitentiary. If you steal his liberty you will be sent to the White House."

working with the mentally disturbed, was leaving for the Philippines to care for the growing number of American soldiers suffering from mental breakdowns. The *St. Louis Post-Dispatch,* in an article headlined "Insanity Among Our Soldiers," described the "neverending stream of worse than dead humanity" returning to the States. In San Francisco there were accounts of horror ships with cargos of "the raving mad and the melancholy mad . . . listless, drooping, dull-eyed, joyless." There were those who were only "a little foolish wandering about, living from hand to mouth and wondering dimly why the world [had] changed."

The army clearly didn't want to discuss the matter, but reporters persisted. Doctors were attributing the "loss of balance" to a combination of sunstroke and malaria. They described men carried in from the field overcome by the heat, purple in the face, swollen and gasping, who had been driven insane. Men could no longer steel themselves as they marched to the front—there was no front, the insurgents were everywhere. No one could catch his breath behind the lines— there were no lines. Guerrilla warfare, as it was now being called, was unraveling the nervous systems of America's soldiers.

General MacArthur explained, "If we were fighting an army the work would be comparatively easy." Instead he was fighting a "secret revolutionary organization." No one was suggesting anymore that the war would be over anytime soon. As Bryan opened his campaign he declared that imperialism was the paramount issue facing America. The question was whether most Americans would agree.

II

In Canton, Ohio, with the sound of a band still quite distant, William McKinley was waiting on the front porch of his newly refurbished house on North Market Street talking to reporters and neighbors. The president seemed relaxed and happy to be home. He was hoping to stay in semi-seclusion until after the election. Secretary Cortelyou assured the press that the president was in close touch with the capital by virtue of a newly installed long-distance phone. As the band grew closer, young boys on bicycles appeared, circling like pilot fish. Governor Theodore Roosevelt was arriving to pay his respects.

The president and his running mate had not laid eyes on each other since an ambivalent meeting at the White House early in the year. When TR finally alighted from his carriage, half the town seemed to spill across the lawn to measure the warmth of the president's greeting. As the two men moved toward each other with outstretched arms, the crowd began to cheer. The president, knowing precisely what was expected, thanked his fellow townsmen for giving the governor such a generous welcome and then shepherded TR into the house. After a family dinner, the press was told that the candidates had settled in the president's study for a private talk.

There was much to be discussed that evening. An irritating series of Republican indiscretions had just surfaced in the press. The chief of the Bureau of Statistics had been caught by a reporter preparing Republican campaign material at government expense; and overeager Republican fund-raisers were being accused of fattening party coffers with illegal contributions from government employees. Every day seemed to turn up another scandal. Mark Hanna was reporting a

On the Fourth of July it was not uncommon to gussy up the family wagon, tie some ribbons on the horses, and head off for the local parade or fairgrounds. By 1900 oxen had all but disappeared and those who survived were seldom decked out in flags.

disquieting apathy among Republican voters and McKinley had learned that Andrew Carnegie was heading back from Scotland to campaign for Bryan. Most serious was the growing crisis in China.

When TR finally emerged from the McKinley home, close to 11 P.M., only a few reporters remained on the lawn. Neighboring homes were dark, the fireflies were out, North Market Street was empty. As the governor headed back to his train he said he was going home to Sagamore Hill in Oyster Bay, Long Island. He had promised his children a belated Fourth of July celebration complete with their own private fireworks display and would say nothing more.

III

In July, concern about the Philippines was eclipsed by the horror of dispatches from China: "Boxer Fiends Render Western Women Limb from Limb" and "Babe Borne Aloft on the Spears of the Chinese." While there were questions about the headlines, there was no doubt that Americans in China were in desperate straits and that thousands were at risk. At the start of the Boxer Rebellion there was a large American presence in China. Protestant missionaries and their families were scattered throughout the interior. American businessmen were settled in Shanghai, and in the foreign settlement at the edge of Tien Tsin, Herbert Hoover, a young Stanford engineering graduate, was just one of a number of American citizens working for Chinese corporations.

His wife, Lou Henry Hoover, an accomplished horsewoman, had been writing a book about ancient Chinese mining practices, collecting antique porcelain, and holding dinners for other Stanford graduates in the city. California papers reported there had been no word from the Hoovers for some time and their families feared for their safety. Ninety miles north, in the ancient Imperial City, Peking, hundreds of Americans, including Major H. E. Conger, the U.S. consul, were trapped inside the American Legation. There were repeated rumors they had all been massacred.

Old China hands had not been much alarmed back in April when Conger first reported that the Boxers, fanatical Chinese nationalists, were threatening to drive all foreigners out of the country. Aware that Conger knew little about China and less about diplomacy, many in the administration thought the consul was overreacting. In 1899, the Boxers had swept down out of the north through Shantung Province, murdering Western missionaries and their Chinese converts. Then the situation seemed to calm down. It was assumed that the central Chinese government had the Boxers under control.

But by the end of May the reports from China were growing more ominous. Boxer troops were again moving south. Refugees reported the murders of Belgian

No group followed news about the Boxer Rebellion more intently than the Chinese Americans in San Francisco, shown here reading bulletins about the war. A number of Chinese men volunteered to fight with U.S. forces but were not accepted.

engineers and English churchmen. German missions in Shantung had been destroyed. Conger cabled Washington that nine Methodist converts had been brutally massacred and the Boxers were now in open rebellion. Hope that the central Chinese military force would gain control was fading. American warships heading for Manila were diverted to the Chinese port of Taku. But the McKinley administration was responding with caution. While it was essential to rescue American citizens overseas, the United States had neither the troops nor the desire to embark on an all-out war with China.

China was potentially the greatest commercial market in the world. Foreign businessmen looked out on the ancient empire with its hundreds of millions of people and envisioned a consumer paradise. For years foreign powers had been trying to carve up the Chinese empire into separate spheres of influence with exclusive trading routes and custom houses. They had fought with each other and on occasion with the Chinese themselves. To protect America's commercial interests and avoid chaos in the region, Secretary of State John Hay had been negotiating an agreement that would keep China's doors open to all foreign powers while at the same time preserve the empire's territorial integrity.

But radical Chinese nationalists were not impressed with these diplomatic niceties. From the perspective of the Boxers, trade would only lead to further contamination of the Chinese people. For decades they had watched as outsiders came in to build and control the railroads and exploit the empire's vast natural resources. They had seen missionaries, in the name of a Western God, meddling in village life, disrupting ancient traditions with the

A member of the Boxers, the radical anti-foreign Chinese society. At the outset of the rebellion, Westerners had no way of knowing whether members of their staffs belonged to the secret organization. In 1900, the Boxers massacred over three hundred foreigners, most of them missionaries.

introduction of Western goods and Western mores. They wanted no more of foreign intruders.

In June of 1900 Boxer forces were heading for the Imperial City of Peking, the heart of the foreign presence in China. This was the diplomatic center of the country. Not far from the Imperial Palace were the foreign consulates, with their luxurious grounds, offices and stables, riding horses, and formal gardens—a city within a city. The entire area was surrounded by a massive wall sixty feet high, forty feet wide, and twelve miles long. Beyond the wall lay the open Chinese quarter with its markets and shops. The wall was impressive-looking but ancient and porous, and Conger, a Civil War veteran, knew that defense of the area would not be easy. The Chinese knew it, too.

Conger was urgently requesting military aid. Every legation had a small military guard, but in the face of any concerted attack the consulates would be outmanned and outgunned. Fifty American marines and a handful of sailors headed north out of Tien Tsin dragging a large automatic gun, but with Boxer troops in control of the countryside it was uncertain they would make it through alive.

In the best of times, the American compound, which included the Conger family, the legation staff, and fifty Chinese servants, was crowded. But now there were also several hundred refugees—American missionaries and Chinese converts—as well as a cadre of visitors from the States. Cecile Payen, a young American artist, had arrived in March "to study the custom and ways of the Chinese people" and would keep a journal throughout the ordeal.

In early June Payen noted that the Chinese guards at the legation gates were turning ugly. A correspondent from *The Times* (London), trying to reach his consulate, was stoned and nearly killed. The same week, several of the Congers' American guests tried to leave Peking, but the rail lines had been severed. Payen wrote: "The fires are encircling us on all sides now; the smoke is so dense and thick the sky is of a pale yellow. . . . About three o'clock this morning, four of the Imperial soldiers who had been placed on Legation Street to help protect us, turned and fired on our men."

Outside of Tien Tsin, Boxer mobs were attacking missionary schools, murdering every Chinese thought to be tainted by foreign contact. Hundreds were dead. Twelve of the Hoovers' fifteen servants had run away. The rail depot had been set afire and columns of rebel troops were reported on the outskirts of the city. In the small foreign quarter at the edge of the city, Hoover and his engineering crew improvised barricades from sacks of rice, sugar, and peanuts commandeered from a nearby warehouse.

The shelling of Tien Tsin began on June 10. Hoover joined a force of Westerners and loyal Chinese fighting fires set by Boxer shells. Casualties were high. Lou Hoover was working in a makeshift hospital set up by a European physician and an army doctor. Bicycling back and forth from home with a pistol in her pocket, one night a stray bullet destroyed one of her tires.

Two thousand foreign troops were facing twenty-five thousand Boxers. American papers reported that the Ninth Infantry was steaming from Manila to join the Allied Expeditionary of British, German, Japanese, and French forces assembling at the port of Taku. But no one in China—or America—could be certain if the relief force would arrive in time.

In Peking, under cover of darkness, the marine guard arrived at the American

The house and chapel in Peking, where seventy Americans—including U.S. Minister Conger, his family, and guests—ate their meals, sleeping on the floor and benches for almost two months. To the left is the Bell Tower with the bulletin boards where all news items and announcements were posted daily.

"The Famous International Gun That Saved the Legations at Peking." The gun, unearthed from a pile of rubbish at the outset of the siege, vintage 1858, rusted inside and out, was restored by an American marine named Mitchell. The carriage was provided by the Italians. The only shells available were Russian and too large, but Gunner Mitchell whittled and filed each down to size and managed to destroy a Chinese barricade with his first shot.

consulate with their automatic gun. Small as it was, the unit was exceedingly welcome. Beyond the legation walls, the streets of Peking were seething with mobs clamoring for the death of the foreign ministers. On June 12, the secretary of the Japanese legation was killed in the streets. When the German minister, Baron Von Kettler, set off by sedan chair with his interpreter to demand an explanation from Chinese officials he, too, was murdered. The Congers tried to console Von Kettler's widow, an American woman from Detroit who had just lost her brother fighting in the Philippines.

Then, on June 20, the siege of Peking began as Boxer troops wearing scarlet sashes entered the city shrieking, "Kill, kill—death to the foreigners!" The Austrian, Belgian, Italian, and Dutch legations were almost immediately destroyed. The Chinese proved excellent marksmen, picking off European guards protecting the wall. Seven of the American guards were killed. The remaining American marines tore bricks from the street to build a breastwork. Inside the compound the women and children were making cartridge belts and sandbags, ripping up draperies, blankets, Mrs. Conger's best table linens, and ancient Chinese embroideries. In one day, with just two sewing machines, they made and filled two thousand bags.

As the fighting increased, Cecile Payen wrote: "We can stand the single shots but these volleys are beyond our nervous strength." Payen passed her time sketching guard posts and buildings that were "a mass of holes from balls and bullets." Couriers from the consulate who reached Shanghai reported that the heads of captured legation guards were being borne through the streets on the tops of spears. Food supplies were dwindling. The few sheep in the compound were reserved for the ill. The Americans were living on rice and horsemeat. All riding horses had been sacrificed except for Mrs. Conger's.

In early July, a Chinese runner disguised as a Boxer reached Shanghai with word that the Europeans could not hold out much longer. One last desperate message from Major Conger reached Washington by a circuitous route: "Quick relief *only* can prevent general massacre." The American papers reported the Western troops in Peking were virtually out of ammunition and hopelessly outnumbered. Following this last communiqué there was only silence and endless speculation.

Theodore Roosevelt, campaigning in Quincy, Illinois, used the news from China as his text, arguing for a militant America. "Yesterday," TR roared, "our fellow citizens were either lying dead or crouched behind the legation walls. . . . The blood of our people runs like water in the streets of Pekin." In fact, for weeks no one would know what was happening in China. President McKinley, who had traveled to Washington for secret meetings, returned home to Canton to wait and to pray. There was nothing else left for him to do.

IV

From early spring until well into fall, the new fast transatlantic steamers were fully booked and had been for months. Seventy-five thousand Americans were sailing for France, clutching cameras and illustrated guidebooks. Aboard the S.S. *Potsdam,* Frances Benjamin Johnston was sorting her photographs on a table in the Ladies Saloon and Smoking Room, while out on deck her mother curled up with a copy of *Huckleberry Finn.* Johnston had been in Europe often. This year, following her speech at the Paris Exposition, she was going on to Russia. But most Americans crossing that summer had never sailed before and were nervously studying the rules of travel.

"Feeing"—or tipping—stewards had become a universal practice. To assure a pleasant journey, travelers were told to take care of the deck steward, the bedroom steward, the saloon steward, the chief steward, the bath steward, and the smoking room steward. If possible, they were to visit the steamer some three or four days before sailing, to arrange with the bath steward for an advantageous place on his schedule. There were cautionary notes about the men who made their living gambling in the smoking rooms and the over-friendly strangers who preyed on the naive.

Rich Americans had no need for these advisories. Tied to Europe by family, culture, and desire, caravans of American millionaires—along with their children, nannies, maids and valets, and eight or ten trunks—arrived on the Continent every year. For the rich, Paris was a grand bazaar where one could buy furniture and art, laces and silks, the finest kid gloves and the sheerest silk stockings. Women waited the winter to buy

Looking through the Eiffel Tower to the Trocadero Palace. Paris was the place to be in the summer of 1900, for everyone except Parisians, who abandoned the town to the tourists. Americans who had never been in Europe before—and there were many— were aided by a large new American Express Co. office, English-speaking guides, the latest American journals, and restaurants that served English and American food.

their gowns at Paquin or Worth on the Rue de la Paix. During these annual treks the children practiced French and refined their manners at a round of summer balls as their parents had before them.

Those with money seldom traveled during the height of the season. In 1900 they arrived in Europe early in the spring, settling into country homes. They would wait to attend the Exposition after the tourists left and the weather had cooled. Henry Adams wrote a friend that the Exposition was a "perfect bake-house of heat," and attendance was lower than expected. Nonetheless, it was not uncommon on a Sunday in August for a half million people to enter one of the fifty different gates to visit "the vastest and the most representative gathering of men and of things . . . in the entire course of history."

The Scottish writer Patrick Geddes wrote, "No man [has] been able to see, much less is any able to show, this vast, indeed too vast, labyrinth of labyrinths, this enormous multitude of collections, this museum of museums." This was the first great Exposition to include large numbers of automobiles, the first to present the steam turbine, X-ray machines, escalators, and wireless telegraphy. There were the most productive apple trees, the newest antiseptics, the latest telephotographic lenses. The ingenuities of American agricultural invention were contrasted with wooden ploughs and jagged sickles, which European peasants had yet to put away.

The fair was a remarkably entertaining melange of advanced technology, high art, and honky-tonk; it was like a gorgeous picnic with band music never out of earshot. One could hire a high, wooden, three-wheeled chair for three francs an hour and be transported from a superb collection of Rodin statues to Al-Rashid's harem. At night the Exposition was ablaze with gaslights and incandescent lights and an electrical searchlight that was so brilliant, it was said to be "like the finger of some Sun God," splashing on the beech trees along the Seine.

At the U.S. pavilion, a much criticized building, exhausted American businessmen found a home away from home, complete with stenographers, typewriters, and daily stock quotations. One night an American band entertained at a small informal dinner for twenty American "colored people sojourning in the city." The guests included the painter Henry Tanner, who was living in Paris studying with Thomas Eakins; Adam Clayton Powell, the well-known minister; Anna J. Cooper, an Oberlin graduate and school principal; Thomas J. Calloway from the U.S. War Department; and his close friend, W.E.B. Du Bois from Atlanta.

Du Bois and Calloway had come to Paris to supervise the installation of the exhibit on the history of the American Negro. Their work was not housed in the main pavilion but some blocks away, in a corner of a large white building devoted to the "science of society." The exhibit was surrounded by some of the more boring displays—the workingmen's circles of Belgium, the city governments of Sweden, and the mutual aid societies of France—but Du Bois was well pleased. There were charts on the increase of literacy and schooling and photographs of "Negro Medal of Honor men" who had fought in the Civil War and the Spanish-American War.

There was material on black inventors—Du Bois quoted a Massachusetts lawyer who had said, "I never knew a Negro to invent anything but lies"—and hundreds of books and periodicals by African-American writers. Du Bois noted, "There are many who have scarcely heard of a Negro book, much less read one." To drill home the point, he included a bibliography compiled at the Library of Congress containing fourteen hundred titles of works written by black writers. And then there were also the stunning photographs by Frances Benjamin Johnston.

Following his stay in Paris, W.E.B. Du Bois attended the Pan-African Congress in London, a meeting of men and women of African descent from all over the world. At the conference Du Bois declared: "The problem of the twentieth century is the problem of the color line, the question as to how far differences of race . . . are going to be made . . . the basis of denying to half the world . . . the opportunities and privileges of modern civilization."

Du Bois thoroughly enjoyed Paris and the Exposition. He and Calloway won gold medals, but both men knew it was a dreadful time to be a black American.

V

On the night of August 15 in New York City, while a sweltering crowd sought refuge from the heat in Central Park, some blocks south in the black neighborhood that ran between Eighth and Ninth Avenues, longstanding hatreds, festering for years, suddenly exploded. It was the kind of incident all too familiar in the South—hard-faced white toughs roaming the streets, attacking every black man and woman they could find—but New York had not seen anything like it since the Civil War. The "Negro Hunt" was set off by the death of a policeman who had been wounded in a scuffle with a black man. *The New York Times* reported that "every trolley car passing up or down Eighth Avenue was stopped and every negro on board was dragged out, and beaten."

Physicians from Bellevue said the scene looked like a battlefield. Sixty wounded men lay on the ground, most of them black. George Walker, a well-known singer of the team of Williams and Walker, and his friend Clarence Logan were pulled off a Broadway car and beaten. John B. Mallory, an engineering student, was rescued from a mob by one policeman and, moments later, furiously beaten by another. While the papers reported that a well-dressed woman had waded into a crowd at Longacre Square to rescue two black newsboys—incidents of common decency were rare.

The police, under orders to use their clubs freely, did precisely that, joining in the "anti-Negro" frenzy. The *St. Louis Post-Dispatch* reported that in New York "to be rescued by the police comes perilously close to being fatal. . . . Every negro 'rescued' was worse lambasted by the police than by the mob." At the station-house, one man was beaten unconscious in front of a group of reporters. The following day a magistrate questioned why so few whites had been arrested, "when the white people who caused this trouble acted like wild beasts."

Thursday evening, again, crowds began to build in the district. Passengers on elevated trains leaned out their windows to catch a glimpse of the threatening throngs below. At Thirty-fourth Street and Eighth Avenue police arrived in the midst of a lynching. The victim was rescued just seconds before strangling to death. The cord had already cut deep into his flesh but no arrests were made. On the third day of the riot, Paul Laurence Dunbar, who had been spending the summer in the Catskills on vacation, arrived in the city.

Dunbar, who was well known in the area, had stopped for a drink at a bar on West 37th Street, and that was the last he remembered. Some hours later he woke in the street, minus his gold watch, a diamond ring, and all his cash, having apparently been fed "knockout drops." Dunbar reported the incident at the West 30th Street police station but was just one footnote on an already overcrowded police blotter.

In the days that followed, black pastors held rallies to protest police violence. Eyewitnesses attested to countless incidents of police brutality. *The World* (New York) acknowledged that the South had every right "to shower biting sarcasm upon the civilized, tolerant, 15th amendment loving people of the North." The mayor of Savannah recommended to the mayor of New York his method for dealing with a race outbreak. "I called out the fire department," he explained, "and ordered every hose turned on the mob. The result was instantaneous. The force of the stream piled negroes up on one another, but it stopped the riot."

Other Stories of Interest

The New York Times, July 9, 1900

Letter to the Editor:

Amazement is expressed at the growth of the Chinese military establishment. . . . This was the work of the powers who scrambled over each other in their zealous efforts to modernize the Chinese soldiery. They detailed skillful officers who carefully drilled and trained the apt Orientals in the business of scientific butchery.

Enterprising manufacturers eagerly supplied vast quantities of Mausers, Krupps, and Maxims to the government . . . and thus the whites in every way facilitated preparations to slaughter every Caucasian in that empire.

The New York Times, July 31, 1900

North Carolina Politics,
Negro Suffrage the Issue

RALEIGH, NORTH CAROLINA—The campaign in the state which ends with the election next Thursday is one of the liveliest and most interesting that ever agitated the "Tar Heel" Commonwealth.

From one end of the State to the other . . . Democratic orators shout "white supremacy" and expatiate on their pet phrase of "Republican misrule and negro domination." And their every word is applauded by Democratic hearers clad in vivid red shirts that have been adopted as official down-with-the-negro uniforms.

In the places where Democratic sway is most violent no Republican or Populist are even allowed to talk in public. Only last week United States Senator Marion Butler made fruitless efforts to be heard in Warsaw and other little towns. . . . At each station he was met by bands of Red Shirts, who forcibly and not too courteously prevented his getting off the train.

The Democratic leaders do not mince words as to their intentions in framing the proposed Constitutional amendment . . . to take away the negro's right to suffrage lawfully or unlawfully; to disguise this act under the pretense of an educational qualification; to allow all white men to vote whether illiterate or not.

The New York Times, August 2, 1900

Riots in North Carolina

CHARLOTTE, NORTH CAROLINA—The Democrats held a rally today at Caesar, in Cleveland County. After the speaking, Bob Brackett, Republican, became engaged in a fight and was cut badly. He is reported to be dying. During the fight, Frank Queen, another Republican, opened fire on the crowd. One ball struck John Bynum Latimore in the thigh. . . . Queen then ran, but is being pursued. It is feared that if caught he may never get to jail.

The New York Times, August 19, 1900

WASHINGTON, August 18—Representative George H. White of North Carolina, the only colored man in Congress, said today: "We are greatly discouraged in North Carolina. . . . In some communities the colored vote is thoroughly terrorized, and everywhere it is demoralized.

The New York Times, August 5, 1900

PARIS—Since the fourth anarchistic attempt to wreck part of the exposition, extraordinary precautions have been taken. The grounds are swarming with secret agents. Nevertheless two more fires started unaccountably. The general presumption is that they were incendiary.

A family farm in Morrison County, Minnesota.

CHAPTER ELEVEN

August

I

In the dog days of summer, Americans exhausted by stories about drought, pestilence, and war found escape in front-page accounts of Josephine Peary and her seven-year-old daughter, Maria, who were sailing for Greenland in search of Josephine's husband. For almost a year now there had been no word from Lieutenant Robert E. Peary, the Arctic explorer, no letters or reported sightings, and his tall and strong-willed wife was setting out in hopes of finding him before another winter closed in. Peary, who had been searching for a passage to the North Pole for ten years, was an uncommonly fascinating figure, but so was Josephine.

Just after the Pearys had married, in the face of widespread opposition, Josephine had accompanied her husband on an expedition to the Arctic, the first white woman in that frozen wasteland. A year later, she had given birth to Maria at Peary's base camp on the northwest coast of Greenland. During the intervening years, she had returned several times. Now, unable to communicate with her husband, she was heading back on the *Windward*, a converted whaler that Peary used as a supply ship. The last she had heard, Peary was not in the best of health.

The search for a route to the North Pole, the last great unconquered land in the North, had become a baffling and dangerous race. So much of the world had been mapped by Western explorers that the North Pole was one of the last remaining prizes. In 1896, the Norwegian explorer Fridtjof Nansen had come close. Traveling by sledge over an ice floe north of Siberia, Nansen had been stopped just two hundred and sixty-one miles away. Then the Italian Duke of Abruzzi bested Nansen's record by twenty-two miles. Ever fearful that one of his competitors would reach the Pole first, Peary mounted one hazardous expedition after the next.

In 1895, after weeks on the ice in northwest Greenland, he arrived back at base camp, his men half-starved and only one sled dog left alive. In January 1899, in total Arctic darkness, he embarked on another maniacal venture. Traveling in −60°F weather, Peary suffered such severe frostbite the team doctor had been forced to amputate seven of his toes. In the summer of 1900, as the *Windward* headed north, it was presumed that Peary was out again struggling against the "immutable forces of the icy north." In fact, he had just completed his most successful expedition to date.

Back in April, hobbling on his mangled feet, he had packed his sleds and, attended by his longtime aide Matt Henson, left the base. In one month's time, he had reached the top of Greenland, the most northernly point of land in the world and, standing where no man had ever stood before, he had built a cairn, a landmark into which he deposited records for whoever might follow. From the coast, with its deeply cut fjords and low rolling land, he had moved out over the frozen sea, praying the ice floe would provide passage all the way to the Pole. But at 83°50′ north, the floe gave way to open water and, for the first time, Peary encountered the awesome Arctic Sea with its rapidly moving mountains of ice.

Again he had been forced to retreat, but while the passage to the Pole continued to

Robert Edwin Peary did not reach the North Pole until 1909. When he finally made his triumphant return from the Arctic, he was informed that Frederick A. Cook claimed to have reached the Pole before him. Cook, however, was discredited and Peary was awarded the rank of admiral by Congress and retired from exploration.

clude him, he had completed exploring the northern coast of Greenland and that alone was an achievement. He would write his sponsors that over the thousand years since Eric the Red first sighted the southern tip of the island, "Norwegians, Danes, Swedes, Englishmen and Americans had crept gradually northward up its shore," and now Greenland's "northern cape has been lifted out of the Arctic mists and obscurity."

About the time the *Windward* was in St. John's, Newfoundland, taking on supplies, Peary, having returned to camp healthy and in good spirits, was out hunting to build his larder for the winter. The musk oxen were plentiful that year, nearly two hundred animals were killed and dressed, the meat stored in well-constructed igloos. On his return to the base Peary wrote his wife that he was planning another expedition for the spring of 1901, and then, God willing, would be coming home. That letter would reach the States mid-November, but Josephine would not be home to receive it.

The next chapter in the adventures of the Pearys would emerge slowly and over time, like a good novel. In August, as the explorer was settling in for another winter, he was quite unaware that just two hundred miles south of his camp the *Windward,* with his wife and daughter aboard, had become mired in early ice, and the ship with its entire complement would be imprisoned for the winter. Among those on board, as Josephine would discover, was Peary's Eskimo mistress, Ally, and their child. It was the first time the two women had met, perhaps the first either had known of the other. They would now spend the next eight months together. Peary would join them the following May. The details of that reunion would never be made public.

———

The same week Mrs. Peary headed north, a flotilla of small boats carrying tourists and reporters assembled on the Lake of Constance, between Switzerland and Bavaria. For weeks the press had been waiting for Count Ferdinand von Zeppelin, a dashing German cavalry officer, to launch what was described as "the most daring and ambitious airship ever conceived." Everything about the machine was oversized, from the floating building in which it was housed to the amount of hydrogen required to lift it off the ground. The craft was four hundred and sixteen feet long. Seventeen separate gas balloons were held in place by an aluminum frame, the whole covered with air-resistant fabric.

Scientific American reported that "the advent of aluminum has been a

The maiden flight of the Zeppelin on July 2, 1900, over Lake Constance was flawed. The motors proved too small, and a guideline got snagged in a rudder, but photographs of the giant craft motoring through the sky signaled that control of the air was now just a matter of time. One observer noted that an airship would have been of immense help in China—resupplying the legations, locating Boxer forces, even carrying Allied troops to the front.

tremendous advance toward producing a ship light and strong enough to be lifted by gas—and gas is, of course, the first essential in aerial flight. Gas will take us up and keep us up, and that is settled." Lighter-than-air craft had been in use for over a hundred years. Large colorful balloons sailing with the winds, carrying three or four people, were a familiar sight at every large fair. But Zeppelin's craft was different; the ship, capable of carrying up to ten tons, could be steered against the wind and carried enough fuel to fly for ten hours.

After several days' delay because of weather, the airship was finally towed out of its hanger on an oversized raft into the center of the lake. The gas compartments were filled with two thousand dollars' worth of hydrogen; the two small Daimler benzine engines were started; the air screws, or propellers, began to turn; and when the final ropes were cut the ship rose gently thirteen hundred feet into the air. From the water spectators could see the two aluminum gondolas swinging from the craft. In the front car was Zeppelin and two other men—an engineer and an amateur balloonist. In the rear car was his friend Eugen Wolf, an experienced aeronaut, along with a machinist.

With the fleet of small boats and tourist steamers following its progress, the ship flew three and a half miles down the lake at twenty-six feet a second. And then Zeppelin hoisted a large blue flag, a signal to those on the water that he was about to descend. Eugen Wolf wrote: "The air ship sank slowly and rested on the water as smoothly as a sea gull. . . . The aluminum cars now performed the other function for which they were intended; and I realized that we were really riding on the waters of Lake Constance."

Naysayers pointed out that the steering mechanism was flawed. On its maiden voyage the ship had only traveled with the wind, but some weeks later, after making minor adjustments, the count took his craft up again and triumphantly flew in an extended circle, six miles long. Charles Stanley, writing for San Francisco's *The Examiner*, was confident that "an air ship capable of carrying the mails and, say, forty passengers at a speed of seventy miles was but a question of months away. The 20th Century will open with the airship," he concluded, "what it will close with no man can predict."

But Zeppelin had other ambitions. Eugen Wolf wrote: "His interest was primarily that of the military tactician seeking a new and terrible engine of war, for it is everywhere recognized that a successful air ship would give a vast advantage to the nation by which it is used." The count was not alone in his thinking. In England, at about the same time, the British writer H. G. Wells, working on a series of essays about the future, envisioned that "aeronauts provided with large scale maps of the hostile country . . . will mark down to the gunners below the precise point upon which to direct their fire. . . .

"Great multitudes of balloons will be the Argus eyes of the entire military organism, stalked eyes with a telephonic nerve in each stalk and at night they will sweep the country with search-lights, and come soaring before the wind with hanging flares. Perhaps they will be steerable." He projected that before 1950 the aeroplane would have been flown and come home safe and sound. "Directly that is accomplished," he said, "the new invention will be most assuredly applied to war." He wrote of a desperate and decisive struggle for command of the sky, of explosive and incendiary devices that would leave no camp or shelter safe, and that "everybody, everywhere will be perpetually and constantly looking up, with a sense of loss and insecurity."

Wells saw "the gray old general with his epaulettes and decorations . . . his spurs and his sword, riding along on his obsolete horse, by the side of the doomed column" vanishing along with the nineteenth century.

———••———

In Dayton, Ohio, inside their not very prepossessing bicycle shop, Wilbur Wright and his younger brother Orville were almost finished building their man-sized glider. They would test the glider after the bicycle business quieted down in the fall. Wilbur had been searching for a location where the winds would be strong enough to lift the craft off the ground and there was sand to break the shock of landing. He had been narrowing the choices from material he received from the U.S. Weather Bureau in Washington.

On August 3, he sent off a note to a local weatherman stationed in a tiny hamlet on the outer banks of North Carolina. With its strong steady winds, the isolated beach at Kitty Hawk seemed a likely site. Wilbur informed his father that even if the experiments were not a complete success, he would at least have a three-week vacation and see a part of the world he had never visited before.

I I

———•◆•———

In the second week of August in Canton, Ohio, the McKinley household was packing up to return to the capital for two weeks. The crisis in China was reaching a climax. The international rescue expedition was only a day or two south of the foreign consulates in Peking. The long tense weeks of waiting would soon be over, but few were willing to predict how the story would end. The rescue operation had begun in July, when a large allied army marching under the flags of half a dozen nations had assembled in northern China at the port of Taku, twelve miles from the besieged city of Tien Tsin.

The battle for Tien Tsin had been nastier than the generals had predicted. On land as flat and treeless as the western plains, American boys had fought for their lives alongside Welsh Fusileers, Sikh soldiers of the British Indian Army, Russians in white blouses, Japanese with bull's-eyes on their caps. The Boxer forces had been entrenched behind mud walls and forts, their large guns hidden by earthen embrasures. The fighting had begun on July 12; the Americans, in an advanced position, were pinned down by heavy fire. Twice the Chinese tried to overrun their positions. Twice they were repulsed; but on July 13, when the Ninth Infantry was finally relieved, eighteen men were dead and seventy-nine were wounded.

The following morning, on orders shouted in half a dozen different tongues, troops, guns, horses, and ammmunition wagons rushed toward the gates of the city. From the mud walls around Tien Tsin, the Japanese provided covering fire and the allies moved in. Back in the States, banner headlines reported the bloody battle and the allied victory, but details were sketchy. It would be weeks before Lou and Herbert Hoover's family would learn that the couple was safe in their battered home in the foreign quarter. One night Lou had been playing solitaire when a shell landed over her head, destroying much of her porcelain collection. Hoover had acted as a guide for an American unit, carrying a rifle he had been given by a wounded marine.

With Tien Tsin in allied hands, commanders wasted no time setting out for Peking, ninety-five miles north. Frederick Palmer, a war correspondent for *Collier's Weekly*, wrote: "The army took the road at dawn, tired in spirit. . . . It was not so foolish as to wonder how it was ever going to stay on its feet until it reached Peking. 'Shall we be there in time?' was the question we were forever asking . . . the hope that we might, spurred on Private as well as General." Following the course of the river, through the flat Pei-Ho Valley, the wagon train stretched out behind the troops farther than the eye could see, a remarkable collection of men and gear that ran five miles to the rear.

There were Russian soup boilers carting giant smoking pots on

An American soldier giving water to a wounded Japanese after the battle for Tien Tsin. U.S. war correspondents, carrying heavy camera gear, provided extensive coverage of the Boxer Rebellion.

wheels, Chinese workers pulling wheel barrows filled with supplies, English marines wrestling giant guns used in the Boer War, Western teamsters driving American wagons as large as prairie schooners. The Japanese had small and agile pony carts, which on the rough terrain were far more effective. In the heat, said to be worse than the Philippines, with the air filled with mosquitoes and poisonous flies, on any given day 10 to15 percent of the men dropped by the wayside. Palmer, accompanying the march, wrote of "the dust and exhaustion of the stragglers of varied colors and races [who] make up the column."

At evening, junks arrived from Tien Tsin with great piles of hardtack, sides of bacon, and boxes of canned goods. The Sikhs, the Bengal Lancers, the Punjabis wandered the embankment looking for water to boil their rice. Palmer noticed that most of the other troops, including the Japanese, favored American cornbeef. Several days out, in a village called Pei-Tsang, the allies encountered their first real opposition. The Japanese were the heroes of that day, staging a magnificent cavalry charge, but their casualties were high and the small field hospital was overrun.

At the end of the first week in August there was a skirmish in Yangtsun. Fifty or sixty Americans were caught in a crossfire between Chinese and British troops. Some of the men had been struck by Chinese shrapnel, more had been hit by friendly fire. The catastrophe was said to have been unavoidable. Leaving a small force to hold the town, the allies moved on. The men were filthy, many were ill, their eyes lined with marks of fatigue. And then came the incident that gave them heart. Some miles north of Yangtsun, a Chinese messenger appeared out of nowhere and produced from the lining of his shoe two small pieces of paper bearing news from the foreign legations. One message was from the American consul, the other from the Japanese—as of August 5 they were alive and had enough supplies to hold out for another ten days.

Suddenly the pace of march quickened. There was a certain jostling for the lead; every command wanted the honor of being first into the Imperial City. A French general, absent for the fighting, suddenly appeared and pressed forward to the front of the line. Not far from Peking, Bengal Lancers in their great turbans broke from the line. Hundreds of Boxers were hiding in the *kowliang*, broomcorn so high it reached the ears of the Lancers' horses. Four miles ouside the city the allied forces broke for the night. Except for an occasional sniper, the countryside was still.

At dawn the troops set out along three separate roads leading to Peking, the men unusually quiet. On the outskirts of the city they were met by swarms of fleas and the sickening stench of unburied dead. In the native quarter there was no resistance. With the exception of a few stragglers, the Boxers had fled. At seven in the morning on August 15, the Sikhs, under the command of a British general, waded up a sewage canal under the Tartar wall and marched into the English legation. Generals, soldiers, and correspondents scrambled up the banks through the filth. The Americans arrived shortly afterward. The siege of Peking was finally over.

Exhausted Sikhs pitched their tents on the lawn of the English compound and studied the damage. The tops of the American and British buildings were badly torn by shells. The rest of the foreign settlement was all but demolished; large elaborate buildings had been reduced to rubble. Troops marveled at the ingenuity of the legation defenses. Every scrap of metal, every candlestick

This photograph was taken as the first American troops entered Peking. Ten minutes later, this unit was engaged in one last skirmish with the Boxers. A popular American officer was killed by a sniper's bullet.

and ornament had been converted to ammunition. Multihued sandbags of silk and satin, filled with dirt, stuffed every niche in the makeshift walls of stone, brick, and earthware. Three hundred and four men, with eighty-five volunteers, had held off thousands of well-armed troops. To be sure, there were fifty-four dead and numbers of wounded, but over seven hundred people had survived the fifty-five day siege.

The New York Times reported that "on entering the grounds of the British Legation [it looked] as if a lawn party was in progress. The British Minister met the rescuers shaven and in impeccable tennis flannels. Mr. Conger [the American consul] was equally presentable. The women were fresh and bright in summer clothing. . . . But on second look it was seen that the rescued were pathetically pale and thin." The rescuers themselves "were haggard and rough-bearded. They dragged along as if ready to drop, their khaki uniforms dripping with perspiration and black with mud." Cecile Payen noted in her diary, "I do not know who was

Legationers cheer the first troops to appear in the foreign quarter.

the happier, the relievers or the relieved, they seemed so proud and happy to find any of us still alive."

In Washington, as the cables arrived announcing the end of the siege, an enormous sense of relief prevailed. But McKinley was barely allowed to enjoy the moment when the situation in China became clouded again. Units of the expeditionary force were reported to have gone on a rampage. The Imperial City was looted, villages burned, innocent civilians murdered. Unspeakable acts of barbarism were being attributed to the Czar's soldiers.

While the United States was opening cautious negotiations with the Chinese government, rumors circulated that the European powers once again were planning to partition China. Additional Russian troops were said to be arriving via the Trans-Siberian Railroad. The president was being urged to protect his country's commercial interests, but at the same time there was no appetite for another foreign war.

An editorial in the *St. Louis Post-Dispatch* warned that "a war brewed in Peking, will be fought in every land and on every sea in the Eastern Hemisphere. Let us pray that the Western world will not be drawn into this sordid and ignoble struggle." In a matter of weeks McKinley would bring home all but a handful of men. The fight to preserve America's position in China would continue, but on the diplomatic front.

III

There was one other crisis that summer, and it, too, began overseas. King Humbert I of Italy was assassinated by a silk weaver named Gaetano Bresci, an anarchist who had only recently returned to Italy from Paterson, New Jersey. Amid rumors that a *grotto* of anarchists buried deep within the city were plotting to assassinate the president as well, detectives poured into the small industrial city of Paterson. Just months before there had been an attempt on the life of the Prince of Wales and then another attempt on the Shah of Iran. Now, once again, there was concern about McKinley.

On August 18, the Secret Service announced that, following a tip from Naples, fourteen suspicious Italian immigrants had been detained as they entered the country. The following day, twelve more men were taken into custody. At the White House security was tightened—two policemen were now stationed at the main entrance; six others were placed on duty around the grounds. Inside the mansion, only prominent politicians and well-known citizens were being granted private interviews. *Harper's Weekly* speculated that campaign rhetoric by Democratic candidates preaching the "gospel of discontent" might be stirring up the "anarchistic cause."

The president seemed indifferent to this new wave of warnings. The Secret Service Bureau had assigned a full-time operative, a jolly little man named George Foster, who was to be at McKinley's side at all times. But back in Canton, the president continued to take his wife for their afternoon drive, and there was no room in the carriage for Mr. Foster. Just about sixty miles from Canton, on his family's farm, a moody young anarchist named Leon Czolgosz also read about the assassination of King Humbert. Later Czolgosz's family would recall that Leon had taken the news accounts of Humbert's murder off to bed with him every night for weeks.

Other Stories of Interest

The Evening Bulletin (Philadelphia),
August 13, 1900

LONDON—Farm workers in England are manifesting violent opposition to the introduction of American agricultural machinery. Some of the farm hands, embittered at the prospect of losing employment owing to the introduction of labor saving inventions, wrecked a number of reapers and threatened vengeance against anybody who should attempt to employ similar machinery.

Mr. P. Anderson Graham, a well-known agricultural authority, said today: "Our present system of handling farm products is altogether too costly. American wheat undersells English wheat in the English market, because of the extensive use of economical machinery in the United States."

The World (New York), August 18, 1900

LONDON—Precautions for the safety of the Prince of Wales during his stay in Homburg, where he arrived today, includes the inauguration of a new system for the protection of royalty from the attacks of the Anarchists.

Under this system every member of a royal family travelling out of his own country has the services of a detective from each European bureau whose special qualification is his intimate acquaintance with dangerous Anarchists.

The detective guard of the Emperor William of Germany has been doubled since King Humbert's assassination, and it is said that the guards have been warned they will be held personally responsible if any preventable mishap occurs to the Kaiser.

Queen Victoria is also more carefully guarded than before the murder of Humbert. During yachting week Cowes swarmed with detectives and the grounds at Osborne House are patrolled by guards night and day.

The New York Times, August 28, 1900
Shah's Throne in Peril

PARIS, August 27—I hear from a thoroughly well informed source* that serious insurrection has broken out in Persia which may in all probability cause the Shah's visit to Europe to be curtailed.

The object of the revolt is to dethrone the present Shah, whose fondness for Western ideas makes him unpopular to Persians of the old school.

*The correspondent did not identify himself and was not identified by *The Times.*

In 1900, Atlantic City was one of the most popular seaside resorts in the East. Those with money came for the entire season. Those who worked came for brief holidays or often just took a train to the shore for the day. The group posing with the donkey has a sign that reads: "I could stay in Atlantic City forever."

CHAPTER TWELVE

September

I

There was not a hint of fall in the still hot sun as Carl Sandburg cycled back to Galesburg, Illinois, the first week of September. The heat-damaged corn was being cut, oats threshed, and the wheat fields plowed as he headed home to his part-time job at the firehouse and his studies at Lombard College. As a boy he had wandered barefoot through Lombard into a world of books and people he little understood but was intuitively drawn to. Now he would report at eight o'clock in the morning for a class in Latin under Jon W. Grubb: "I had seen him milk a cow and drive her to pasture. I thought it would be interesting to study Caesar's *Commentaries* with a professor who could wear overalls and milk a cow."

In 1900 only the rich or the most determined went to college, but Lombard made it easy. Like so many of the small prairie colleges in the West—the most democratic institutions in the country—the small co-ed college accommodated those with part-time jobs and checkered school careers who had gone to work too young. Sandburg was taking a mix of preparatory and college courses and would have to leave class when the fire whistle blew, but one way or other he was going to get an education. He remembered a friend saying "you could never get enough of it."

If there was any one thing most Americans agreed on in 1900, it was the need for schooling. Fifteen million children now attended public school, in many states for nine months a year, absolutely free. Illiteracy had dropped to an unprecedented eleven percent, and outside the South the record was far better. It was expected that every child would learn to read, write, and do arithmetic with "readiness and certainty," and most did. In much of America the common school was a triumph. It was there that Sandburg, the son of an immigrant father, found common ground with the mayor's daughter and with "a brown-faced mulatto girl who held her own in classwork."

They had all used the same primer, the same kind of slate, memorized the same poems and discovered together that the earth was round. In eighth grade they had heard Miss Hague question the stupid pages in their history book that described the Red Man as "crafty and cruel." Miss Hague knew books were essential but not infallible. She knew her history. Along with the basics, they had all been drilled in the habits "of doing right, being kind and respectful." No one seemed to question the superintendent's use of a thick, brass-edged ruler on the open palm for a misdemeanor. An educated conscience was every bit as important as an educated brain, and most parents expected their children to acquire both.

But in 1900 as students headed back to school, from kindergarten up the consensus over the American educational systems was unraveling. Beyond the basics, there was little agreement over what children should be taught or how they should be taught. Educators were embracing new gods, preaching the doctrine of individuality. Philosopher John Dewey had triggered a revolution with the publication of *My Pedagogic Creed* in 1897, in which he declared that education must begin with "insight into the child's capacities, interests, and habits." Education was to grow out of a child's world, arithmetic could be absorbed more readily by studying carpentry or sewing than sitting before a blackboard covered with abstract numbers.

Followers of Dewey decried cramming information into the minds of children like "sausage meat into skins," teaching by rote the endless lists of names and dates signifying little and quickly forgotten. In Washington, D.C., at the beginning of the year, a Senate investigative subcommittee, charged with overseeing District schools, held hearings on the new teaching methods. The local school superintendent was reassuring. Over the past ten years, he said, Washington schools "had changed as radically as streetcar transportation, and all to the good."

Children in the third grade were now well grounded in fractions, fifth-graders were able to read the newspapers and follow the news of the day, and overall, students had developed such an interest in their work that discipline was no longer necessary. Dime novels, which had so often been brought surreptitiously to school some years back, were said to have disappeared entirely. But skeptics on the Senate committee questioned whether children could learn multiplication tables without being drilled, and whether they would ever learn to spell. It was a criticism one heard across the country. Wasn't there a value in facing up to drudge work, in dealing with distasteful tasks as a matter of duty? Wouldn't those taught along the lines of least resistance end up flabby of mind and will?

Dewey had said that a community's paramount duty was to support education, which was all very well and good, but the fripperies being added in 1900 were expensive—the field trips, the apparatus for physical culture for girls as well as boys, the employment of all kinds of special teachers. Did a democratic education

Schoolchildren on a trolley in Washington, D.C., photographed by Frances Benjamin Johnston.

truly require classes in fruit growing, stenography, or metalwork? Was there really a need for girls to learn basketball? Should citizens be forced to pay for music and art classes as well as textbooks and school luncheons? In a nation with such enormous diversity, who should pay to educate *other* people's children? And that turned out to be the most difficult of questions.

Generations earlier Americans had accepted that universal education would be the great equalizer, essential in a democratic society. That worked pretty well as long as most of the children were Anglo-Saxon, but in the last years of the nineteenth century an astonishing mix of children were turning up at public schools, and the best and the worst in American attitudes suddenly collided. Members of all-white legislatures in the South had no desire to spend money on poor black children. In Boston and New York, where tens of thousands of children from eastern Europe and Italy were arriving at overcrowded schools, there was little appetite to increase the budgets.

But for all the shortfalls nationwide, almost all children in America were going to better schools than their parents had. And for parents who had never dreamed of being able to acquire an education, the free schools were one of the great American blessings. Even in the South, impoverished and race riven as it was, illiteracy had diminished. In the port cities of the East, there were intensive courses for children who didn't speak English, night school for adults, extended kindergarten days for the children of the poor, special classes for the disabled.

Mary Antin, who arrived in Boston from Russia as a child in the 1890s, never lost her sense of wonder that in America education was free. Her father's greatest hope had been free schooling for his children. It was "the essence of American opportunity, the treasure no thief could touch . . . it was the one thing he was able to promise us when he sent for us; surer, safer than bread or shelter. . . . No application made, no questions asked, no examinations, rulings, exclusions; no machinations, no fees. The doors stood open for everyone of us."

One of the noisier debates in the fall of 1900 was over the role of organized sports in schools and colleges. Even the smallest schools now had basketball teams and baseball teams, and over five thousand high schools and almost every college had a football squad. The president of Yale declared that team sports were the best hope of counteracting "the selfish, individualistic tendencies of the age." But at many colleges students were said to be more passionate about athletics than academic pursuits. At what point did good sound physical training become an unhealthy mania?

It still felt like summer when young men in britches and some in leather helmets began loosening up for the bone-crushing game of American-style football. The superintendent of the Kansas City school system wrote about the "orgies that return every autumn under the head of 'Football Slaughter.' " J. M. Greenwood wrote: "Men—university and college presidents and professors—call these brutal contests high educational aspirations. To kill, maim, debase, kick up the devil . . . and call it manly education is to call *Hades—Heaven!*" But Greenwood was fighting a losing battle.

The game, which had evolved over twenty years or so from English-style rugby at Harvard, Yale, and Princeton, had become a national passion. College football was covered by every major paper. There were codified rules and well-defined plays; every man on the squad now had a specific assignment; the larger, rounder rugby ball had been replaced by a slim, spherical model designed to reduce air resistance and make kicking more accurate. The attacking team was allowed three tries, or downs, to advance the ball a minimum of five yards. Pre-season articles described, somewhat fuzzily to be sure, the "scientific" principles of the sport, but in the end, what drew the crowds was the promise that two teams of strong young men would go at each other with maximum and sometimes killing force.

The first fatality in 1900 came early in the season. A ball carrier for Lake Forest University in Illinois died after he had been tackled and both teams piled on top of him. A young man no longer had to go to war to prove his manhood—football turned out to be a reasonable substitute. Somehow Theodore Roosevelt had found time that fall to write an essay, called "The American Boy," in which he advised young men that "In life, as in football, the principle to follow is: Hit the line hard; don't foul, don't shirk, but hit the line hard."

The big games between traditional rivals—Army-Navy, Stanford-Berkeley, Harvard-Yale—which were held around Thanksgiving, drew enormous crowds. During the Harvard-Yale game, in 1899, Helen Keller, studying at Radcliffe—Keller was both blind and deaf—could feel the reverberations from the stadium, blocks away. "We could hear the yells," she wrote, "of the boys and the cheers of the lookers-on as plainly in our room as if we had been on the field. There were about 25,000 people at the game and when we went out the noise was so terrific we nearly jumped out of our skins, thinking it was the din of war and not of a football game. . . . But in spite of all their wild effort, neither side was scored." This November, the game between Harvard and Yale would be the match-up of the season.

In September, Yale was described as "the mightiest football combination ever formed." Their forwards were heavy six-footers, "lusty, stout-waisted, and agile." To make sure they would be properly fed and cared for, the university was opening special dining facilities for the players and hiring additional trainers. Overall the Harvard team was less experienced and lighter, but the men were said to be "shifty and nervy," and the quarterback, Charles Dan Daly, was "the greatest . . . who ever played the game." Daly had wrenched his knee in an early practice session, but that only intensified interest. The press would follow Daly closely.

Football was now big business. The Harvard-Yale game alone would bring in $40,000 and both athletic departments were looking forward to another lucrative season.

———— •·•·• ————

The beaches were crowded well into September, during the long hot summer of 1900. At Atlantic City, New Jersey, tourists included numbers of Southerners escaping the heat.

II

In that curiously hot September, along the Atlantic seaboard from Bar Harbor south, summer resorts were extending their season. Labor Day was now a legal holiday in many states, and on Monday, September 3, excursion trains were jammed as tens of thousands of people escaped to the seaside. In Atlantic City, while hotels were no longer forced to set up cots in hallways and parlors, the boardwalk and beaches were still surprisingly crowded. Out in the ocean the water was warm and experienced swimmers were enjoying an unusually high surf. The newspapers noted a tropical storm building somewhere in the Caribbean.

In Galveston, Texas, down at the Pagoda Bath House, hundreds of bathers were enjoying the waves. All the bathhouses and tourist hotels were filled that week. On Wednesday morning, as gale force winds reached the Florida Keys, the surf became wilder, but the weather had been so oppressive no one wanted to get out of the water. Visitors from Kansas, checking into the Hotel Grand, were grateful for the strong ocean breeze. Back home, just days before, the thermometer had climbed to 115 degrees.

All week, Isaac Cline, station chief at the Galveston Weather Bureau, had been monitoring the weather as the hurricane moved north, lashing Miami and Palm Beach with winds reported up to one hundred miles per hour. Down at the port, Wednesday and Thursday, the warning flags were flying. Early Friday morning Cline was alerted that the storm had shifted course and was heading west across the Gulf of Mexico. He immediately went down to the docks to warn the captains of outbound freighters to stay in port. In 1900, the National Weather Bureau was a much respected service, in contact by telegraph and telephone with three thousand weathermen—professional and volunteer—from Canada to the Caribbean.

In the Galveston harbor more than one hundred ocean-going vessels lined the modern stone-capped piers. The deep-water port was among the finest in the nation; the federal government had spent eight million dollars building a pair of jetties that ran over five miles out to sea. By noon Friday, it was clear that the storm had again shifted course. With heavy swells building in the Gulf, seamen began securing great steel cables strong enough to withstand the strongest winds and tides. Gulf coast stations reported that the wind was intensifying, but the day was clear, and throughout the city there was no concern.

Galveston sat on a narrow sand island thirty miles long, off the southeast coast of the state; the thirty-eight thousand people who lived in this city of broad clean streets were used to keeping a sharp weather watch. All but the youngest had lived through many a gale. Washed by Galveston Bay on one side and the Gulf of Mexico on the other, water regularly made its way across the city, but Galveston was a city of substance. Only fifty years old, its enormous ornate homes and giant cathedrals, the large and elaborate public school buildings, had been built for the ages.

In 1900, in spite of the drought, a record-breaking grain crop was arriving daily over the three long railroad bridges. Drays of cotton were being carried from the mainland across the longest wagon bridge in the world. On Friday night the tide was at an unusual height, but the sky was reasonably clear and the brilliant moon was reassuring. During the night the wind began to blow, and by early Saturday morning water had begun seeping into the southern portion of the city—but there still was no alarm. The people of Galveston had seen it all before. In the early morning, gardeners mowed lawns, maids scrubbed porches, housewives serenely ordered their dinners.

A little before nine it began to rain as Southern Pacific freight trains continued pulling in by the wharves. Workmen moved bales of cotton inside the large covered sheds that ran alongside the piers. The three grain elevators were already filled to capacity. While there had been none of the usual portents of a hurricane—the brick dust sky was not in evidence—it was becoming clear to Isaac Cline that a severe storm was on its way. He went down to Strand Street to advise merchants to place their goods at least three feet off the floor, and then, harnessing his horse to a two-wheel cart, drove along the beach urging homeowners and tourists in small cottages to seek secure places for the night.

By noon on Saturday Galveston was struck by gale-force winds, the water was rising on both sides of the city and in the streets, and whitecaps danced on the surface of the water. The public was warned that the worst was yet to come, but young men were seen wading, laughing at the unexpected, and ferrying women and children in skiffs from one house to the next. A little after noon the last train arrived, and then the bridges to the mainland were submerged. Hundreds of people now began descending on the weather office for advice; refugees were crowding into every building of substance. At St. Mary's Orphanage, the Sisters of the Incarnate Word gathered ninety-three orphans in the girls' chapel on the first floor of the building. Most of the children were four to six years of age.

At three thirty, Cline sent a final message out of Galveston: "Gulf rising, water covers streets of about half city." Moments later, he noted that the last electric streetcar attempting a run was hurled off its tracks. Just before his anemometer blew away, Cline recorded wind gusts at 102 mph. Later Father James Kirwin described slates from the roof of St. Patrick's Cathedral flying through the air like hail—"more deadly than mauser bullets." The city built on the sand-spit by the sea was now entirely cut off from the mainland. It would be days before the outside world could piece together what happened to Galveston between Saturday afternoon and early Sunday morning.

Within the city two great forces were colliding. From the southwest, hurricane-force winds were driving giant waves onto the beach, while a gale from the northeast was roiling the waters in the bay and turning the Gulf into a maelstrom. No one had ever seen anything like it. Along the beachfront, the cottages, elevated on stilts above the sand, battered by waves and wind from both directions, were the first to go. By midafternoon, telegraph poles, roofs, and timbers were being tossed through the air and the water kept rising. Around four o'clock, as Isaac Cline was making his way home to his house on Rosenberg Avenue, the water in the streets was waist-deep and running like a millrace. By six-thirty, when his brother Joseph finally reached the house, the water was up to his neck.

As darkness fell, fifty strangers huddled on the second floor of the Clines' new house, along with Isaac's wife and their three children. From the windows they could see homes ripped from their moorings being driven into others, which collapsed like dominoes. In an apartment building called Lucas Flat, at St. Mary's University, and in the Rosenberg Public School refugees tried to block out the sound of the shrieking wind, the shattering of glass, the groaning of the timbers. At seven-thirty, with the debris around Cline's home piled eight to fifteen feet high, the sea rose four feet in as many seconds. Over one terrible extended moment, a tidal wave swept in from the Gulf, swallowing much of the city.

Later, in his official account, Cline wrote that "the force of the waves acted as a battering ram . . . my residence went down with about fifty persons who had sought it for safety, and all but eighteen were hurled into eternity. Among the lost was my wife." Momentarily knocked unconscious, Cline surfaced clinging to his youngest child. His brother surfaced with the two other children. Together they drifted on debris in the wood-clogged sea for hours, landing just three hundred yards from where the Cline home once stood. As they staggered ashore, the water was falling fast and the cloud-hidden moon had reappeared.

In the early hours of Sunday, survivors struggled to make sense of the world around them. Dawn had found a thousand people wandering naked, the seas having torn the clothes off their bodies. Stunned and wounded, men and women drifted through the streets aimlessly searching for loved ones. Dislocated dogs stood howling over bodies. The half-dead lay in the streets. Nearly half the homes in the city had been swept out of existence. Where twenty thousand people had lived just the day before not a house remained. The city was all but impassable, clogged with the remains of buildings and people and the carcasses of animals.

And in this madness Galveston was trapped in total isolation, desperate for help, unable to call out. Midmorning, a team of volunteers left for the mainland, seeking aid. They sailed across the still hazardous bay, choked with sunken vessels, debris, and corpses. Two newsmen, Richard Spillane and Tom South, made their way by foot, by coach, and finally by train to Houston, arriving before dawn

The devastation in Galveston, Texas, was almost incomprehensible. Over a third of the city had been swept out of existence. Most photographs of the aftermath were taken by local photographers. City leaders tried to stop off-islanders from photographing scenes like this one for fear of discouraging those who might invest in rebuilding the city. A Thomas Edison film crew, however, snuck a motion picture camera past the authorities to produce the most dramatic footage that had been filmed to date.

on Monday Spillane, ankles swollen, no longer able to walk, reported that Galveston was a city "whose very cemeteries had been emptied of their dead as if to receive new tenants." On a strip four blocks wide and three miles long, not a timber remained from over three thousand homes. Later he wrote of "streets choked with debris sandwiched with corpses; a city lifeless and bloomless . . . and over all, a thick, noxious slime, the vomitings of a maddened, retching ocean."

At the time no one knew the casualty figures. Initial estimates ran from five to six hundred. Each day the estimates rose. Incoming vessels found bodies floating one hundred miles out in the Gulf, and search parties on the mainland discovered the dead entangled in brushwood seven miles inland. In time it would be accepted that over six thousand people had died, five thousand had been injured, and ten thousand made homeless. The country had never known a greater disaster. At St. Mary's Orphanage the ninety-three children and ten Sisters of the Incarnate Word had perished, tied together in groups of eight.

Hundreds were dead in the Lucas Flats. The Pagoda Bath House had been swept out to sea. The Rosenberg school had collapsed. Down in the harbor, the steel cables that had held the great freighters to the wharves had snapped—the ships had been tossed like rowboats against the new piers—or carried to shores miles away. At the rail yards, of the hundred freight cars waiting to be unloaded most had been thrown off their tracks. Few houses of worship were left untouched. The magnificent St. Patrick's Church was ruined. Every single black church in the city—fourteen in all—had been leveled.

Amid the carnage were miraculous stories of survival. Two little girls were found five miles from their home in the branches of an uprooted tree. William Nisbett, a cotton broker, was buried in the ruins of the Cotton Exchange saloon. When he was dug out the following morning Nisbett was fine but for a few bruised fingers. Eight people swept across the bay were picked up alive, but most of the missing were never seen again and almost every family in the city was in mourning.

At two o'clock on Sunday afternoon in the Tremont Hotel, with water still sloshing on the floor of the lobby, in a remarkable meeting city leaders assembled to sort through the myriad crises facing the city. Men who had lost everything but the clothes they were wearing, stunned by the deaths of friends and loved ones—the mayor, bankers, agents for the railroads, cotton brokers, lawyers, and a rabbi—responded to a disaster they had yet to comprehend. Thirty-two thousand survivors were without food or water; the city was without light or power or communication systems; the streets were clogged with debris. Most of the horses in the city had been killed. The sewers were backed up; the cisterns filled with filth.

All that remained of St. Patrick's Church, a city landmark, were four small stained-glass windows, a few statues, and two altars. Even before the bodies had been removed from the rubble, services were being held at one of the surviving altars. Only three of the many churches in the city escaped without serious damage.

Some unable to face the horror drifted away, others found a druglike release in a maniacal pursuit of work. By evening, paths were being dug through the rubble, food had been commandeered from wholesale grocers, and drayloads of foodstuffs were being hauled around the city. Commissaries were set up in each ward and supplies were given free to those without money. Shelter was being found for the homeless, makeshift hospitals and morgues were set up. The top priority, most difficult of all, was burying the dead, and that work began immediately. Standard procedures were waived; there was no time or means for inquests or death certificates or even the comfort of burial ceremonies.

By Monday morning volunteer grave diggers were overwhelmed. Every able-bodied man was pressed into service. In the continuing heat, bodies could not be held an hour longer. Orders were given to load the corpses onto barges and take them out to sea. On the fly-swept piers in the bright morning sun, piles of bodies of human beings were dumped alongside carcasses of animals. But this order was not pursued for long. The sanity of the people could not endure the sight of overburdened wagons carting cargoes of the dead through the city. In the end, the only solution was immediate burial or incineration. Within hours, adding to the horror was the smoke from funeral pyres burning in the streets all over town.

That day an abbreviated edition of *The Galveston Daily News,* printed on a handpress, reported that food, water, and volunteers were on their way from Houston. Over a hundred men were at the waterworks, frantically trying to uncover machinery buried in the debris. Some hours after news of the disaster had

Small homes had been torn from their moorings, picked up like toys and dropped blocks from where they once stood.

---

reached Washington, the governor of Texas received a telegram from President McKinley offering condolences and the promise of aid. A military contingent was heading south, with rations of food and tents. A tug from Houston arrived in the city with two thousand gallons of water. It was not enough, but the pumps at the waterworks had been uncovered and were being repaired.

On Wednesday, the Relief Committee ordered whiskey for men on the burial crews. The stench of the bodies had become unbearable. A bargeful of disinfectant was ordered from the mainland. On Friday, telegraph service was restored—although all but three of the city's telegraphers had died. Word was received that ten doctors and twenty nurses from Bellevue Hospital in New York were on their way. So was Clara Barton, now the president of the Red Cross. Eleven days after the disaster the first train arrived, linking the city with the outside world.

Journalists began filing heartbreaking stories, which were published on the front page of papers across the country. Americans were now so closely tied together by the press that anguish in one city could immediately be shared by citizens thousands of miles away. The response to the disaster was without precedent. Millions of Americans contributed to the relief effort. Boxcars of supplies—medicine, food, water, clothing—began pouring into Galveston. Suddenly there was food for the taking. Over a million and half dollars in relief would be raised in little more than a month.

On the fourteenth day after the flood, Isaac Cline filed his formal report, later published by the U.S. Weather Bureau. He carefully laid out his professional notes—the barometric readings, the velocity of the winds, then, in a cool, almost detached way, described his personal experience. He ended the essay by reflecting on the mood of the people in the city, two weeks after the disaster: "Notwithstanding the fact that the streets are not yet clean and dead bodies are being discovered daily among the drifted debris, the people appear to have confidence in the place and are determined to rebuild and reestablish themselves here."

The bridges were to be built ten feet higher than before and Cline reported that the Southern Pacific Company was planning to "construct the wharves [to] withstand even such a hurricane as the one we have just experienced." A colonel from the U.S. Corps of Engineers recommended building a seawall twelve feet high and thirteen miles long. Others, encouraged by the Europeans who were firing cannon at hailstorms, suggested orders be given that forts along the seacoast "fire at any approaching storm or cyclonic disturbance."

But as restoration began, *National Geographic* questioned whether it was wise to rebuild on a vulnerable sandbank, or right for the city to subject its people—and the country—to another disaster. Galveston would forever be exposed not just to the vagaries of tropical storms but to the sea's unremitting appetite for land. For some time now, scientists had been recording the steady erosion of beachfront property on the Atlantic and along the Gulf. Homes and estates valued at thousands of dollars were being lost every year.

In Louisiana, Lafcadio Hearn wrote, "the sea is devouring the land. . . . Far out you can see through a good glass the porpoises at play where of old the sugar cane shook out its million banarets, and shark fins seam deep water above where pigeons used to coo. . . . Grand Isle is going, slowly but surely; the Gulf has eaten three miles into her meadowland." Galveston "had been planted on the last of the great natural embankments of the west coast [of Texas] remaining unsubmerged."

But the people of Galveston were not to be deterred. Galveston survived because it was meant to survive. Beyond the spiritual imperative was one simple geographic fact: like most great cities, Galveston had been built on the site of an exquisite natural port. Three and a half million people in Texas and Oklahoma Indian territory, and as far north as Kansas, were directly or indirectly dependent on Galveston's harbor. There were other southern ports but they were farther away. Galveston would not be allowed to die.

Within weeks, those who had emerged from the storm without a home or single earthly possession were being provided the means to start over. There were stipends from the Relief Fund for repairs, home furnishings, and tools. Small cottages were being mass produced for $315 apiece. Two weeks after the storm the grain elevators were loading cargo in the harbor, cotton was arriving for shipment overseas, stores and offices were reopening, construction companies were booming. At the Fancy Groceries and Liquor Store, proprietor Henry Toujouse acknowledged that he had sold only one bottle of champagne during the troubles—but his stores would keep; he was in Galveston to stay.

III

Several days after the hurricane battered Galveston, on an isolated barrier island off the North Carolina coast, Bill Tate, postmaster, fisherman, and political boss for the county, his wife, and their three children waited to welcome a visitor from the mainland. Not many travelers found their way to the tiny hamlet of Kitty Hawk. There was nothing much there—a handful of unprepossessing homes, a church, a store, a weather bureau, a life-saving station on the coast. There were no bridges from the mainland; the only way in was across the Albemarle Sound. A few years earlier a young poet named Robert Frost had stumbled on the island with a group of inebriated duck hunters, but by the fall of 1900 that visit was probably long forgotten.

On September 11, Wilbur Wright found himself bailing water in a leaky flat-bottomed scow, on an uncertain thirty-five-mile journey down the Pasquotank

River and across the sound to Kitty Hawk. The waves were running high, the wind was strong, and the boat almost swamped. The sails on the schooner were rotten; early in the trip the foresail tore loose, then the mainsail gave way. Wright later wrote his sister that the cabin was so dirty and vermin infested he kept out of it from first to last. He landed at Kitty Hawk, drenched, exhausted, and grateful to the Tates for their warm welcome.

For about two weeks, while waiting for Orville to join him on the island, Wilbur boarded with the family, and to the wonder of everyone in town began assembling his flying machine, a prefabricated glider, in the Tates' front yard. The

William Tate and his family on the porch of their home, which also served as the Kitty Hawk post office. Wilbur reported that the Tates had "no carpets, very little furniture, no books or pictures." But they were hospitable people and helpful. Orville reported that Bill Tate "attempts to do a day's work in two or three hours so that he can spend the balance with us and the machine."

notion that any man thought he could fly both amazed and irritated some of the islanders. If God had intended man to fly he would have given him wings. Using Addie Tate's sewing machine, Wright spent his days tailoring panels of French sateen fabric to cover the wings of the glider. When complete, the craft would have a span of seventeen and a half feet and weigh just under fifty pounds.

Wilbur wrote his father: "I have my machine nearly finished. It is not to have a motor and it is not expected to fly in any true sense of the word. My idea is merely to experiment and practice with a view to solving the problem of equilibrium. . . . I hope to find much in advance of the methods tried by previous experimenters . . . when once a machine is under proper control under all conditions, the motor problem will be quickly solved." Wilbur assured his father he did not expect to rise many feet above the ground and did not intend to take dangerous chances.

When Orville arrived with food, cots, an acetylene lamp, and his mandolin, the brothers pitched a large tent a half-mile from the Tates' home, on the godforsaken stretch of beach they would come to know so well. They had gone to Kitty Hawk for the sand and the wind, and had found both. There were nights when sudden squalls blowing off the ocean threatened to tear their tent from the ground, and there were days when the sand nearly blinded them and battered their machine.

Around October 3—they were never certain of the date—with the help of Orville and Bill Tate, Wilbur pulled himself up onto the double-decker glider for the first time, stretching out flat, his hands on the elevator control. With Orville and Tate racing alongside, playing out the guidelines attached to each wingtip, Wilbur was lifted off the ground, reaching an altitude of perhaps fifteen feet before the craft became unstable. The flight lasted only seconds, but in that brief time Wilbur gained a clearer understanding of the requirements for controlled flight, and control was everything.

They went back to flying the craft as an unmanned glider, testing its strength and resilience, making minor changes, flying the glider in winds of different velocities, with and without weights. Mid-October they had yet to spend even a second in free flight. Then, the morning of October 20, on the top of a large dune called Kill Devil Hill, Wilbur lay down on the glider, while Bill Tate and Orville each grabbed a wingtip and ran down the hill, holding the craft until it was airborne with Wilbur in control. The first few flights were cautious, no more than five or ten seconds long, and only a foot off the ground.

But Wilbur was flying, balancing the craft with the forward rudder, then landing gently and safely in the sand. He began to make glides of three to four hundred feet, lasting as long as fifteen seconds, holding the craft about five feet off the ground. Wilbur was now controlling the craft, it was not controlling him. Over the course of a total of two minutes' flying time, the Wrights had learned what they needed to move on. A few days later, they left for Dayton, abandoning their now battered glider in the dunes. Wilbur was well pleased "to be able to return without having our pet theories completely knocked in the head by hard logic of experience, and our own brains dashed out in the bargain."

Before it could be claimed by the sea, Mrs. Tate retrieved the French sateen fabric that covered the glider's wings, to use in dresses for her daughters. The Wrights would return to Kitty Hawk again and again, but it would be years before the world understood what the brothers had accomplished on the barren dunes, just a few miles past Bill Tate's home in the fall of 1900.

This photograph of Wilbur Wright was taken just as he was landing the 1901 glider on the sands at Kitty Hawk. No photograph exists of the manned flight in the fall of 1900.

Other Stories of Interest

The Washington Post, September 1, 1900
Text Books in the South

ATLANTA, GEORGIA— The Grand Army of the Republic at Chicago, Wednesday, adopted resolutions condemning the school books alleged to be used in the Southern schools as calculated to perpetuate prejudice against the Federal government over events of the Civil War. Gen. John B. Gordon, commander-in-chief of the United Confederate Veterans says he does not believe any respectable Southern teacher is knowingly using any book that is tended to perpetuate prejudice. . . .

"Every recommendation made by our historical committee has been to find and sustain only such books as gave the truth of history without the slightest tinge of passion and prejudice against either North or South."

The New York Times, September 8, 1900
The Wonderful Wizard of Oz,

by Frank Baum With pictures by
W. W. Denslow. Illuminated title page.
Pages 230. George M. Hill Company.

In "The Wonderful Wizard of Oz" the fact is clearly recognized that the young as well as their elders love novelty . . . something new in place of the old, familiar, and winged fairies of Grimm and Andersen.

The story has humor and here and there stray bits of philosophy . . . the Wonderful Wizard who turns out in the end to be only a wonderful humbug. A scarecrow stuffed with straw, a tin woodman, and a cowardly lion do not at first blush promise well as moving heroes but in actual practice they take on something of the living breathing quality that is so gloriously exemplified in "The Story of the Three Bears" that has become a classic.

The book has a bright and joyous atmosphere, and does not dwell on killing and acts of violence. Enough stirring adventure enters into it, however, to flavor it with zest, and it will be strange if there be a normal child who will not enjoy the story.

Harper's Weekly, September 15, 1900
It is still under discussion whether the Nicaragua or the Panama route is better for the ship-canal that seems inevitable between the Atlantic and the Pacific.

Wilbur Shober and Booth Grunendike, in Springfield, Illinois, posed for Booth's mother, Mary Booth Grunendike. An obsessive photographer, Mrs. Grunendike took well over four thousand photographs. Her family owned a drugstore and she probably had access to the store's darkroom.

CHAPTER THIRTEEN

September–October

I

On a fall morning along the Shiawassee River in the small town of Saginaw, Michigan, Theodore Roosevelt was greeted by a crowd much like the one that had seen him off in Bay City just a half hour before. As he grabbed for every outstretched hand he was also trying to conserve his voice. He had been campaigning for some weeks now, and as his doctor had predicted his throat was raw, on the verge of giving out, yet there were two more months to go. As the procession fell into line mounted members of the local Rough Rider Club took the lead, followed by six bands, twenty carriages, and several hundred people marching afoot.

There was nothing more entertaining than a presidential rally on a pleasant fall day, the seductive sound of the trombones, the whinnying of the horses, the joy of being part of a partisan convocation, a Hallelujah chorus singing out the designated refrain, "Teddy, Teddy, Teddy!" God how Roosevelt loathed that name. No one but a stranger ever dared to use it, but like so much else these days, it was beyond TR's control.

By September the people in Saginaw, as in much of America, had caught election fever, the quadrennial disease that only the more cynical managed to resist. In the center of town on a flag-bedecked stand in the middle of a square at Jefferson Street, TR spoke to a crowd so large most people, including a reporter for *The Washington Post,* could not hear a word he said. But those beyond the reach of his high, piercing voice followed the cheers of those closer in, applauding in all the proper places. At the end of a very abbreviated speech, just five minutes long, Roosevelt and the crowd locked in a wild and noisy embrace. As TR headed off for Owosso, the next town down the line, the people of Saginaw ambled back to work, pleased by the morning's diversion.

From Labor Day on, both TR and William Jennings Bryan had been campaigning flat out, traveling in palatial railcars, star performers in the most expensive and exhaustive presidential contest America had ever seen. Both men were drawing large and eager crowds. TR was the greater novelty, a political newcomer on the national landscape, but Bryan was sure to be entertaining. At a rally in Parkersburg, West Virginia, questioning America's title to the Philippine islands, he asked rhetorically: "Who says the Lord gave them to us?" When someone in the crowd shouted, "Mark Hanna," Bryan shot back, "While I am not prepared to deny that God does speak through the human voice, I do think that when he gets ready to speak to the American people he will choose some other mouthpiece than Mr. Hanna."

In the campaign of 1896 Bryan had traveled nineteen thousand miles, making five hundred and ninety-nine speeches. In the summer of 1900, Mark Hanna, chairman of the Republican party, anticipating that Bryan would take to the road once again, had asked Roosevelt to counter with a tour of his own. TR had hated the idea of touring the country like a huckster, selling himself to the people. But once he committed to this "rapid transit" tour, he astounded his handlers by charging onto speaker's platforms as though the fate of the nation was carried in his arms.

A dozen or more times a day TR warned voters that Bryan's policies would lead to "panic in the business world . . . and prolonged misery among all our people." An ardent defender of America's expansion into the Philippines, Roosevelt waved the flag in almost every speech: "I do not want this flag to come down where it is planted, where our men have fought and shed their blood for it." By mid-September the press was covering the campaign as though it were a horse race, measuring the candidates by their stamina. At the end of his first full month on the road, TR's secretary told reporters that TR had covered almost thirteen thousand miles, delivering two hundred and ninety speeches, and there were six weeks left to go. Bryan was known to be in great physical shape, capable of running on limited sleep, of delivering pre-breakfast speeches at dawn, but he was beginning to tire.

The only evidence of fatigue anyone could point to in the governor of New York was the wavering in his voice. In a note to his sister, however, TR acknowledged he was "having a very hard trip." He had been moving nonstop through the "open-hearted, wide-awake . . . cattle and mountain countries in the Northwest." Except for a half-dozen "first-class horse-back rides," he said, "I do nothing but fester in the car and elbow to and from stagings where I address audiences." Nothing in TR's experience had prepared him for the tour, not the madness at the convention in Philadelphia, which had lasted less than a day, or the periodic outpourings of support he so enjoyed as governor. Always in the past, after he had had his fill of admiration, he had been able to go home, back to the leavening influence of his family and the privacy of his study.

Stumping the West, Theodore Roosevelt was reported to have made forty separate appearances over the course of one day, before winding up with his usual long address at night.

The moment he was nominated he knew he had lost his independence, but he could never have imagined the extent to which he would be captive to the demands of others. For every appearance he made, every delegation he received, every interview he granted, hundreds of others were rejected. Everywhere he went now, whether it suited him or not, reporters were bound to go, and always somewhere out of view was an aide with a watch in his hand. In an essay for *Scribner's* on "How a President Is Elected," A. Maurice Low wrote that from the moment a man is nominated "he lives in a glass house with an X-ray machine at every corner of every room. . . . Poets, warriors and matinee heroes may enjoy some privacy occasionally when they cease to be rare china. . . . But a presidential candidate belongs to the public, and the public will not surrender one jot of its ownership."

Although TR was not a presidential candidate he had become the most sought after man in the country and everything he did now was news or was shaped to make news. When a reporter described him sitting on the train mentally refreshing himself with essays on "questions of metaphysical and psychological importance," it was hard to know where contrivance ended and the genuine began. But in fact TR may well have been studying a paper on metaphysics. What was astonishing about this very public man was the stubbornness with which he pursued his private passions.

Over the course of one day on the tour, following breakfast and a speech at seven-thirty, he took off a half hour to read a "historical work." Between nine and noon there were two more speeches, a couple of meetings, an hour spent on correspondence, and then at midday he set aside another half hour, this time to read an "ornithological work." Lunch was squeezed in between two more speeches, and then at two-thirty he settled down with a volume of Sir Walter Scott. Before the day was over, TR gave three more speeches, met with the press, answered telegrams, and still managed to preserve three more reading periods as well—the last a full hour before he went to bed at midnight.

In contrast, President McKinley was spending a quiet fall in Canton. When he took his daily walks and drives he saw McKinley-Roosevelt placards in shop windows, but there were no visiting delegations this year, no front porch speeches or impromptu parades down North Market Street. McKinley had asked Republican leaders to respect his need to work on presidential matters and they had dutifully complied. Only an occasional reporter lingered on the lawn. No one doubted McKinley was dictating Republican strategy, but that was not the stuff that made a journalist's heart beat faster. The headliners were half a continent away, and so was the press corps. If the president was discomfited reading about Teddy every morning, no one knew it. The tension in his face reflected a host of other concerns.

Bryan was proving to be more effective than Republican strategists had projected, and in the eastern states where anti-imperialists continued to make headway, some were now predicting heavy Republican losses. The polls showed a disquieting number of undecided states, and in the second week of September, after a month of speculation, it looked as though the anthracite miners in Pennsylvania were finally going out on strike. There had been thousands of strikes in 1900, but a full-scale walkout by the miners could affect the fortunes of the entire country and the election. A sympathetic lot, the strikers could play directly into Bryan's hands and influence the course of the election. Mark Hanna had quietly been trying to pressure the mine operators, but they were proving to be an obdurate bunch.

For weeks John Mitchell, the young president of the United Mine Workers, had been requesting a meeting between the operators and the union. Now he told the press the union had done all it honorably could do to avoid a conflict: "We have reached the point where we must either advise the miners . . . to continue working under these unjust and tyrannical conditions or counsel a strike." He appealed to the American people and the American press for support, acknowledging that a walkout could reach well beyond the coalfields, affecting "the great manufacturing industries of the East, the wholesale and retail business establishments, the great ocean, lake, canal and railroad interests, laboring men and capitalists."

On September 13, miners assembled by the thousands in Hazleton and Wilkes-Barre, Shenandoah and Shamokin, in coal towns and villages in northeast Pennsylvania, awaiting the order they had all been expecting. "Do not wait for any further notice to strike, but cease work in a body on and after Monday, September 17, 1900." The timing was perfect and Mitchell knew it. There were a hundred and fifty thousand men working in the region. If they could be persuaded to walk out in concert, the UMW would be the strongest labor force in the country, capable of bringing industrial America to a standstill on the eve of the election.

In Chicago, Mark Hanna, chairman of the Republican National Committee, convened an emergency meeting at party headquarters. From Hanna's perspective, the strike could not have come at a worse time. Photographs of hollow-eyed children could too easily be used to mock McKinley's slogan of the "full dinner pail." Across town, at Democratic headquarters, an official declared that the strike "will aid us to demonstrate that combinations of capital are dangerous and constitute a standing menace to labor."

As the deadline approached, mine owners were blaming the troubles in the region on a handful of hotheads and outside agitators. With four days left before the deadline, no one knew what to expect, including UMW president Mitchell. Of the hundred and fifty thousand men working in the anthracite mines, only nine thousand had joined the union.

II

Before dawn, on Monday, September 17, in the coal town of Shenandoah there was an uneasy, almost unpleasant quiet. The air reeked of coal, and "as far as the eye could see," wrote one reporter, "mountain and plain were grimy with the dust of coal; even the streams were black, jet black, with the color of it." Journalists new to the area were stunned by the loneliness of the landscape, the deadness of the vegetation, the great abandoned gullies. Every half-mile, huge ungainly buildings known as breakers rose into the sky, and everywhere one looked were "great pyramids" of refuse coal. By six that morning, white plumes of smoke began rising from the collieries surrounding the town, as firemen started up the boilers, a signal that the mines were opening as usual.

The streets were still all but empty except for union representatives who had arrived in town the night before. Along Centre Street, trolley cars waited. In every cottage and shack the men were up now, along with their wives and children. In just half an hour, almost every miner in the region, one hundred and fifty thousand of them, would have to walk out the door of his home and declare his position. Many had been through other strikes and few had been successful. Strikers had often found themselves not only out of a job but blackballed throughout the region. There wasn't a household where someone didn't know a man or a woman who had been roughed up, or killed by the Coal and Iron police.

In the strike back in 1897, a small contingent of Polish, Slovakian, and Lithuanian miners had marched toward the town of Lattimore in hopes of urging other men to join them. The group was neither large nor militant. In their white shirts, formal hats, and jackets, they looked for all the world like members of a fraternal organization. But at the edge of the village, sheriff's deputies, angered because the demonstrators did not disperse, leveled their pistols and Winchester rifles and fired directly at the marchers. The first man to fall was carrying an American flag. Nineteen in all were killed and at least thirty-two were wounded. It was three years ago, almost to the day. The memory of the Lattimore massacre was goading some into action, but it was also frightening others.

Ever since the strike order had come down, the miners had been talking among themselves and with their wives. There was hardly a man who had any savings to speak of and once the strike began there would be no more credit at the company store. The men from Scotland reminded each other of the saying back home, "A man must eat, musn't he not? And his children must eat, musn't they didn't?" There was rent to be paid and with winter not far off the children would be needing boots—particularly the boys working in the breakers, who often sat in wet coal up to their knees. And when the weather turned as it now threatened to, they would need to buy fuel, a galling bit of business for those surrounded by banks of refuse coal, as large as the breakers. Any child caught picking bits of coal, even the size of buckwheat, on company ground, could be charged with larceny.

By Friday, in every town, strangers had begun to appear in the streets—journalists, union officials, Pinkerton men, and company spies. Suspicious miners kept to themselves. In Hazleton that morning, the UMW was setting up headquarters in two large front rooms at the second-rate Valley Hotel. The rolltop desks were being moved into place, the typewriters had yet to arrive but Mitchell—Johnny d'Mitch as many now called him—was expected within hours. Union officials told reporters that within days, "a great coal famine would sweep the nation." That afternoon, an unusual number of women were seen laying in supplies: flour, dried beef, and oatmeal.

On Saturday afternoon at two-thirty, as men emerged from a mine outside of Hazleton, clusters of reporters waited to gauge their disposition. A company sign on the pay car read, "Work Monday September 17," but as the men waited in line for their wages, few were willing to talk to reporters. At UMW headquarters, Mitchell was now receiving regular bulletins from all over the region. At a few collieries the men had walked out early. In Shamokin, there was tension between the foreign workers who were supporting the union and the better-paid, English-speaking miners who were disinclined to strike. Mitchell feared similar trouble at other mines, in other towns.

A fault line fell between those men known as "Americans," the English speakers—the Welsh, and the Scots, and the Irish—who held most of the skilled jobs, and the "Polanders," or "Huns," who came from a mix of Slavic countries, knew little English, and were given the lowest-paying jobs. In the past, all attempts at organizing the anthracite workers into one effective union had been wrecked by ethnic hatred. If the men began fighting each other now, the UMW was headed for disaster. Solidarity was essential but considered unlikely.

For months Mitchell and his organizers had been urging the miners to bury generations of mistrust, arguing that cave-ins and explosions and "rotten gas" were not selective. At the end of a year of the hardest, meanest, most dangerous work on earth, "Americans" and "Polanders" alike were seldom better off than when they had started. For the most part they shared the same hardships and the same grievances. Wages were of course the central issue. The UMW was asking for a flat 20 percent hike across the board. Mitchell was quoted as saying that on average the men were getting only $250 a year. Skilled miners were probably making around $400, maybe more, but there was little argument that by any standard, with few exceptions, the men were underpaid.

There was no American industry in which workers were subjected to more outright cheating. Ostensibly, miners were paid for every ton of coal hauled to the surface, but every cart of coal also contained a certain measure of rock and dirt. In the anthracite fields, to be paid for one ton of coal, miners were required to deliver over three thousand pounds of material, in some as much as four thousand pounds. In many mines, a man's haul was rated by a company dockage boss, often not the most reliable of men. At other collieries, men were paid for filling a standardized cart, but reporters found carts that had been illicitly enlarged. On some, the sides had been extended; others had been fitted with ingenious flexible rubber bottoms to accommodate 15 percent more material, adding to a man's labor but not to his pay.

On Saturday afternoon, as sober-faced miners clustered in the streets, it was still impossible to guess their intentions, but reporters noted that at the Yorktown mine, and there were others, the men had brought their tools out at the end of the last shift. The operators continued to express the greatest confidence that if a strike should occur, it would not last long. But at the same time they were preparing for the worst. Barbed wire was being strung up around the breakers, guards were patrolling at night, and at the Hazleton depot trainloads of Pinkerton men were arriving, two hundred and fifty men at a time—menacing reminders of violence past.

Owners of the gun shops reported a run on revolvers. Mitchell cautioned the

Working in the breaker where coal was shattered and sorted, the "breaker boys" worked ten- to twelve-hour days, removing rock and slate from an endless stream of coal. Many of the boys were under the legal age of twelve; some were as young as eight or nine. Most were foreign born. Forbidden to use gloves, which would impair their sense of touch, the boys' fingers cracked and bled until the skin hardened. Many youngsters took to chewing tobacco in hopes of preventing coal dust from going down their throats.

miners not to allow themselves to be provoked into "quarrels and violations of the peace." It was, he said, "one of the most common methods used . . . to destroy the public sympathy and defeat our cause." Mitchell understood as well as any politician "the irresistible power of concentrated public opinion," and how quickly that sentiment could be turned if the miners were seen as lawless.

After Sunday mass, in Mountain Carmel, Mother Mary Harris Jones, the aging patron saint of America's coalfields, told the women attending a rally that "together they could do anything." The widow of a miner, Mother Jones, now about seventy years old, was a fearless organizer who had been on the UMW payroll for years. She spoke of the lives of the breaker boys, the dead-eyed children, some as young as eight, who for ten hours a day straddled moving troughs of coal removing the slate and flint. There were tens of thousands of boys under legal age working in the anthracite mines, scrawny pale-faced youngsters making no more than $1 or $2 a week. Ever since knockoff time on Saturday, packs of boys, feeding off the excitement, had been racing through the towns, tumbling down refuse dumps, unmindful of the tension of their elders.

When the work whistles sounded on Monday morning, as each man opened the door to his home, everyone—neighbors, union officials, reporters, shopkeepers—knew his decision: whether he stood with the union or against it. In a world in which men had but two sets of clothes, those dressed in the black coats and hats reserved for Sunday wear were on strike. Those in work clothes were headed back to the mines. In every town in the region it was the same, two streams of men moving in different directions. Given the level of tension and the numbers of men involved, to everyone's surprise, each stream passed the other with remarkable restraint. No violence was reported that morning.

It would be some hours before the counts were in, but from first light it was clear that an extraordinary number of men were idle. In a few towns the strikers were the English speakers, but in Shenandoah, and almost everywhere else, it was the "Polanders" who had elected to go out on strike. By midmorning district telegraph offices were jammed with reporters filing dispatches. In Shamokin, where almost every mine was affected, a journalist for *The Philadelphia Inquirer* reported the walkout had come as a sudden blow to operators and merchants: "The men have been so quiet . . . ," he wrote, "the real depth of their feelings has not been known even to their greatest intimates." Even Mitchell was astounded. By nightfall, at least ninety thousand men had joined the walkout.

Coal operators told reporters they were still confident the action would end in failure and the complete destruction of the UMW. One mine official declared that the operators would not rest "until there does not remain a single union man from one end of the anthracite region to the other." With many predicting that the strike would end in violence, the reporter added a personal note: "You are likely to hear of many stories to the effect that men have broken the law, but it is only fair that before any stock is taken in such tales that they be thoroughly investigated first. I have thus probed the truth of two such stories today and found them both without any foundation. . . . Two or three days will bring matters to a crisis, one way or other."

On Tuesday, on a road above Hazleton, Hungarian strikers were out before dawn. The fences and roads were covered with frost, and the walking wasn't easy. There were stones and hollows in the mountain roads. In the half-light the men were chanting a Hungarian marching rhyme when up the hill out of the mountain mist came a group of men in work clothes carrying their dinner pails. The strikers surrounded the workers, and one by one exhorted each to join the walkout. A few were turned back, but most held their ground and were allowed to pass unmolested. With variations, the scene was repeated all over the region. There were moments of tension, but to Mitchell's great relief, for the second day in a row there were no serious incidents.

On Wednesday, ugly rumors sent union officials racing to a small town on the Susquehanna River, following reports that a conflict was imminent between union men from the colliery in Lykens and twelve hundred non-union workers in nearby Williamstown. The strikers were quoted as saying they would drive the men out of the Williamstown mine even if they had to "drown them out" by destroying the water pumps. The clash was averted, but with each passing hour the chance of violence seemed more likely.

By Thursday, the fourth day of the strike, only fifteen thousand men remained at work, but owners were more intransigent than ever. A number were threatening to go out of business rather than deal with the UMW. Some were already timbering their mines and bringing the mules to the surface. The newspapers were now predicting a long and bitter struggle. The ripple effect Mitchell had foreseen was setting in. Coal stocks were already dwindling; orders were no longer being filled. In towns around the area, businesses were affected. Shop clerks were discharged, rail crews laid off, and in Scranton the theatrical companies were not meeting their expenses. But small business owners, in spite of their losses, seemed to be supporting the union.

It was clear to everyone that only intercession by outside forces could bring the companies to a settlement. While there were hundreds of mine operators and owners, most of them, 70 percent or more, were either owned or controlled by the railroads—and the railroads in the region were in large measure controlled by a group of New York financiers led by J. P. Morgan. Any agreement would have to involve the presidents of the rail companies—they were, in fact, the invisible coal barons. In New York, *The World* reported that at Mark Hanna's behest, Morgan had already tried to intercede but to no avail. Matters would have to become a great deal worse before the presidents of the coal companies could be convinced to negotiate.

From Mitchell's perspective, it was all just a matter of time. Magazines and newspapers were running stories about the dismal conditions in the coal towns and public sympathy was with the miners. Most important, the men themselves were in good spirits. Their fears of blacklists, dismissals, and violence had begun to fade. There was almost a holiday atmosphere in some towns. Baseball games were being organized and men were hiking up into the mountains to chop wood for their stoves. One union official told a reporter that the strikers were prepared to stay out all winter if they had to.

On Friday the twenty-first, Mitchell, exhausted but confident, went into seclusion, locking himself up in his office for the day, refusing all appointments. He had been working seven days a week for almost a year, seldom getting home to see his wife and four children; he scarcely knew the youngest. The demands were unrelenting, he was traveling constantly, speaking at meetings, rallies, and press conferences, and the owners had launched a personal attack on him, questioning his honesty, hiring detectives to follow him night and day. He confided to a friend, "The nervous strain under which I am laboring is fearful." It was at that moment the news arrived that threatened to unravel all he had accomplished.

Earlier that Friday morning, at an isolated colliery outside Shamokin, a watchman had seen a man moving toward the engine house. There was an exchange of fire and the guard was wounded. A few hours later Mitchell was told of the tragedy at Shenandoah. The first accounts described "blood flowing in the streets." A nine-year-old girl and two men were reported dead and at least twenty-three others were said to be grievously wounded. The governor was calling out three regiments of infantry along with a battery equipped with Gatling guns and a troop of cavalry. The entire county was described as terror stricken. News spread by telegraph and telephone and the informal chain of connections that linked one coal town to the next.

Strikers and officials milled around in front of union headquarters waiting for details, but it would be hours before the truth could be untangled. Mitchell immediately dispatched a telegram demanding that local leaders maintain order and asking "honest strikers to aid the authorities." It was precisely the kind of incident he had sought to avoid—a clash between the "Polanders" and the "Americans."

When the walkout had begun in Shenandoah on Monday, enough English-speaking miners had remained in the pits to keep the mines working. In the days that followed, the strikers had begun pressuring the workers. By midweek, six of the collieries in the region were closed. By Friday, of the thirteen thousand miners in the Shenandoah Valley only six hundred remained at work, mostly English speakers. That afternoon a band of strikers—who would be variously described by the press as Polanders, Huns, Lithuanians, and Hungarians—gathered at the gate of the Indian Ridge colliery waiting for the workers at the end of the shift. Mine officials called Sheriff O'Toole and his posse to escort the workers home.

As the deputies led the miners down Centre Street, the strikers followed, hurling "sticks and stones and curses." In a section known as the "bloody first ward," the street jammed with spectators and children, the strikers overturned a trolley car in which some workers were riding. Sheriff O'Toole gave the command, and his deputies drew their guns and began firing. Later it was said that five hundred shots were fired. Centre Street was turned into a sea of glass. The windows and town lamps were shattered; the swinging doors of the saloons looked as if they had been used for rifle practice. When Captain Christian of the Coal and Iron police arrived, the crowd scattered.

Contrary to early reports, in what all agreed must have been a miracle, only one person was killed and only a handful had been wounded. Annie Rogers, the child who had been mentioned in all the dispatches, had been shot but was "in a fair way of ultimately getting well"; and Eddie Coyle, who was hit below the heart while dragging his children from the street, was pulling through. But Mitchell knew, as he had from the outset, that if the miners turned to violence they would lose all outside support. Publicly he blamed the sheriff for his ruthless disregard for the lives of others; privately he was concerned about the men remaining "steady and patient." The papers were already reporting that sympathy for the strikers had diminished and their position had been weakened.

Late that afternoon it began to rain in Shenandoah. A correspondent for *The New York Times* reported that the Hungarian who had been killed "was permitted to lay in the gutter where he dropped." *The Times* reporter went on to explain, "Foreigners of the class employed here say a dead man is of no use, and they refuse to care for the body." It wasn't true, but there was much written that day that wasn't true.

———

Sunday morning, when Stephen Bonsal, a war correspondent for *Collier's Weekly*, arrived in Shenandoah, he found the hotels crowded with twenty-five hundred National Guardsmen. With eight men to a room, it was, he said, not hard to get back on a wartime footing. Reports had described Shenandoah as a city under siege, but Bonsal found the mood between the townspeople and the military surprisingly friendly. Soldiers were being invited home for dinner. *The New York Times* reported that the English-speaking strikers were in favor of going back to work and that the coal operators in the valley were expecting that come Monday morning the collieries in the area would be in full operation.

The operators told Bonsal that the rough treatment the strikers had received had broken the back of the strike. He quoted one operator as saying, "I shall have forty percent of my men at work on Monday morning. The rest will come sneaking back in a day or two, and then I will take whom I have chosen. We have got them beaten." Early Monday morning before sunup, the correspondent was out on a hill overlooking the town, waiting, as he said, to record the death of the strike. When the boilers started up he could see the shafts of smoke against the sky. As the sun grew stronger, reporters, strikers, union officials, and mine owners waited, as they had on the first day of the strike.

In the minutes following the sounding of the whistle not a door opened, not a man appeared. Bonsal noted that at seven o'clock and again at seven-thirty, "the coal hills and the washed-out hollows resounded with the inviting and warning whistles but not a miner stirred, not a door opened wide, not a window shade was drawn." Again the strikers had caught the press and the operators by surprise. The response seemed unanimous, and Bonsal realized there must have been an understanding between them all, the "Americans" and the "Polanders." "After half-past seven," he wrote, "steam was turned off . . . the fires were allowed to go out, and soon no more smoke came from the chimneys. The soldiers for the most part were withdrawn . . . and the bosses and the superintendents hastened with black looks to telegraph New York and Philadelphia of the complete failure of their attempt to resume work."

A few hours later five thousand people gathered for the funeral of Anthony Axaloboce, the miner killed on Friday. The American flag was furled and draped with crepe and as the Lithuanian band played a death march, a long dark line of men slowly moved down Centre Street to the small redbrick chapel of the Russian Church. Not a soldier or a policeman or a deputy sheriff was in view. There was no need. On Cemetery Hill, Mother Jones urged the men to resist but not to be the aggressors. "Success," she said, "would be their reward for good."

Before September was over, there were reports that the coal barons were finally coming around. Mark Hanna was seen entering J. P. Morgan's marble office building on Wall Street, along with the presidents of the railroad companies. When he emerged from the meeting, reporters asked if it were true that the McKinley administration was trying to bludgeon the owners into an agreement by threatening to lift the tariff on foreign coal. Hanna categorically denied the charge and refused further comments, but the press knew the Republican chairman was under enormous pressure.

As Hanna and McKinley had feared, the miners' cause had become a major political issue. An editorial in one Democratic paper declared, "No really permanent prosperity can rest upon the degradation of so many thousands of people. The American people will come to this conclusion and express their opinions by their ballots in November." At a rally in Nebraska, Bryan challenged the Republicans to take "their full-dinner pail arguments into the coal fields." He went on to say, "Whether a man is a laboring man, a farmer or a merchant, he must see that the opportunities are constantly narrowing under this trust system." Mills and factories were running low on coal. If the strike continued much longer, there would be nationwide layoffs.

Mitchell too was feeling the pressure. Daily the papers were running accounts of brawls in the coal towns. The strike fund was running low and the men were

The Pennsylvania Eighth Regiment marching down Centre Street in Shenandoah, Pennsylvania, surrounded by miners in their suits and bowlers. It was assumed by coal operators that with the arrival of the troops many of these men, guaranteed protection, would return to work, but the operators had underestimated the strength of the union.

stretched. There were stories of farms outside Wilkes-Barre being robbed, of corn, meat, and potatoes lifted in the night. A cow had been butchered and sheep stolen. In conversations with Hanna by long-distance telephone, Mitchell learned that the coal trust would offer a flat 10 percent raise across the board—some of the companies had already made the offer, but they had no intention of recognizing the UMW and were refusing to deal with the other issues on the table.

The question was, could Hanna do better, and how long could Mitchell count on the strikers holding out? He sensed their restlessness at every meeting. Thousands of men, desperate for work, had already been forced to leave the area. He would have to begin to prepare the membership for a compromise. At an enormous rally in Shenandoah he warned the men that in the end they could not expect to "eradicate all the evils and injustices heaped upon you for forty long years." Hanna, too, was working under limitations, but he knew that Mitchell needed more than a 10 percent raise to convince the miners to go back to work. By mid-October, the Republican leader told a reporter a compromise could be reached within a day or two. He was not far off.

On October 25, Mitchell was able to announce that the pay hike had been guaranteed at least until the following April and that the owners had also agreed to abolish the much hated sliding pay scale. It was less than he had wished for, but as much as he could get. He told the miners, "Your victory is so nearly complete, that no good can be served by continuing the strike any longer." Most important, he said, "you have established a powerful organization, which will . . . make your employment less hazardous and more profitable than before the strike began." The coal owners had not recognized the union, but the miners had. The "Americans" and "Polanders" together had proven the power of collective action, and Mitchell could boast that the strike had been "the most remarkable contest between labor and capital in the industrial history of our nation."

In the end, the coal barons remained in control, and as the presidential election moved into its closing weeks, it was not lost on the press that the Republicans, not the Democrats, had engineered peace on the labor front. But the celebrations in the coalfields went on for days. In Shenandoah, the breaker boys marched down Centre Street cheering Mitchell. At the last great demonstration, two thousand boys in miner's caps gathered to present him with a magnificent solid gold badge. The presentation speech was made by a ten-year-old worker named Vinnie Phillips. Mitchell was so affected it was moments before he could pull himself together to thank the boys for their honor.

Other Stories of Interest

The New York Times, September 25, 1900
Song and Dance for Montana

CHICAGO—Senator Clark of Montana has sent to Chicago for a full corps of sketch artists and vaudeville "headliners." The Senator is going to use them in the Montana campaign and the voters are going to be given amusement together with the speeches for anti-imperialism, anti-trusts and free silver.

Before going [the players] told friends they had been guaranteed $1,500 a week each by Senator Clark.

The Examiner (San Francisco),
October 11, 1900
Danish West Indies
May Soon Be Bought

LONDON—Referring to the mooted purchase of the Danish West Indies by the United States, the Copenhagen correspondent of the "Daily Telegraph" says: The renewed negotiations will result, I believe, in the purchase. The opposition in the Danish Parliament favors the transaction but urges the Government to obtain a larger price than the United States previously offered. It is understood that America wishes to use St. Croix as a naval coaling station.

*The Freeman, An Illustrated Colored
Newspaper (Indianapolis),*
October 27, 1900
The Duty of the Negro Voter

It ought not to take a Negro a great while to make up his mind as how he shall vote this year. The division of the vote is hardly to be considered at this time. It is the duty of the Negro to vote for the Republican party.

It will be quite time to consider the advisability of dividing the vote . . . when shotguns are dropped from the assassins' hands, when mob fires cease to be funeral pyres, when the accident of birth-nature ceases to amount to a crime, when color and oppression are no longer synonyms, when the laws of this fair land are administered to all alike.

The Democratic party has spoken. It is not misunderstood.

The McKinleys at a small private dinner at the home of Senator Mark Hanna (left), in Cleveland, Ohio. The president, disregarding custom, always insisted on sitting next to his wife, even at state dinners, for fear she might suffer a seizure.

CHAPTER FOURTEEN

October–November

I

The back roads leading out of Canton quieted down in the afternoon, the drays and wagons, filled with produce, all but disappeared. The McKinleys' coachman could allow the horses to amble as they moved out into the country. Ida McKinley had an obsessive need to pull her husband away from the telephone and the daily boxes of correspondence. All the pressures of the White House seemed to have followed the president to Canton. There was still fighting in China between the allies and the Boxers, and the dispatches from the Philippines brought more bad news. But once in the carriage no one could reach him, no senator could demand his attention. The McKinleys never seemed more at peace than when they settled in for one of their isolated drives.

But for much of October, Secretary Cortelyou and Detective George Foster watched the carriage leave North Market Street with a sense of foreboding. On October 2, Foster received a warning, for the third time in as many months, that "the president's life was in peril." The western branch of the Secret Service, based in Chicago, had informed the agent that three men—presumed to be anarchists, two Italians and one tall fellow "who dresses like an old soldier"—were on their way to Canton to kill the president. The assassins were said to be planning to waylay the carriage on the outskirts of town. The police were alerted to watch for all suspicious strangers, and two policemen were assigned to guard the McKinley home at night.

In the days immediately following the warning, Cortelyou tried to keep the president at his desk. A second Secret Service agent was sent out from Washington to back up Foster. Following the murder of King Humbert in the summer, the president's aides had grown increasingly apprehensive. On October 10, word arrived from Rome that a suspect being held in connection with the death of Humbert had bragged to police: "Anarchists have killed kings and queens: now they should kill a president of a republic." Mark Hanna feared that the intensity of the campaign rhetoric might inflame some lunatic: "There are many diseased minds in the country," he said.

For months the Republican press had been accusing the Democrats of "inciting class hatred," and Hanna lambasted Bryan for appealing to "working men with the doctrines of the Socialist and Anarchist." But the president would not allow himself to become a prisoner in his own home. By mid-October, the McKinleys once again were driving along lonely country roads in their carriage, with its distinctive emblem on the back.

In the closing weeks of the campaign, the president was more confident about the election. The Democrats were stalled. At the public betting centers across the country the odds were running four to one in favor of McKinley. The contest was not over, but the major issues had been so thoroughly aired that a correspondent for *Collier's Weekly* wrote: "The people had become sated with dry discussions. They wanted excitement, the glare and din of pyrotechnics. . . . They were to have enough." Where a hundred torches had been the norm, there were now a thousand. Where fifteen hundred small flags had once sufficed, the order was tripled, the rallies if possible were larger and more elaborate, the pace of the candidates even more frenetic.

To keep up his strength, Bryan was eating six meals a day and and was indulging in a rubdown after every appearance. In New York City on October 16, in the kingdom of Richard Croker, thousands of Tammany Hall minions were dressing the city for what was to be the most elaborate reception of the campaign.

Booming cannons would announce the arrival of William Jennings Bryan and a fusillade of rockets and Roman candles from atop the tower on Madison Square Garden would signal his passage through the streets. One aide was in charge of nothing but fireworks. Another had responsibility for the calcium lights that were to blaze from every rooftop along the way. The boy in Croker imagined how he and Bryan would ride together in an open carriage, swept from one location to the next on an ovation of such intensity that the cheers would overwhelm the Republican strongholds upstate. Croker promised reporters that no less than a hundred thousand people would be out on the streets.

And from the moment the two men met in Grand Central Station it had all gone pretty much as Richard Croker had planned, except for a dramatic change in the weather. At the last minute a cold front had moved in and to his great disappointment Croker was forced to bundle Bryan into a closed carriage. As the entourage made its initial stop at Tammany Hall, the wind picked up and a storm broke over the city. Croker managed to contain himself, but all who knew him could see in his eyes projections of disaster. The crowds already were not as large as he had wished, and the cold driving rain would send even more people home.

But as suddenly as the storm had arrived, the sky cleared and a rainbow appeared. This may have been the omen that led Croker to push his luck, or perhaps his political instincts were muted by the excitement he had so artfully contrived. He now began to push himself, to shadow Bryan, to never be more than an arm's reach away. And Bryan, in a speech at Cooper Union, deviated from his script and with a bow to his host, expressed his gratitude, saying: "Great is Tammany and Croker is its prophet."

That brief moment of grace did neither man any good. Bryan would almost immediately regret the statement. He was trounced by the Republicans for his unseemly association with the Tammany boss. That Bryan was a man of probity, and had met Croker only once before, made no difference. He had paid homage to a man said to be a grafter and a crook. Croker was now tied to every sin in the city. *Harper's Weekly* declared that in the three years of his reign, crime, prostitution, and homicides had all greatly increased. And the wild extravagance of the New York demonstration raised questions about his fund-raising tactics. According to *The New York Times,* the Tammany boss had tapped every Democratic candidate running for local office, every contractor desirous of doing business in the city, as well as every municipal worker.

Croker, of course, had not invented these tactics. He had been schooled as a young precinct captain in a long, if ignoble, tradition. Anyone who wanted to work for the city, in any capacity, had to support the party in power. A city employee was expected to contribute 5 percent of his annual salary or risk losing his job. Earlier in the campaign the Republican fund raisers in Washington had been engaged in similar practices. But Richard Croker landed in the national spot-

Throughout the election campaign, Harper's Weekly *alternately lambasted New York City's Democratic leader, Richard Croker, and the Democratic candidate, William Jennings Bryan. When Croker hosted Bryan in the city, it was a splendid opportunity to tie Bryan to signs of corruption (October 13, 1900).*

light at a time when the subject of campaign financing was under scrutiny. For months Bryan had been accusing the Republicans of using corporate funds to buy the election.

The 1900 presidential campaign was the most ambitious and expensive in history. Both parties had vowed to reach every voter in the land and the cost of their transcontinental campaigns was enormous. A November article set the cost of the presidential contest at an unbelievable $5 million. If one included the congressional campaigns, the bill would come to about $20 million. In Chicago, both parties had established headquarters rivaling in size and complexity the operations of any major corporation, with sophisticated communication systems and armies of clerks and analysts, schedulers and writers.

From early spring, large news bureaus run by experienced political writers had been working around the clock supplying partisan material to hundreds of small papers around the country. The foreign language press was courted and often subsidized in circuitous fashion. Thousands of subscriptions were purchased by the headquarters' staffs. The literary bureaus were churning out speeches and carefully tailored materials for special interest groups in every language. Daily, mountains of pamphlets were being bundled and shipped to precinct captains across the nation. The Republicans had sent four million documents into New York State alone. Following Bryan's appearance in the city new materials were required to counter his comments.

Throughout the campaign, speakers were hired, the most effective commanding as much as $1,000 a week. W. Bourke Cockran, a former New York congressman who had switched his allegiance from McKinley to Bryan, demanded that the Democrats soothe the hardships of his speaking tour by providing a private parlor car, a dining car, and accommodations for both his manservant and personal cook. A relatively modest rally now cost $4,000. Add a torchlight parade with a sufficient number of bands, calcium lights and stereopticon displays, advertising, handbills, and well-known speakers, and the affair could run as much as $20,000. Croker's New York extravaganza undoubtedly cost far more.

It had come as no surprise when early in the campaign the Democratic party announced it was running low on funds. A similar Republican shortfall had not been expected but was easily remedied. Mark Hanna simply turned to sympathetic corporate leaders, as he had in 1896, and in a reasonable time raised an additional $2.5 million. For the Democrats, it was harder going. There were only three basic sources of funding: business interests, rich men "anxious to secure political prominence," and officeholders eager to hold on to their jobs. The election process had become more and more dependent on the rich and the powerful, which in 1900 gave the Republicans a considerable advantage.

An increasing number of Americans, including Theodore Roosevelt, expressed concern about the growing alliance between politics and business. But, one analyst concluded that even "if a presidential candidate was nominated only to reform this very system, his managers to elect him would have to spend millions of dollars." Reform seemed unlikely.

The campaign ended not a day too soon. Both William Jennings Bryan and Theodore Roosevelt were

New York Republicans hastily scheduled a Roosevelt rally following Bryan's appearance in the city. A local party headquarters called for volunteers to march in what would later be described as a spontaneous tribute to TR.

exhausted, and TR's voice was all but gone. Both men, declaring that victory lay ahead, boarded regularly scheduled passenger trains and headed home. The statisticians computed that while Roosevelt had visited twenty-three states, covering over sixteen thousand miles, Bryan had won the marathon. Political writers immediately analyzed the long and often brutal contest. Under the pressure of a dozen or more appearances a day, neither man had been at his best. *Collier's Weekly* declared that TR had "permitted his admiration for war and soldiers to grow into a mania so that many who once thought well of him would dread to see him in the President's place."

The magazine stated that "if it were certain, or even probable, that Mr. McKinley would not live out his term, and that the Vice President would succeed him . . . the Republican success would be in greater danger than it is. . . . In all other respects," *Collier's* concluded, "those who know Governor Roosevelt must believe that he is much better fitted for the Presidency than is Mr. McKinley." The assumption was that TR had all but buried his virtues "under a sort of thrasonical swashbuckling militarism."

II

On election day 1900, Americans who had once waited days for the outcome of a presidential election now wanted the results "without an instant's delay." San Francisco's *The Examiner* had installed seven new telephones in the city room and boasted direct communication with "the two great news centers in the East and Middle States, New York and Chicago." As results reached the pressroom, they would be fed by telephone to operators stationed around the city, who in turn would program giant "stereopticon bulletin boards" set up along Market Street and at six locations in the outlying districts. San Franciscans would receive the latest news almost as fast as the paper. *The Examiner* assured its readers that telephone repairmen would be on duty all evening in case of any trouble with the lines.

In Chicago, *The Tribune* would relay information by color-coded fireworks every hour from eight in the evening until two the following morning. The paper promised its rockets would be exploded at an altitude high enough to allow everyone in Cook County to follow the results. In many major cities, telephone companies had hired hundreds of additional operators to provide reports to telephone subscribers holding election night parties. One company boasted it would be able to send a bulletin to four thousand residences within a minute of its reception. From the Atlantic to the Pacific, Americans would all be connected in one gigantic communications web.

On election day morning, almost every city in the country was reporting clear skies, which both parties immediately heralded as helpful. In Galesburg, Carl Sandburg turned up before dawn at the Brooks Street polling place where he had been hired as an election clerk, at $3 for the day. He probably had a good idea

In 1900, San Francisco's Examiner *had seven telephones in daily use. An additional thirteen instruments were installed before the election both to collect returns and pass on information to operators in the outlying districts. In spite of the paper's pride in its telephonic systems, the bulk of the returns were still received by telegraph wire.*

how his neighbors were voting. Many were still talking about the day TR came to town, and pro-McKinley sentiment was runing high. But when it came to marking his own ballot, Sandburg could not get himself to "put an X before the name of either Bryan or McKinley or any other candidate for President. In my first vote . . . I was an independent, tied to no party." Sandburg was not alone in his ambivalence. For all the passion expressed during the campaign, in many towns voting was lighter than expected.

In Lincoln, Nebraska, William Jennings Bryan, after a breakfast of tenderloin steak and onions, escorted by a small group of friends, set out to vote at a firehouse some blocks from his home. Carriages of newsmen following the procession noted that an unusual number of men in the streets were wearing blazing yellow Republican badges. Bryan elected not to notice. On his return home, however, he stood on his porch and delivered a curious passage from a speech of Abraham Lincoln's. "Many countries have lost their liberties," he read, "and ours may lose hers, but if she shall, may it be my proudest plume, not that I was the last to desert her, but that I never deserted her."

In Canton, the mood was different. As the president made his way down North Market Street he stopped every few feet to exchange personal greetings with his neighbors. He invited two friends to come back to the house after they voted and urged others to drop by that evening. Clearly in jubilant spirits, McKinley made no statements either at the polling station or back home on his porch. His smile said it all.

In Oyster Bay, Theodore Roosevelt voted at Fisher's Hall, above a barbershop. The governor was accompanied by his coachman, his gardener, and an elderly servant, Pop Davis, who had driven TR to the polls when he had cast his first vote twenty years before. One reporter described the governor as rattled, racing into the polling booth without picking up a ballot. TR told reporters he intended to spend the day at home with his family, unless there was trouble in the city.

Early in the morning New York was awash with rumors. There were stories of intimidation at the polls, of a conspiracy to import ringers from New Jersey, of questionable men in the voting lines. Weeks earlier, during registration, photographs had been secretly taken of men suspected of signing up more than once. The photographs of these "repeaters" were distributed to inspectors at key polling places, and numbers of men were taken off for questioning. But on the whole, the process seemed orderly enough. On the Upper West Side the lines were long, and in the silk-stocking districts the rich were out early and in force. On Sixth Avenue, in a florist shop of small dimensions, a reporter spotted an almost shabbily dressed man waiting in line with his son: John D. Rockefeller and John D. Jr. But the key to how the election was going was not here, where voters were predictably Republican, but in all the polling places in middle- and working-class districts.

It was assumed that the city would go for Bryan—the questions was, by how much. The Republicans were firmly entrenched in the rest of New York State. To swing New York to Bryan, Croker would have to bring out over a hundred thousand Democrats in the city and its environs. In Tammany territory, on the Lower East Side, the streets were filled with people. Small boys huddled around bonfires, the bread sellers were doing a brisk business, and outside every polling place there were long lines of voters. But it was impossible for reporters to tell if the lines were longer than usual, and the Tammany hacks, busy coaching new voters, were not reliable sources of information.

And then around noon, reporters discovered that stockbrokers with midtown offices at Astor Place were making preparations to stay open all night. Delivery wagons were arriving with cases of champagne and elaborate platters of food. For months trading had been light as investors waited for the election. On Monday, there had been a brief flurry as speculators bet on a McKinley victory, but most people had chosen to play it safe. The brokers, however, mindful that they had been caught short when the market soared following McKinley's victory in 1896, had no intention of being caught again.

They had arranged to spend election night with their clients, monitoring returns off the ticker tape machines. At three o'clock in the morning, New York time, when the London exchange opened, the brokers would be able to begin trading via cable. Given the advantage of the time difference, if McKinley swept the country as they now expected, they would have their buy orders in long before prices could rise in New York. If the impossible happened, and Bryan won, they would dump their clients' holdings before most Americans were even out of bed. They would be limited, of course, to those stocks sold on both sides of the Atlantic, but even that would be a substantial advantage.

Long before any results were known, crowds began gathering in City Hall Park. The first election bulletin was provided at 3:10 in the afternoon, by *The World* on a giant screen outside the Pulitzer building. A small town in Massachusetts had voted for the president, 174 to 150. Within an hour or so, the streets were so clogged the trolleys were having trouble getting through. The first returns were scattered, and while there was no discernible voting pattern anyone could get a hold of, at Tammany Hall Richard Croker was hiding behind his paper, unwilling to engage in conversation, even with his closest allies.

By early evening in Canton, the McKinley home was filled with friends, relatives, and neighbors. The president had settled in the library with his gentlemen guests, the ladies remained in the parlor with Ida McKinley. Periodically Secretary Cortelyou appeared first in one room and then the other to read the latest bulletin. By six-thirty the returns from New York suggested McKinley was ahead and would take the state by a healthy plurality. At eight, there was a personal wire from a New York Republican leader assuring the president that he had been reelected. The press was back, camping on the lawn. McKinley could hear the crowds and see the red fire torches reflecting against the windows in his study. The news was coming faster than anyone had expected, but McKinley would bide his time. He would not be pressured into a premature announcement.

In Oyster Bay, up at Sagamore Hill, the Roosevelt family had gathered in the reception room in full evening dress to read the bulletins that were being sent over from the telegraph office three miles away. TR was the only major political figure who had neglected to have his home specially wired for the occasion. At ten o'clock, a newsman knocked at the door to inform the governor that victory was assured. Roosevelt had won the office he had neither sought nor wanted. He told the reporter that the returns proved the American people wanted "the good times to continue," and then sent off congratulatory messages to both McKinley and Mark Hanna.

In New York City, the brokerage offices were crowded. Clients were arriving in a state of euphoria. The champagne was opened and luncheon served to fortify the traders for the long vigil still ahead. Waiting for the London exchange to open, traders warned their clients against reckless buying, but investors were unwilling to be cautious any longer. The following day, one paper reported that the traders had bought somewhere between three and five hundred thousand shares of stock. The figures may have been overstated, but trading was heavy and the bulls were out in force.

Across the country in San Francisco, with the results no longer in doubt, *The Examiner* flashed McKinley's and Roosevelt's pictures on huge stereopticon screens, and from the roof of the Hearst building, flares of blue stars filled the night sky. From the Palace Hotel to Grant Avenue, traffic was suspended. The Republicans had won all but four states outside the solid Democratic block in the South. Bryan had even lost his home state of Nebraska, and in his own precinct had been outvoted by the men with the yellow badges. It was an overwhelming victory for William McKinley. TR had supplied youth, flashes of brilliance, and

In New York on election night—as in many other cities—stereopticon slides were used to deliver up-to-the-minute news to the crowds who had gathered in the streets.

patriotic fervor, but it was the president who had carried the day. Even in seclusion he was able to provide the sense of security and steadiness Americans so desired.

Voters had not forgotten the panic that gripped the country before McKinley had taken over in 1896. Those who had been out of work for months, even years, had felt a hopelessness they never wanted to feel again. Bryan had campaigned on behalf of the average American—but he never won their confidence. He had been eloquent about the Philippines, but few voters cared about Filipino rights, and those who did worried far more about his economic theories. Even Andrew Carnegie, the most impassioned anti-imperialist of them all, in the end had voted for McKinley. Just before the election, he wrote: "Mr. Bryan is much too earnest, too sincere and true to be entrusted with power, filled as he is with ideas subversive of economic laws."

When the votes were officially counted analysts uncovered an unsettling fact. Over a million more people were eligible to vote in 1900 than in 1896, but fewer had gone to the polls. *The Daily Picayune* (New Orleans) explained the stay-at-homes: "There was a great body of citizens who saw too much Socialism in Bryanism and too much imperialism in McKinleyism, to be able to choose between them." What the paper did not mention was the almost total absence of black voters in the South. One state after the next—Mississippi, Louisiana, South Carolina—had imposed convoluted laws designed to keep black men from voting. The statistics told the story. In 1896, in Louisiana, 130,344 African Americans were registered voters; in 1900, only 5,320 remained on the rolls. The disenfranchisement of African Americans in the southern states was now all but complete.

III

The morning after the election, the McKinleys' home had a storm-swept quality. In the library, hundreds of open telegrams and handwritten messages awaited the president's attention. The famous lawn was littered, the chrysanthemums in the big iron vase were broken and dying, but as the carriages were being packed and the McKinleys said their good-byes, it didn't seem to matter. At the depot, the president and his wife, along with Secretary Cortelyou, Dr. Rixey, George Foster, the maid, the valet, and the McKinleys' nearest friends, boarded two private railcars to return to the capital. They had been away from Washington for almost four months.

As the train pulled out of the station, in deference to Mrs. McKinley's nerves there was no noisy demonstration. But at Dueber Heights, the president was given a twenty-one-gun salute while columns of workmen from nearby shops and factories stood along the tracks in a continuous line for over a mile. There were victory celebrations at every stop across Ohio. In the factory town of Salem, a vast concourse of people waited to watch the president's car go by. The train rolled through Leetonia and Columbiana, and in a drizzling rain which did not deter the crowds, moved on through East Palestine and New Galilee as the light began to fail.

In New York City when the stock market opened, the rush of business was so great that by midday the clerical staffs were overwhelmed, unable to keep up with

Richard Croker at Tammany headquarters. Following the election, the papers reported the party chief had quit talking even to the party faithful. Croker's political life was coming to an end. A reform mayor would be elected in New York City in 1901 and Croker would live out his days breeding horses in Ireland.

the orders. One paper reported, "Wall Street Has No Bears." Money that had been hoarded by small investors during the campaign was pouring into the market. Over the next four days, the price of Standard Oil jumped $130 a share and the value of John D. Rockefeller's personal holdings increased by over $21,000,000. Reporter Lincoln Steffens, who had spent the fall campaigning for McKinley and Roosevelt, wrote his father: "Well we've won, didn't we. The hypocrites have beaten the fools. . . . Stocks are booming and a lot of new trusts are about to be formed. Everybody is making money. The Street is going wild and the keenest of the big criminals down there say that we shall have such a boom as we have never had before."

Richard Croker had remained a true believer to the end. Convinced Bryan would win and the market would collapse, Croker had sold all his holdings just before the election. He was off now for an extended vacation in Europe, where it was said that he was planning to retire.

IV

In Oakland, California, Jack London wrote a friend that the election had turned out pretty much the way he had expected. He would have voted for

McKinley, he said, if he had thought Bryan had a ghost of a chance, but as it was he had cast a straight Socialist ballot, voting for Eugene V. Debs for president. The Socialists had made a good showing with over 96,000 votes. In Massachusetts two Socialists had been elected to the state legislature. London predicted that in time the Democratic party would fade away and there would be a "capitalistic" party and a socialist party.

Over the past year London had tried to bring order to his life. He had made a marriage of accommodation. Bessie Maddern was a strong and practical woman. Jack and Bessie had been friends for years, but they were often at odds. Bessie had little patience with his friends—the rowdy collection of sailors, Klondikers, writers, and soldiers of fortune who turned up every Wednesday, eating and drinking and arguing, often late into the night. But Jack was not about to change. He was blessed and cursed with friends and as compulsive about these relationships as he was about his work.

Although he had acquired a generous advance on his first novel and no longer had to trek down to Traeger's to pawn his bike, he was as driven as ever, writing a minimum of a thousand words a day, revised and typed. Anna Strunsky later wrote that Jack "mortgaged his brain in order to meet the market demand." Over the course of 1900 he would publish twenty-seven manuscripts, including sixteen short stories and a number of essays, and begin collaborating with Anna on a book called *The Kempton-Wace Letters*. The project had grown out of a long-standing argument on the subject of love. Years later, Anna explained that "Jack held that love is only a trap set by nature for the individual. One must not marry for love but for certain qualities discerned by the mind."

In the book London and Strunsky assumed the voices of two fictional characters, Dane Kempton and Herbert Wace, who were carrying on an argument via an extended correspondence. The letters from Dane Kempton, a poet and a teacher at Stanford University, were written by Anna; London assumed the persona of the pragmatic Herbert Wace, a graduate student in economics. Years after the book was published, Anna insisted that Jack had presented his argument so "brilliantly and passionately as to make one suspect that he was not as certain of his position as he claimed to be." And then, too, she knew what a romantic he was at heart. In one of his first letters he had written:

> I shall be over Saturday night. If you draw back upon yourself, what have I left. Take me this way: a stray guest, a bird of passage, splashing with salt-rimmed wings though a brief moment of your life—a rude and blundering bird,

used to large airs and great spaces, unaccustomed to the amenities of confined existence.

London argued that the harshness of his childhood had taught him that reason was mightier than imagination. But Anna did not believe that, either.

Other Stories of Interest

The World (New York),
November 11, 1900

Cocaine fiends are increasing at an alarming rate in New York. Strange as it may appear, the users of this drug are the most intelligent and well-to-do people of the town.

A few years back there was only an occasional call for cocaine, but recently one Tenderloin drug store's sales have increased to such an extent that the drug is kept prepared for its customers.

Cocaine is much in demand among semi-professional people who wish to nerve themselves for a special venture. . . . The true fiend uses a cocaine solution and injects it with a hypodermic needle. Others take the powder. . . . Some of the hypodermic needles are made to order and are very valuable.

An ordinary needle, or "gun" as it is known, can be bought for $3. The true fiend will pay $50 and $100 for a work of art, gold mounted and chased. As he becomes broken the "gun" goes in the pawn shop and the proceeds are spent on more powder. Eventually the user of cocaine becomes a wreck and finishes his days in an asylum, begging piteously for the drug.

The New York Times,
November 11, 1900

GALVESTON, TEXAS—After spending nearly two months in relief work among the sufferers in Galveston . . . Miss Clara Barton feels there is no longer a necessity of her to remain in the field.

The work of relief will be continued, however, during the entire Winter. . . . Miss Barton stated that the thousands of dollars . . . set aside for repairing damaged buildings and constructing others amounts to much less than 5 per cent of the actual needs of the people. . . . She added that the coming winter cannot fail to bring untold hardships and suffering.

The Examiner (San Francisco),
November 14, 1900

NEW YORK—There was not any holly decking the United States army transport Kilpatrick when she sailed to-day from the foot of Pacific Street, Brooklyn for Manila, but she was a Christmas boat just the same, with her hold full of boxes each bearing on its lid a soldier's name.

The hold full of boxes are to be Christmas presents for the American troops in China and the Philippines, where holiday presents are not indigenous to the soil.

The elegant Casino Theater Bar and Café at Broadway and 39th Street in New York City.

CHAPTER FIFTEEN

November

I

In November, as the weather turned raw, and every home in the North was either too hot or too cold, Americans read about a heating apparatus that in the future would be set at seventy-two degrees and ignored for the rest of the winter. Hot and cold air would be piped in from central power plants, adjusted by spigots, like water for a bath. The electrified home, the house without a match, without a single pair of stairs, a dish towel, or a chimney, was a comforting thought to those hauling coal and ashes and coping with soot-stained walls. With the twentieth century now just weeks away, writers, engineers, artists, and politicians were once again conjuring wondrous portraits of the future.

The Ladies' Home Journal prophesied that ready-cooked meals would be bought from establishments similar to bakeries, delivered by automobile wagons or even pneumatic tubes. With wireless telephones and telegraph circuits spanning the world, the magazine projected a husband aboard ship in the Mid-Atlantic would be able to call his wife in Chicago and she in turn would be able to call China as easily as someone in New York City could telephone Brooklyn. By the year 2001, grand opera would be telephoned to private homes and sound as

KEY TO TOPOGRAPHICAL
MAP OF NEW YORK IN 1999.

1—Tunnel from Hackensack to
Jersey City.
2—Suspension bridges across the
Hudson to Peekskill—city
limit.
3—Bridges across Long Island
Sound.
4—Public parks and recreation
piers.
5—Eight new bridges across
Newark Bay to Bayonne.
6—Cantilever bridge from New
York City to Staten Island.
7—Two suspension bridges
across the Narrows.
8—Bridges and tunnels across
East River and Blackwell's
Island.
9—Canal connecting Newark
Bay and New York Bay.
10—Canal connecting Long Island
Sound and Jamaica Bay.
11—Bridges across the Kill von
Kull. Two tunnels between
Staten Island and Brooklyn.
12—Electric railroad across Jamaica Bay.

The World, *December 30, 1900*.

NEW YORK CITY
AS IT WILL BE
IN **1999**

COPYRIGHT 1900 BY THE PRESS PUB CO.

SUPPLEMENT TO THE N.Y. WORLD DEC 30, 1900

PICTORIAL FORECAST OF THE CITY
AS APPROVED BY
ANDREW.H.GREEN, H.H.VREELAND,
and JOHN.B.McDONALD.

MADISON SQUARE TODAY—1900

THE MADISON SQUARE OF A CENTURY HENCE — 1999.

THE PICTURE OF NEW YORK IN 1999.

By Andrew H. Green,
Father of Greater New York.

"I believe that this picture of New York in 1999 gives withal a conservative idea of how the city will look in that year. It would not be bold to predict that long before that time some mode of aerial transit will be the vogue."

By H. H. Vreeland,
President of the Metropolitan Traction Company.

"I unhesitatingly approve of this picture of New York as it will appear in 1999. While prophetic, it is based on reasonable imagination."

By John B. McDonald,
Contractor of the Rapid Transit Subway Company.

"I approve of this picture as being a carefully conceived representation of what New York will look like in 1999."

ANDREW H. GREEN

HERBERT H. VREELAND

JOHN B. McDONALD

harmonious as it did in the concert hall. Photographs would be telegraphed from any distance and reproduced in color. "If there be a battle in China a hundred years hence, snapshots of its most striking events will be published in the newspapers an hour later . . . and in all of nature's colors."

In the twentieth century, man would be able to see around the world. "Persons and things of all kinds will be brought within focus of cameras connected electrically with screens at opposite ends of circuits, thousands of miles at a span. Americans . . . will view the coronation of kings in Europe or the progress of battles in the Orient. The instrument bringing these distant scenes to the very doors of people will be connected with a giant telephone apparatus transmitting each incidental sound in its appropriate place. Thus the guns of a distant battle will be heard to boom when seen to blaze, and the lips of the remote actor or singer will be heard to utter words or music when seen to move."

All year there had been a stream of predictions about modern railroads and ships and automachines. *The Ladies' Home Journal*'s experts envisioned passengers traveling on trains artificially cooled, racing through hot and dusty country with the windows closed. Electric ships would cross the ocean in two days. Traveling above the waves, they would be supported by runners "with apertures expelling jets of air." The projections that seemed closest to fruition involved the automobile. The magazine predicted that by the end of the new century, the horse in harness would be as scarce as the yoked oxen in 1900.

In just a matter of months, the automachine had become firmly planted in the popular imagination. For years, self-propelled carriages had been the playtoys of the rich, but by the fall of 1900, articles were being published about autocars for the average man and woman. On November 5, when the Automobile Club of America's first motor show opened in New York City's Madison Square Garden, tens of thousands of people came to study machines they could not yet afford but dreamed of one day owning.

In 1899, the sight of a mechanical carriage west of the Mississippi was a rare and much heralded event. By the end of 1900 most Americans living in a major city had seen self-propelled vehicles maneuvering through horse-clogged streets. In recent months, in Boston, New York, and Washington, the occasional electric cab had multiplied to hundreds. Automachines were now delivering ice, newspapers, and merchandise. Chicago had its first motorized ambulance. However, it was not the commercial wagons that were exciting most Americans, but the machines designed for personal use, which promised a kind of independence and freedom never known before.

Many visitors at the New York Automobile Show, in November 1900, had never been in a machine before. Free instruction was offered, and to illustrate the comfort and safety of the vehicles, families were encouraged to participate.

Trains kept their own schedules and never took you quite where you wanted to go, and horses got hungry, cold, and tired. The auto was nothing but a dumb machine, but that was part of the joy. In his *Experiment in Prophecy*, H. G. Wells explained that with a privately owned motor, "one will be free to dine where one chooses, hurry when one chooses, stop and pick flowers, turn over in bed of a morning and tell the carriage to wait." True, with a horse you could relax your attention now and then, the responsibilities for a drive were not entirely yours. A smart four-footer sensed the perils of the street, and he knew his way home. But a woman in St. Louis wrote that "the sensation of gliding along at any speed and for any distance without feeling you are punishing your horse, is so fascinating."

There was also a sense of danger, which made motoring no less fun. A magazine writer named Cleveland Moffett told of being driven down Fifth Avenue at a time of heavy carriage traffic. He held his breath "as the young man steering threaded his way between wheels and horses, shot down lanes of vehicles where an inch's wavering or a second's hesitation meant collision." The week of the auto show, William K. Vanderbilt drove full tilt into a fish-delivery wagon at 51st Street and Fifth Avenue. Vanderbilt had already been arrested for speeding in

Massachusetts and probably held the record as the automobilist with the most accidents to his name.

On one occasion he had driven straight into a stone wall, and spent a month wearing a court-plaster. Taking his father for a spin down the main street in Newport, he almost killed them both in another collision. Following the accident with the fishwagon, Vanderbilt, who was accompanied by his footman that day, was reported to have said, "I'll settle for everything, my good fellow." Unfortunately that meant paying for the disposal of one horse and the purchase of another.

Fatal encounters with pedestrians were becoming so common there were demands that vehicles be fitted with "man-catchers" in front of the wheels and *The New York Times* was calling for driver education. One manufacturer said it was time to correct the "tommy-rot ideas in the heads of buyers, that all they need do was turn on the power and the thing was done. Even if he bought a horse, he would not take chances driving him through crowded thoroughfares without first having learned something of his disposition."

The automaker believed that drivers, like musicians, needed practice. "The carriage moves so swiftly and noiselessly under the slightest touch of the lever that many fail to understand the tremendous speed at which they are traveling." The simplest machines and the pleasantest to drive were the electric carriages. One owner wrote, "There is no fire in it, no smell about it, nothing to break or get out of order; no gauges to watch, no tangle of oily, grimy parts." Ready to start at a moment's notice, the electric vehicle was considered ideal for city use.

But batteries needed to be recharged every twenty to forty miles, and outside the largest cities, recharging stations did not exist. At the motor show an imaginative entrepreneur demonstrated a coin-operated machine that supplied electricity the way a hydrant supplied water. Wealthy owners were building their own recharging plants, but for most people, the electric carriage was too expensive and impractical. Gas-driven autos were the most adaptable vehicles. Unlike electric carriages they could run over rugged roads, through sand, mud, or snow, and did not balk at hills. An automobile carrying two people could travel twenty-five miles on a gallon of fuel, for a cost of just ten cents. But they were noisy machines that rattled the teeth and reeked of fuel.

Cleveland Moffett wrote: "Every visitor to Paris where gas-driven machines swarm on all the boulevards, will remember how his nostrils have been offended, as these panting machines sweep past, with that sickening smell of imperfect combustion. . . . True, this unpleasant feature affects those in the carriage less than those behind it." But, Moffett added, "once a rider is accustomed to the piston-beat and the rattle of gears, he minds them no more than the pounding of horses' hoofs in ordinary driving."

As for steam-driven autos, Mary Booth explained in *Good Housekeeping* that running such a vehicle was "not as difficult in practice as the operation of a sewing machine." The notion of sitting atop a boiler did not appeal to many, but Booth assured her readers that the danger of an explosion was about "as imminent as that of one's house tumbling down about one's head." For those needing to build an auto room, she recommended using the cellar with a graded entrance from the garden. One of the newest New York apartments had built a compartment in the basement for machines, and in other cities there were "repositories much like livery stables."

One writer cautioned that while the auto was a machine "of Titanic promise . . ." it was still "a little too new for utility, a trifle too exacting for pleasure, a shade too crude for elegance." And while in New York City there were now six factories employing five hundred people, autos were still handmade and most manufacturers had yet to make a profit. All across the country companies were going out of business. Among the failures that November was Henry Ford's Detroit Automobile Company.

But Americans were impatient. Whatever problems existed, the desire was so overwhelming that solutions would simply be willed into existence.

II

When the Paris Exposition closed in mid-November, Americans felt a curious sadness. Even those who had never crossed the ocean had collected souvenir photos and stereoviews as mementos. The great French fair had become a symbol of 1900, extravagant and optimistic, and the scene of countless American triumphs. American athletes, painters, photographers, and firemen had all gone to Paris to compete in international competitions and come home with medals and memories. But the magnificent Italian Palace, with its murals and mosaics, the Swiss Village, the Palace of Electricity, the ingenious moving sidewalk, the buildings along the Quay of Nations were all scheduled for the rubbish heap.

Around the same time, American papers reported that "the genius of decadence," Oscar Wilde, the brilliant Irish writer, author of the best-selling novel *The Picture of Dorian Gray,* had died in a hotel on the Left Bank in Paris. Wilde had a following in the United States; Americans enjoyed his work and he had lectured in the States. The obituaries were disapproving of his "unwholesome affectations," but not specific about those "affectations." There was no mention that his two years in an English prison had been punishment for his love affair with Lord Alfred Douglas. The papers did report that Wilde had retreated to Paris, in ill health and bankrupt. One story noted that his former associates had shunned him, and "his publisher had withdrawn his books from their shelves."

As the United States commissioners were packing to leave Paris, Americans at home were already shifting their attention to the next great international fair—the Pan American Exposition, scheduled to open in the spring of 1901 in Buffalo, New York. The exposition was being held to "bring into closer communion the peoples of the Western Hemisphere." America was not popular with its southern neighbors. Ever since the Spanish-American War, the United States had been seen as a bully, imposing its will on the former Spanish colonies of Cuba and Puerto Rico. Brazil, Chile, and Argentina were said to be ready to defend themselves if necessary, against the aggressive North Americans.

The United States government was accused of unfair trade practices, asking "How much can we sell to them?" and too seldom asking "How much can they sell to us?" It was hoped that this bow to those of "Spanish" blood would help offset ill feelings between America and its neighbors to the south. *Harper's Weekly* wrote: "This new world has made strange bed-fellows. The problem confronts us now, and extends indefinitely into the future, for it grows out of the juxtaposition of races that have difficulty understanding each other, yet somehow must reach an *entente.*" But as Americans headed into the winter season, they were far more interested in the monster sports stadium rising in Buffalo and the new Music Temple than in hemispheric politics.

Among those planning to visit the Pan American Exposition the following summer was Frances Benjamin Johnston. She would time her visit to coincide with the arrival of President and Mrs. McKinley.

III

Winter came early in 1900. By mid-November it was bone-chilling cold when crowds began to line the streets near St. George's Church in Stuyvesant Square. It was early in the New York social season for an occasion of such import, but nothing would compare that year with the wedding of Louisa Pierpont Morgan to Captain Herbert Satterlee. J. P. Morgan, for one unusual moment, was concentrating on family matters. Louisa's wedding was said to be the most magnificent

John Pierpont Morgan bellowing at a photographer. Morgan lived a regal life, collecting paintings, sculptures, rare books, and homes. In addition to the house on Madison Avenue, he owned a country house in upstate New York, a city and a country home in England, a suite in Paris, and another in Rome. His 302-foot steam-powered yacht, the Corsair, *served as a magnificent sea-going palace. And for those occasions when Morgan was in Egypt, a private steamer awaited him on the Nile.*

marriage celebration in the history of New York. But in spite of the stir created by the press, the banker was going to considerable lengths to protect the privacy of his beloved oldest daughter. One hour before the wedding, he drove down to the church to check on final arrangements with majordomo J. Johnson, hired for the occasion.

Assured that as per his directives a squadron of compliant city police would keep the curious fifty yards or more from the church, the banker returned home. At the Morgan residence on Madison Avenue, a seventy-five-foot extension, fifty feet wide and two stories tall, had been added to the conservatory just for the wedding feast. The marquee had been built like the palaces at the Paris Exposition to shine for one brief festive moment and then be gone. The ceiling was concealed by white bunting and the temporary walls, painted Turkey red, were draped with priceless tapestries featuring sixteenth- and seventeenth-century love scenes. It was said to be the most beautiful and costly room ever designed for a wedding collation in the city, and it was to last for only one day.

Earlier in the week, Miss Morgan's wedding presents had been placed on display for her friends: one million dollars' worth of diamond jewels; oriental rugs; gold plates and tableware; loving cups made from a shell taken from a captured Spanish war ship; oriental rugs and paintings; silver candelabra and silver mirrors. Then all was sent off to bank vaults for safe keeping, except for some of the diamonds Louisa would wear for the wedding.

At 3:35 P.M., with Morgan lackeys standing guard at the church, the bridesmaids arrived, the ostrich plumes on their red panne velvet toques brushing the frames of the carriage doors as they were helped out onto the sidewalk. The Morgan equipage pulled up with its prancing bay horses, decked out with white rosettes. Satin streamers fluttered from the coachman's whip and the buttonhole of his bottle-green coat. As Morgan had ordered, the curiosity seekers who had braved the blustery weather to see the bride were held at such a distance that they could glimpse little more than a flicker of white.

Waiting in the front pew of the church was the long-suffering Mrs. Morgan. Pierpont and his wife were seldom seen together anymore; his attentions had long since strayed. The ceremony was brief, and then "the great concourse of fashionables regained their carriages" and headed north for the reception.

At the mansion, the crush was so great, reporters were amused to note, that a number of guests were forced to use the servants' entrance. Fifteen hundred invitations had been issued and almost no one had declined. Every room was a bedazzlement of flowers: massed orchids and garlands of smilax entwined with ropes of roses and tendrils of asparagus fern. At the entrance to the marquee was a curtain of dark red roses, caught back by apple-green satin ribbons. Neapolitan musicians were playing ragtime and selections from grand opera, chosen by the bride. Mr. Morgan was everywhere, directing the proceedings. An orderly and systematic man, he may have been irritated to read that the height of the crush was like a political rally at Madison Square Garden, but Morgan was never ruffled. He marshalled his staff, and fifteen hundred people were seated for a light but elegant five-course luncheon.

In the evening paper, next to the story about the most lavish wedding ever held, was an impassioned defense of the rich that had been delivered the day before by the Episcopalian Bishop William Lawrence of Massachusetts. Lawrence explained that while history seemed to support the suspicion that wealth contributed to the fall of Rome, he had come to the conclusion that there was another side to the story. "In the long run it is only to the man of morality that wealth comes. . . . We, like the Psalmist, occasionally see the wicked prosper, but only occasionally. . . . Godliness," he said, "is in league with riches."

As to the Bible, "While every word that can be quoted against the rich is true, other words are as true and strike another and complimentary note. We are released from the subtle hypocrisy which has beset the Christian through the ages, bemoaning the deceitfulness of riches, and at the same time working with all his might to earn . . . a fortune if he can." In closing, Lawrence claimed that material prosperity was helping make "the national character sweeter, more joyous, more unselfish, more Christlike. That is my answer to the question as to the relation of all national prosperity." It was a comforting time to be rich.

Theodore Roosevelt, the vice president–elect, had just invited Morgan for dinner. TR explained to a friend that the invitation reflected an effort on his part to become "a conservative man in touch with the influential classes." As for Morgan, he could only have assumed that the new Republican administration would continue to take a benign view of the growth of big business. He would soon make the largest deal in industrial history.

For over a year, the banker had been jousting with Andrew Carnegie. When Morgan's company began producing finished steel tubes, Carnegie ordered the construction of a plant to produce steel tubes. When Morgan's Federal Steel Company began to challenge Carnegie Steel, the old Scotsman threatened a price war to undercut his competitors. When the Pennsylvania Railroad, which was controlled by Morgan, raised its rates, Carnegie let out word he was planning to build his own competing rail line. All thoughts of retirement seem to have faded from Carnegie's head. Morgan could see nothing but chaos ahead. "Carnegie is going to demoralize the railroads," he said, "just as he demoralized steel." He would have to be stopped. Competition was a wasteful business.

The Southampton town football team in Long Island, New York.

IV

The afternoon before the Harvard-Yale game, New Haven was football-wild, as fans, anticipating "the greatest and most sensational gridiron contest in the annals of sport," gathered in smoking rooms, saloons, and hotel lobbies to argue the relative merits of the Crimson and the Blue. Both teams were undefeated for the season and the contest for the intercollegiate championship was described as the game of a lifetime. Every seat in Yale Field could have been sold many times over. In New York City, the Knickerbocker Athletic Club, taking pity on those unable to buy tickets, arranged for a telegraph line to provide play-by-play descriptions while the game was in process.

Harvard and Yale were old rivals. At their first game, in 1876, they had lined up like English rugby teams, with forwards, halfbacks, and backs. Walter Camp, who had played for Yale and was now considered the godfather of modern American football, recalled that in the first season "for a crowd simply to get around the ball and kick indiscriminately and let it roll out where it would did not at all suit the American idea of order and preparation." But though football was now far more complex, it was still a kicking game. The punter was considered as important in football as a pitcher in baseball. Over the year there were how-to articles on the science of the punt, the drop and the place kick.

In a November article in *Outing*, Percy Haughton, a former Harvard player, laid out the fundamentals of punting. Speed was essential. Using a stopwatch, Haughton found it often took a man a full three seconds from the time the ball reached his hands until it left his foot, a maneuver he believed should take one and three-quarters to two seconds, at the most. He emphasized launching "non-catchable balls," high "whirling" punts with a spiral twist. He berated players for wearing boots, thought shoes "should be pliable enough to allow the toe to be pointed with ease." One of the leading kickers in the country played in his slippers.

More attention these days was being paid to protective gear. Football's reputation as a man-killing sport had not diminished. A University of California freshman had recently been paralyzed and both the Yale and Harvard teams had been plagued with injuries. Earlier in the month, Daly, the Crimson captain and quarterback, had been carried off the field with a wrenched knee and was forced to stay in bed for days.

There were now ingenious devices to protect the walking wounded. Hammered aluminum shields with padded edges were wrapped around men with bruised thigh muscles or injured collarbones. Those with bad backs were encased in a belladonna plaster wrapped over a substance that burned "like a flame, producing a strong stimulus to the nerves." Leather helmets protected the ears of plunging linebacks.

Purists opposed the use of "armor." It was said to cause more injuries "than is consistent with the best interests of the game," but when Daly led the Harvard squad out into Yale stadium, the men were said to look like "armor-clad warriors on the battlefield," and the crowd roared. In spite of Daly's bad knee, the sportswriters and coaches insisted that the captain was in peak form, and psychologically he was. Charles Dan Daly, the All-American boy, who looked like a model for a Charles Dana Gibson drawing but without the arrogance, had never been more joyful. In his kit bag he had a letter from Congressman John Fitzgerald confirming his appointment to West Point. At the age of twenty-one, Daly had received many honors but none as important to him as this.

Entering college at sixteen, he had distinguished himself at track and on the football squad. An engaging man, his ambition to enter the Point had been supported by the president of the University, but Daly had been passed over by Senator Henry Cabot Lodge, perhaps because he did not have the proper social standing. With time running out—the cut-off age at the Point was twenty-two—he had gone to see Fitzgerald in the summer of 1900. The two men had much in common. Both were sons of Irish immigrants, both had attended the prestigious Boston Latin School and both had been accepted by Harvard. When an unexpected vacancy opened up at the Point, the congressman gave the appointment to Charles Dan Daly.

As the quarterback entered Yale Field, he received an enormous welcoming cheer. The sky was an icy gray; there had

Charles Dan Daly, captain of the Harvard football team.

been flurries in the morning, but the playing field, which had been covered with straw, was in perfect condition. Daly won the toss and the Crimson band played "Fair Harvard." In the first couple of plays the teams seemed well matched, but then Yale's powerful backs and strong and heavy line began pushing the Harvard team down the field. At the three-yard line, the Yale quarterback fumbled; the Crimson recovered the ball and the Harvard stands went wild. But within minutes Yale was back on the Harvard one-yard line and the team moved forward, scoring the first touchdown.

Harvard's eleven struggled manfully, but observers noted that Daly lacked "the speed, the quickness and snap for which he was famous." The Crimson missed key tackles, and their backs were unable to gain ground. The Yale line would not go down, they kept pushing, squirming, wriggling, always forward. An error, curiously enough, led to Yale's second goal. The team's left end and left halfback collided racing for a high punt, but on a dead run, the Yale quarterback was able to scoop up the ball and keep going. On the next play, Yale's captain, Gordon Brown, overran three Harvard tacklers, and sixty-five yards later the score was 12–0 and the half was over.

It was a disconsolate group of Crimson players who trotted back for the second half, with Daly clearly limping. Minutes later Yale made their third touchdown, and Daly, barely able to walk, took himself out of the game. As one Harvard man after another was carried off the field, the Yale grandstand began to sing, "Here's work for the undertaker. A nice little job for the casketmaker." Only three of Harvard's original team were left when time mercifully ran out. The Yale fans were singing, "At the local cemetery they are digging a new grave, no hope for Harvard." The final score was 28 0.

Later that night, as the Harvard team arrived in Boston, Captain Daly was on crutches, his left leg hanging limp. But in 1901, playing for West Point, Daly would be elected All-American quarterback.

Other Stories of Interest

The Examiner (San Francisco),
November 22, 1900

ST. PETERSBURG, November 21—Alarm is growing over the Czar's condition. Not withstanding the bulletins of a favorable character sent out from Lavidia, it is believed that the patient is in the gravest danger.

LONDON, November 21—The anxiety over the condition of the Czar is not allayed but rather aggravated by the conflicting reports of its nature. . . . It is the persistent rumors of poison and vague allusions to weakened heart action in the bulletins that cause doubt and misgiving. The Russian rule has sometimes been characterized as a despotism tempered by assassination, and people in the present crisis are talking suggestively of that ominous maxim. Three distinct kinds of poison have been mentioned in the Czar's illness. One said that it was tainted milk. Another that the cause was bad fish, and the third plainly said that the Nihilists in the Czar's household had been administering to him some form of slow poison in his daily food. . . .

It is these unexplained facts, coupled with the grave doubts as to the succession and the danger to peace in Europe in case of the Czar's death, that are causing so much anxiety and doubt in the European capitals.

The New York Times
November 24, 1900
Lieut. Churchill to Lecture

Winston Leonard Spencer Churchill, M.P., recently with the British army in the Transvaal, is to lecture 100 times in America. His first appearance will be in the Waldorf-Astoria on Dec. 12, after which he will make a tour of the country.

Lieut. Churchill is the son of Lady Randolph Churchill. He is first cousin to the Duke of Marlborough. While an officer in the Transvaal the Lieutenant was the correspondent for The London Daily Mail, and since his return from the war he has been lecturing in England.

New York Evening Journal,
December 2, 1900

LOWELL, MASSACHUSETTS—Louis Gilmore, captain of the Lowell High School football eleven, died today from injuries received in a game with the Beechmonts on Thanksgiving Day. Young Gilmore was trying to break through the line when his spine was fractured or displaced and he collapsed. . . . He was eighteen years old.

CHICAGO—William Bartlett, aged sixteen, and captain of a neighborhood football team is in dying condition today as a consequence of the game. . . . It was thought the victim was kicked at the base of the spine.

May Adelson, known as the "Belle of San Francisco," just before her appearance in an amateur musicale.

As so many had predicted, the old-time Christmas no longer seemed quite good enough for modern youth. With a dozen presents at his feet, young Syl Dankoler, in Sturgeon Bay, Wisconsin, still seemed discontent.

CHAPTER SIXTEEN

December

I

Christmas came early in 1900. In the larger cities, shopping started right after Thanksgiving. Americans were on a buying binge the likes of which no one had ever seen. Ministers warned that the holiday had become too commercial and the frequent use of the word "Xmas" in advertisements underscored the loss of Christ. But religious leaders were fighting a battle that had already been decided. It was estimated Americans would spend $50 million on Christmas this year. The cathedral of choice was now the merchandising palace. Customers stood ten and fifteen deep before windows designed to arouse "cupidity and longing." Commerce had never been more creative—or successful.

The author of *The Wonderful Wizard of Oz* had been the first to transform the pedestrian window display into an art form. Frank Baum, a traveling salesman in the 1890s, had found work as a window trimmer in Chicago, and discovered an inborn talent for using smoke and mirrors to delight and deceive. He created window displays that were so seductive they touched off desires consumers didn't know they had. Window trimmers all over the country began using Baum's techniques. Years later, the writer Edna Ferber said, "It is a work of art that window, a breeder of anarchism, a destroyer of contentment."

Men and women who had felt blessed as children if they were given one store-bought present each Christmas were being urged to compare the "marvels of modern genius with the crude toys" of their youth. There were dolls that talked and dogs that walked and "automobiles that ran just like the big ones." There were complex train sets with four-way switches and express locomotives that ran at different speeds and electrified doll houses with lightbulbs the size of a pea. Fathers who were handy were building electric elevators for miniature mansions. There were telephone sets for children that could be used over a distance of about a thousand feet. Those on a budget could buy the components at an electrical supply shop.

By the first week in December the peddlers along New York's Sixth Avenue, their carts decorated with Christmas bells and sprays of holly, were offering a variety of inexpensive machine-made toys—miniature upholstered furniture, tin soldiers, and "invalid dolls" from Japan and Europe that had been damaged in shipment. Buyers were mesmerized by demonstrations of mechanical elephants, camels, and beetles. In the midst of the bazaar, Salvation Army soldiers, standing by their kettles, tried to reach the conscience and move the spirit with anthems of the season. Caught in the confusion of this unfamiliar celebration, young Marcus Ravage longed for home, lonely for the smells of Vaslui, Romania, and holidays he knew—the Feast of the Maccabees, the Feast of Weeks. How would he ever know, in this strange land, when Purim was coming?

His father had written urging Marcus to save money he had yet to earn. He was living off the kindness of others. He could not go on forever without a proper meal, and his "traitor shoes" from home did not keep out the snow. He had been staying with his cousin, Mrs. Segal, the proud possessor of a five-room apartment on Allen Street that by day looked like a proper American home but at night was transformed into a sleeping camp. In the parlor, four men slept broadside on the sofa, their legs extending out onto chairs. Up to nine sleepers found places on the floor, the lucky ones resting on feather-bedding.

People slept atop bureaus and on the dining chairs set in a row against the wall. Two bedrooms became female dormitories, the third was rented by a family of five. Mrs. Segal and the baby rested atop the washtub in the kitchen, while the other children were splayed around on the floor beside them. In December, with the windows sealed, the night air was rank with the smells of food and bodies and overused clothes. Marcus was fascinated by the morning ballet, which began with the clattering of the el train that raced past the window. The men flew into their clothes before the women could emerge and then everyone in the apartment competed for access to the sink and the one dank towel. When the furniture was restored to its proper places and the bedding was tucked away, the whole colony sat down for coffee at the round table in the dining room. Breakfast and laundry were included in the rent.

Marcus's share of the couch could bring fifty cents a week; it was time he start paying his share. He was still a greenhorn, but his cousin said he was "bleaching out." In the midst of the Christmas crush Ravage embarked on his first commercial venture, selling chocolates for a penny apiece at the corner of 14th Street and Fifth Avenue. Mrs. Segal had provided the initial capital—$1—and the loan of her brass tray. But although Marcus had selected a busy spot, "No one in that whole rolling sea of humanity seemed to be fond of chocolates." And then another peddler, an elderly man selling Oriental spreads at a nearby stand, bought a candy but warned Marcus he was charging too little. "Your American," he said, "likes to be charged a stiff price; otherwise he thinks you are selling him trash."

Marcus raised his price and was stunned to discover that people would pay five cents for what cost him less than two-thirds of a penny down on Orchard Street. At the end of his first day, he had supper in a Romanian restaurant on Allen Street: chopped eggplant and a bit of pot roast with mashed potatoes and gravy. Within days, the candies gave way to a tray of toys, sheet-metal acrobats that did not spoil when business was slow. For the first time in America old dreams began to surface, set off by the sight of boys his age carrying bags filled with books. Were they all going to become doctors?

Learning English was now a necessity, but Marcus lived in a world where people spoke Yiddish and Romanian, and Americans turned out to be so "loquacious." How to learn such phrases as *give in, give up, give way.* The dictionary and English Bible he had bought were less help than he had hoped. Without proper shoes or English he would never find a job, and peddling was an uncertain business. He found himself thinking more and more of home, and then Couza, the townsman who had lured him to America in the first place, interceded once again. Suddenly Ravage found himself in a starched white apron working in a saloon with a beautiful oak bar. This was not the ideal job, but it came with three meals a day, a clean bed at night, and three dollars a month.

By Easter, another holiday that was not his own, he would be able to buy American shoes and an American suit and a derby "which played queer tricks with his face, but made [him] feel like a man." In time the bar would give way to a job in a sweatshop, the sweatshop would provide money for school and Marcus would then write home, urging his brothers to join him. Later he would return to Vaslui, and then come back to America for good, where by then he belonged.

Twenty blocks or so uptown, and more than a world away, Ida McKinley was selecting fine linen handkerchiefs in her six-room suite in the Manhattan Hotel. Tradesmen had been arriving from shops all over the city with goods for her consideration. The First Lady had come to New York to complete her Christmas shopping, accompanied by family and friends, servants, and Dr. Rixey, but without her husband. At the train station, reporters noted there was no need this time for an invalid chair. The president's wife had gained ten pounds and was in excellent health. Dr. Rixey attributed her well-being to the triumph of the election. Mrs. McKinley spent several days finishing her shopping and then returned to Washington for the start of the winter social season.

1900 had been a wonderful year for Ida McKinley.

Ida and William McKinley.

II

In the coal region of Pennsylvania, the month began with a Christmas miracle. Ever since the strike, the miners had been working flat out. At a number of collieries, the men had voted not to work Christmas Day, an extravagance that in other years would not have been considered. In early December, shopkeepers were filling their windows with oranges and nuts, ornaments and candy canes. But then, on Wednesday, December 5, at the old, overworked Nay Aug colliery in the small town of Dunmore, not far from Scranton, the land around the mine gave way and a massive cave-in completely blocked the exit, trapping thirty-two men one thousand feet below the ground. As teams of rescue workers began digging through the rubble the earth continued to shift. Huge ugly fissures ripped the surface of the land.

Within minutes of the disaster, the wives and children arrived—alerted by those sounds that always signaled trouble. The old hands had little hope of reaching the miners alive, but held their tongues. Inside the mine the imprisoned men were better off than any knew, for the moment at least. In total darkness—their lamps had been extinguished by the rush of air—they had established that, miraculously, all thirty two members of the crew were alive and uninjured and that the air was pure and they could relight their lamps. Surrounded by rubble and shaken by the fall, some counseled remaining in place until help could reach them. But then the pillars behind them began to crack, and every man knew time was running out.

Mine foreman John Gibbons, the most experienced man in the lot, crawling over rubble on his hands and knees, set out to find an escape route. Gibbons squirmed through crevices barely wide enough to tolerate his body. By inches, he reached an area he knew to be some fifteen feet from an air shaft, which opened out to the exit. Returning to collect the men, he led them over the short but exceedingly difficult and dangerous route. Moving on their stomachs, dragging crowbars, picks, and shovels, the miners inched through spaces that seemed too narrow for the narrowest among them. Every unexpected sound, every falling chunk of shale, was heard as warning of another fall to come.

The shaft, Gibbons told them, had been carved through solid rock and would probably provide a clear passage to the exit, if they could only reach it. On the surface now, a full hour after the cave-in, the roof of the mine was still working, and over an area of five acres the land had continued to settle. Tons of additional rock were threatening to drop at any moment. It seemed beyond reason that the miners could be reached in time. But inside the mine, the men—all thirty-two—had made it through the rubble and by turns were trying to dig an escape route to the shaft. They could still hear the shifting of the roof and the working of the timbers and knew that with each lunge of a pick they might unleash another fall.

Two hours and fifteen minutes after the cave-in—it had seemed a great deal longer—the miners broke out into the air shaft, which as Gibbons had promised was as clear as the day it had been built. One man after the next scrambled into the shaft, then out the exit into an unbelieving crowd. The men were torn and shaken—but alive. In the coal towns that night the story of the escape from Nay Aug was told and retold as nothing less than a New Year omen. At a union meeting an organizer predicted that within five years miners would only work a six-hour day and all the demands that had been rejected in October would be raised again in the spring. If necessary there would be another strike.

That same week, a seismic shift of quite a different nature was taking place in a boardroom some hundreds of miles away. J. P. Morgan was tightening his hold on the anthracite region. Morgan and his associates had taken control of the Erie Railroad, and in the future not a chunk of hard coal would move, east or west, without his agreement. Morgan also bought up the large and profitable Pennsylvania Coal Company. In the future, he would be able to dictate production and prices. Back in the fall, the Morgan cartel had been caught unawares by the strength of the miners. Now they would be in a far stronger position to deal with the union.

It was clear that both sides were gearing up for another fight. At UMW headquarters, John Mitchell had been considering moving on. He was tired of "doing three men's work, for one man's pay." He wanted an elegant home, the big house on the hill and all the trappings of the good life. He was being tempted by a lucrative job with an insurance company in Philadelphia, but in the end concluded "my whole heart is in the organization which I have seen grow from few in numbers to its present magnificent status." Mitchell would stay on to face Morgan once again.

III

In a land of desire, J. Pierpont Morgan was perhaps its most insatiable consumer. Nothing seemed beyond either his pocketbook or his reach. Morgan's agents were dispatched around the globe, spending months, sometimes years lying in wait to purchase an eighth-century illustrated gospel or a copy of the Gutenberg Bible. Once, when he had tarried awhile in England, Mark Hanna suggested Morgan was getting up a syndicate to buy the British Empire. But now, at the end of 1900, the financier was on the eve of consummating the greatest deal of his life—in fact, the largest deal in the history of the industrial world.

He was moving to take control of the steel industry; creating a financial mechanism to buy out ten corporations, including the works of Andrew Carnegie. For some weeks Morgan had been forced to wait while Carnegie wavered. But in the end, the Scotsman had scribbled Morgan a proposal, written in pencil on an ordinary scrap of paper. He would accept $480 million dollars for Carnegie Steel. When the deal was finally concluded and the two men shook hands, Morgan said, "Congratulations, Mr. Carnegie, you are now the richest man in the world." Unsaid was that Morgan was one of the most powerful.

With the founding of the United States Steel Corporation, Morgan had assembled the first billion-dollar business in history. He had also raised a defining question for the new century: Who would run America? Had the great financiers finally become more important than the government? Brisben Walker, editor of *Cosmopolitan*, wrote that with the formation of U.S. Steel, "the world . . . ceased to be ruled by so-called statesmen. True, there were marionettes still figuring in Congress . . . but they were in place simply to carry out the orders of the real rulers—those who control the concentrated portion of the money supply." The president of Yale, Dr. Arthur Hadley, declared that if the trusts were not brought under control, there would be "an emperor in Washington in twenty-five years."

In Germany, the Kaiser raised a curious question: "Suppose, that a Morgan succeeds in combining under his flag several of the oceanic lines?" What would happen if one of his ships was involved in an international incident? Because Morgan "did not occupy any official position in his country outside of the influence derived from his wealth," the State could decline any responsibility. "To whom could one turn?" the Kaiser asked. The German emperor was not alone in his concerns.

IV

After five months in the doldrums, on December 1, Washington was finally coming back to life. When Congress closed down in June, the diplomats, the socialites, and the lobbyists had fled. For months the city was a social desert; the only event of note was the funeral of George Washington's great-grandniece. But with the McKinleys in residence, and Congress about to go back into session, the avenues were thronged. The hotel lobbies were filled with smoking, gossiping men, who returned like the swallows whenever the legislators came back to town.

Republican leaders were making the required pilgrimage to the White House, not only to congratulate the president but to remind him how, by their eloquence and wiles, each had contributed to the party's triumph. But McKinley had been sobered by his reelection. He cautioned his fellow Republicans that he had not been elected by one party alone, and that "the new problems were too exalted for partisanship." A political correspondent, Walter Wellman, reported the president warned congressional leaders to avoid any expression of extravagance, militarism, imperialism, or favoritism to special classes.

The Democrats, however, dismissed the talk of moderation as nothing but talk. They were convinced, Wellman said, that the Republicans, "puffed up and insolent with success," would once again prove that they were "the party of the corporation, the trusts, money, plutocracy." Wellman also noted that "no sooner is one Presidential campaign out of the way than the scheming and planning is begun for the next. Before 1900 has passed we are looking forward to 1904."

But on December 3, when Congress reassembled after the long hiatus, politics were briefly suspended. The Senate chamber that morning looked like a flower garden. Only an occasional sighting of one pudgy hand indicated the presence of Mark Hanna. The Republican leader was totally hidden behind a mass of blossoms. This was not the first time the legislators had received flowers. It was common practice for friends, and those who wanted to be friends, to send floral tributes on opening day. But, consistent with so much else in 1900, the offerings this year were excessive.

Over in the House, the Republican side of the chamber looked like a huge chrysanthemum show. On the floor, the scene was more like a club reunion than a meeting of the legislature. Men who had been defeated during the last election were embraced with expressions of collegial understanding. The only essential business of the day, President McKinley's message to the Congress, was read by a clerk while most members went to lunch.

Among those who had announced their coming retirement—the current session would end in March—was John Fitzgerald, who was considering a run for mayor of Boston. His colleagues were sorry Fitzgerald was leaving, and so were reporters. The congressman from Boston was always entertaining. When the House, under pressure from the prohibitionists, outlawed the sale of intoxicants on military bases, Fitzgerald rose to suggest that the House might also want to ban the sale of liquor in the capital: "Members should do a little penance," he said, "after such a virtuous vote for the soldiers of the regular army." With hoots of amusement, Fitzgerald was ruled out of order.

On the other side of the aisle, George White, a Republican from North Carolina, was also ending his congressional career, but for very different reasons. White had been in politics for over twenty years. An imposing man, more than six feet tall, a lawyer and former school principal, he was the last African American left in Congress. At one time there had been twenty black representatives and two senators, but for four years, as White felt impelled to remind his colleagues, he had been the sole spokesman for nine million black Americans—and soon he would be gone. In 1900, there was no future for a black politician in North Carolina, or anywhere in the South.

During the summer White had reported that a violent campaign had been mounted to frighten black men from going to the polls. Thousands of white Republicans had turned against their party and joined the Democrats' race crusade. White's own family had been attacked, his wife's health was broken, and his daughter, an Oberlin College student, had been falsely accused of smuggling guns to black voters. In recent years he had watched as the legal rights of black Americans were systematically erased. By law and by violence, North Carolina had now made it all but impossible for most black men to vote.

In the House, White had heard African Americans described as members of an "ignorant, debased, and debauched race." Representative David A. De Armond from Missouri had declared that "Negroes [were] almost too ignorant to eat, scarcely wise enough to breathe, mere existing human machines." White had had enough. But before retiring, he was championing one last bill—to reduce the size of the congressional delegations from those states that had disenfranchised black voters. Except for the sponsor of the bill, Elmer D. Crumpacker from Valparaiso, Indiana, out of the three hundred and fifty-six members of the House, White found only one other ally—John Fitzgerald from Boston.

Speaking on behalf of the legislation, Fitzgerald condemned the new voting laws; he pointed to the men in the black regiments who had served with bravery and distinction in Cuba alongside the Rough Riders, and suggested their white comrades "would protest with mighty vigor against the disenfranchisement of a race that produced such brave and noble souls." Then Fitzgerald went on to say, "I am absolutely opposed to any discrimination on account of race, color, or religion."

In his final address to the House, George White declared: "This Mr. Chairman, is perhaps the Negroes' temporary farewell to the American Congress. But let me say, phoenix-like, he will rise up someday and come again. These parting words are on behalf of an outraged, heartbroken, bruised and bleeding people, but God-fearing people, faithful, industrious, loyal people—rising people, full of potential. . . . The only apology I have to make for the earnestness with which I have spoken is that I am pleading for the life, the liberty, the future happiness, and manhood suffrage of one-eighth of the entire population of the United States."

It would be twenty-eight years before another black American would be elected to the United States House of Representatives, and sixty-seven years before there would be a black American in the Senate.

V

On December 12, when President McKinley's carriage appeared at the White House gate, tens of thousands of people were waiting on Pennsylvania Avenue. All business in the city had been suspended for the celebration of the 100th anniversary of the nation's capital. The weather was brisk, and the horses were fractious. As the president made his way to the reviewing stand in his open victoria, riders were finding it difficult to hold the animals in line. To guard themselves against the wind, older marchers had resurrected uniforms not seen in years. Veterans of the Grand Army of the Republic wore tall black shakos and heavy military overcoats with dark blue capes flung over their shoulders.

Lieutenant General Nelson Miles, commander of the United States Army, the chief marshal of the parade and an expert horseman, rode with soldierly deportment, looking neither left nor right. As he reached the reviewing stand in his splendidly embroidered uniform, Miles saluted the president with a broad sweep of his sword, and then, the unthinkable occurred. The general—who was credited with destroying the village of Crazy Horse, with capturing Chief Joseph, with accepting the surrender of Geronimo—was suddenly unhorsed. Frightened by the sound of a band, his horse rose on his hind feet until his body was perpendicular with the ground, and in front of the president of the United States, both horse and rider fell to the asphalt.

Only Miles's pride was injured. The horse and the general regained their footing quickly, and Miles remounted without aid. But the general suffered one more indignity that day. The papers reported that Theodore Roosevelt received more enthusiastic cheers than Miles. Wearing an unfamiliar silk topper, TR, who was riding in a carriage in the governors' parade, was not immediately identified. But once he was spotted, word was passed along the line that Roosevelt was coming, and from that moment on, TR received one unbroken cheer all the way to the Capitol.

What was not apparent to the crowd was that ever since the election, TR had been restless and melancholy. While he was trying to assume a vice-presidential posture, he was wistful about giving up a life he so enjoyed. He wrote a friend in England, "Two happier years could not be imagined than Mrs. Roosevelt and I have passed, during the winters here at Albany and during the summers at Sagamore with all our children well and about us. . . ." He explained that the office of the vice presidency was like a "fifth wheel to a coach . . . it is not a stepping stone to anything except oblivion. I fear my bolt is shot."

He was being asked for favors he had no power to fulfill. He had been given twelve tickets for the inaugural ceremony, enough for his immediate family, his sisters and their husbands, but he could not invite their children. He needed a holiday where he would not be tempted to eat too much; he felt "as old as Methuselah, fat and stiff." Early on, exercise had become a part of his life. The gymnasium in Albany had been as much for TR as for his children.

As a boy, when he had suffered from asthma, his father had encouraged him to take hold of his body, to build his strength, to "prepare to do the rough work of the world." And whenever he had been troubled—when his father died, when his beloved first wife and mother died on the same day—he had headed west where he could throw himself into the strenuous life. "Black care," he wrote, "rarely sits behind a rider whose pace is fast enough." He would not sit around now and brood or attend innumerable boring dinners, waiting for the inauguration in March. On New Year's he would become a private citizen again. Then he would be off for the mountains of Colorado to hunt mountain lion and bear.

The decision made, he wrote to Philip Stewart, who was arranging the trip. "I feel like a boy again and am just crazy to get out." He had a Winchester .33. Did he need a revolver? What about bedding and German socks? New York was a poor place to buy winter footgear. But first there was Christmas at Sagamore Hill. The children would be coming up to sit on the bed to open their stockings, and then after breakfast they would all go to the gun room where the larger presents would be laid out on the table. As for the future, he said, he had no expectation of going any further in public life, after the vice presidency.

In Washington, the evening of the Centennial, the president, TR, the cabinet, members of Congress, and the diplomatic corps attended an unusual ceremony held in the House of Representatives. In the brilliantly lit hall, one speaker after another recounted the triumphs of America over the past hundred years. Governor Shaw of Iowa declared: "The close of the most remarkable century in the flight of time finds Americans the best housed, the best fed, the best clothed, the best educated, the best churched, the most profitably employed and the happiest, because [they are] the most hopeful of any people at any time or under any sky."

As the president returned to the White House with his cavalry escort, at 15th Street a searchlight fastened to the Treasury building focused on the presidential party, who appeared out of the darkness into a bold but pleasing blaze of light.

VI

It may have been the story of General Miles that lingered in his mind, or simply that Paul Laurence Dunbar had little experience on horseback. Whatever the reason, when a courier arrived from the White House with an invitation for Dunbar to ride in McKinley's inaugural parade in March, the poet declined. But as Dunbar later told the story, the messenger was hardly out of the house "when my wife and mother made siege on me, and I ran down the front steps in my house jacket and slippers and told him that I had changed my mind." Dunbar would escort his mother in her new silk evening dress to the inaugural ceremony.

Matilda Dunbar's passage into the twentieth century would be happier than her son's. In the weeks before Christmas, Paul was taking time off to "smoke and read and play cards and make the night hideous with my violin." How long this idleness would last, he didn't know. It had not been an easy year. Professionally, both Paul and Alice had been singularly successful. She had just published a one-act play in *Smart Set* and was working on a novel. Paul's reputation had continued to grow; his books were selling well, but emotionally and physically he was frail, his marriage tense, and he had been drinking again.

Paul Laurence Dunbar.

During the summer when he blacked out in the midst of the race riot in New York, he had told the police, the press, and his mother that knockout drops had been put in his beer. More likely, Paul had been drinking and simply passed out. He disappeared for days that time, and Alice was crazed with worry. A few weeks later in Evanston, Illinois, he arrived for an appearance, late and drunk, and the incident was reported in the papers. The consumption had returned. Paul was hemorrhaging again and was probably using morphine to still the pain of coughing and drink to mask his fatigue.

He wrote to Alice: "Sweetheart: I have treated you shamefully . . . and I have no excuse for my silence except that I have nothing good to write. I know that you by this time know that I have been playing the devil as usual. So no more of that. . . . I want to see you, dearie, very much. Will you promise not to scold me much, my own?" Neither Paul nor Alice was approaching the New Year with many illusions. Dunbar was clinging to his beautiful wife, but she had already begun to pull away. In one of his poems he defined "Life's Tragedy":

> *To have come near to sing the perfect song*
> *and only by a half tone lost the key . . .*

VII

On Christmas Eve, the weather was warm even for Galveston, when Santa Claus, sweltering in his robe of furs, climbed through a window at the newly repaired Mason's Temple. The tree, said to be the largest in town, had been decorated by the local electrical shop. If the carols and the presents did not assuage the sadness of children newly orphaned, it was not acknowledged. In the shopping district that night, the stores were staying open late. The people of Galveston seemed startled by their own behavior, but there was an abiding need for continuity, for the comfort of tradition.

With bodies still being found in the outlying districts and thousands living in temporary shelters, it had been assumed the holiday this year would pass almost unacknowledged. But as Christmas had approached one could sense a shift in mood. Memories were stirred by fresh fir trees from Maine. Pages of advertisements in *The Galveston Daily News* were running under a banner that read, "Still Doing Business at the Old Stand." Thomas Goggan & Bro. were selling pianos and organs on easy terms for those unable to pay cash, and Stewart & Gonzales were recommending that parents buy their sons double-barrel shotguns: "Every boy should learn to shoot." At Loughin's there were fancy fruits, Smyrna figs and Turkish dates and plum puddings in a variety of sizes.

The physical and commercial resurrection of the city was nothing less than astonishing. From an economic perspective, Galveston had had a good year. The personal toll was another matter. In the days immediately following the disaster, witnesses had written in a psychic fury of "cemeteries emptied of the dead," of a city "covered by the vomitings of a maddened, retching ocean." In September, there had been no restrictions on words; they were often as wrenching as the sea. But now, in the aftermath, when reality was setting in and the loss was most intense, language was more guarded and the words no longer seemed to come. Mourning had become a private affair.

On Christmas Eve, in the longstanding custom of the South, crowds turned out with tin horns of the latest design, wooden whistles, and pasteboard criers. The fireworks would be set off later that evening. As the promenade made its way up one side of the street and down the other, confetti and rice were scattered by the wind.

The Roosevelt children—Ethel, Theodore, Alice, Quentin, Kermit, and Archibald—with a few of their more domesticated pets.

Philadelphia, Pennsylvania, December 31, 1900.

CHAPTER SEVENTEEN

New Year's Eve

I

At six in the morning, on December 26, Jack London sat down to write to Anna Strunsky—it was to have been her Christmas letter; the last letter for the year. He told Anna she had been a delight to him, a trouble—and a glory. That same day in the *St. Louis Post-Dispatch,* a well-known literary critic predicted it was just a matter of time before London was recognized as a writer as forceful as Rudyard Kipling. London had studied Kipling's "plain style," and admitted there was a lot of Kipling in his own work. At the end of 1900, he was being compared to Kipling—one of the most masterful writers in the world. He could see success now, almost take its measure, but his personal life was out of kilter. He wrote Anna:

> Just when freedom seems opening up to me, I feel the bands tightening and
> the rivetting of the gyves. I remember now when I was free. When there was
> no restraint and I did what the heart willed. . . .

Surely, sitting here . . . writing stories for boys with moral purposes insidiously inserted . . . surely, this is not all. What you have been to me? I am not great enough or brave enough to say. This false thing which the world would call my conscience, will not permit me. . . . A white beautiful friendship?—between a man and a woman?—the world cannot imagine such a thing. . . .

Anna and Jack would remain friends for the rest of his life—although in time, both would go on to marry other people. *The Kempton-Wace Letters* would be published in 1903, and be followed shortly after by London's most popular book, *The Call of the Wild*. In an astonishingly brief time, he would write two hundred short stories, four hundred nonfiction pieces, twenty novels, and three full-length plays. His work would be translated into eighty languages.

He had postponed writing poetry until fame and fortune were made, but, as Anna would write, "Death came before he had remembered his promise to himself. Death came before he remembered many other things. He was so hard at work—so pitifully, tragically hard at work." London died in 1916.

II

In the bitter wind and cold, on the days just after Christmas in Kansas City, Missouri, the superintendent of streets, Tom Pendergast, had double-sized crews clearing the snow-covered streets. He dared not wait until the day of New Year's Eve—when the city might be locked in ice. The "Central City" in the West, the upstart city on the plains, was planning to hold the largest, most lavish celebration in the entire country. *The Kansas City Journal* declared that the Century Ball would "set the pace for the rest of the world." The gala had caught the attention of the national press, and even the London papers. The city had been much in the press this year, but too many of the stories reflected an eastern condescension—snide items about rough western dress and rough western ways. Not a word about the public library or fine schools or concert halls.

The Century Ball would prove once and for all that Kansas City was more than a "little Chicago," more than a commercial hub with gambling halls. The people of Kansas City had refined their ways. Men who had been dismissed as lard kings or princes of the stockyards were ordering pink and magenta knee britches and powdered wigs from New York for the ball. It was said that there wasn't a historical costume left in all of St. Louis or Chicago. A dance instructor from Leavenworth had been teaching society leaders the minuet, and sixty men from the Kansas City Symphony were rehearsing Strauss waltzes, the Virginia reel, and the two-step.

Some felt it had been an act of wild imagination to designate the Convention Hall, a vast and uncharming space, as the setting for a fin-de-siècle ball. But it was the only place large enough to accommodate ten thousand dancers, and more important, there was an emotional tie between the city and the hall. The pride of the prairie, the most perfectly constructed auditorium in the world, the building had been funded entirely by popular subscription. It was the hall that had led the Democrats to choose Kansas City as the site for their presidential convention. The announcement back in February that over twenty thousand free-spending, glad-handing, spirited delegates would be arriving for a week or so had warmed the hearts of every merchant, theater and hotel owner in town.

Then in April, three months to the day before the convention was to open, the hall had caught fire. Fanned by a strong wind from the plains, it had burned with such fury that in less than thirty minutes it was totally destroyed. But as the

There was a timeless quality to Roy and Mabel Wood as they made their way to the Grand Century Ball in Kansas City, on New Year's Eve, 1900.

roof with its great steel girders crashed to the ground, civic leaders moving through the crowd were soliciting donations to rebuild the auditorium. At dawn the following day, calls had gone east with orders for new steel supports. Before the ground had cooled, crews were set around the clock to clear the site and a new hall had risen quite literally out of the ashes. Three months later, missing only an embellishment or two, the building reopened with flags and banners flying and almost every seat in place.

The hall had come to symbolize the spirit of the Middle West. After events of the spring, transforming the space into a garden of earthly delights seemed a relatively easy challenge. Twelve hundred fir trees from Louisiana were carted into place. The dance floor was to appear like a placid lake in the midst of a forest. Armies of electricians and carpenters, floor finishers and florists had been working for days. A false ceiling was created out of thousands of yards of muslin. In the last hour before the turn of the century, an enormous electrified hourglass would dominate the scene. The top half of the glass was filled with sixty golden lightbulbs. With the passing of each minute, a bulb in the top half of the glass would die, and as the crowd of thousands chanted, the lower half of the glass would begin to fill with "the sands of time."

Everything seemed on schedule. If only the temperature would ease a bit—if only it wouldn't snow anymore.

It was quieter down the line in the town of Independence. With Christmas over it was too cold to linger in the square. But at the end of 1900, people in Independence were feeling good about themselves and good about their future. *The Independence Sentinel,* in a burst of optimism, predicted that the changes in the next one hundred years would probably exceed even the most extravagant expectations. "The 20th century should silence all the crockers," the paper declared, "and demonstrate to all that the world is getting better instead of worse." Harry Truman, a senior now in high school, and his friend Elmer Twyman were working on their class yearbook. "Progress," Twyman wrote, "is the cry on every hand. . . . Truly we are wizards performing miracles. We lack nothing but the airship . . . or, perhaps, the 'fountain of youth.' "

Over the course of 1900, almost without their knowing, Americans had been moving across an unseen divide, from one age to the next. There had been no single event, but a series of incidents that seemed to signal the coming of the future. In Boston, on December 30, the last horse-drawn trolley made its way to Back Bay and was replaced by a twelve-passenger, electrified omnibus, without any fanfare. Seven thousand horses were sent into retirement—or worse—and no

The town square in Independence, Missouri.

one seemed to mourn their going. The papers that week reported that Marconi had "sent intelligence through space"—without wires. Men were now intruding in the province of the wizards. Scientists in America and Europe were searching the heavens for a message from Mars. And Nikola Tesla, the famed electrician and inventor, was convinced that "ere long all human beings on . . . will [be] thrilled by the glad news: 'Brethren, we have a message from another world.' "

Reality and fantasy continued to blur. In *The Washington Post,* Henry Litchfield West recalled that Jules Verne had conjured a voyage to the moon. "If that still remains a bit of fiction," he wrote, "there would seem to be no good reason why it should not some day be transformed into result." What had yet to be done, would be done.

III

The White House was quiet on New Year's Eve, 1900. A large crush of people was expected for the reception the following morning, and to conserve her strength, Mrs. McKinley had retired early. Christmas always left her feeling sad and tense. Around eleven o'clock that evening, Secretary Cortelyou found the president in his office reading a book about the American Revolution. Whether William McKinley was reflecting on how his administration would be judged in the future will never be known, but as almost every paper made clear that day, those that supported him and those that did not, McKinley had presided over a remarkable turning point in his country's history.

When he came into office in 1896, Americans were an inward-looking people. The nation was depressed, close to drowning economically, victim in part to its own abundance and industrial genius. Following the war, an aggressive export campaign had turned the economy around, but prosperity had been acquired at a price. While the China market seemed to be secure, the war in the Philippines continued and America's commercial success had created tension among the European powers. At the end of 1900, the Frankfurt *Zeitung,* in Germany, stated that "ever since the war with Spain the United States has pursued undeviatingly a policy of world conquest."

Historian Brooks Adams, in an essay for *The Atlantic Monthly,* declared: "Americans must recognize that this is war to the death—a struggle no longer against a single nation, but against a continent. There is not room in the economy of the world for two centers of wealth and empire. One . . . in the end will destroy the other." Adams believed western Europe was in decline, and that in the future, Russia and the United States would be the only great powers left. In its year-end supplement, *The Courier-Journal* of Louisville, Kentucky, was troubled by Russian aggressiveness. The Russians had overrun Central Asia right to the Chinese border and the edge of India. *The Courier-Journal* reported, "Europe is not yet all Cossack, but the danger seems as great as it did to Napoleon."

An editorial in *The Washington Post* reminded its readers that for "all our progress of luxury and knowledge . . . we have not been lifted by so much as a fraction of an inch above the level of the darkest ages. . . . The last hundred years have wrought no change in the passions, the cruelties, and the barbarous impulses of mankind. . . . There is no difference in the matter of inhumanity—no change from the savagery of the Middle Ages. We enter a new century equipped with every wonderful device of science and art . . . [but] the pirate, the savage, and the tyrant still survives."

When asked about the one change he would most like to see in the coming century, Andrew Carnegie declared, "The earth freed from its foulest stain, the killing of men by men in the name of war." There had been fifty major wars in the nineteenth century and countless smaller conflicts. Ministers spoke of the need for world unity. A number of writers evoked the peace conference that had been held at The Hague the year before. Oscar Strauss, a former minister to Turkey, believed that in the future, mediation would be the "controlling moral power." And in Independence, Missouri, seventeen-year-old Harry Truman sat down and copied lines from a poem by Tennyson, which he would carry in his wallet for the rest of his life.

> Heard the heavens fill with shouting, and there rain'd a ghastly dew
> From the nations' airy navies grappling in the central blue;
>
> .   .   .   .
>
> Till the war-drum throbb'd no longer, and the battle flags were furl'd
> In the Parliament of man, the Federation of the world.
> There the common sense of most shall hold a fretful realm in awe,
> And the kindly earth shall slumber, lapt in universal law.

As the year ended, William McKinley believed, with all the optimism with which he was endowed, that the United States could be a force for peace in the world, that commercial supremacy did not require the nation to abandon its moral principles. Just before midnight, he was joined by his brother Abner. At the sound of a few warning shots from a distant cannon, the McKinley brothers, along with Secretary Cortelyou, threw open a window onto Pennsylvania Avenue. As bells and trumpets announced the century, the president allowed himself a few minutes for sentimentality and then went down the hall to retire.

———•••———

As the bells and trumpets faded and Americans were waking in the twentieth century, an English novelist and scholar, Sir Walter Besant, turned to the people of the United States with a question he described as old as history itself: "Whether political society is to be a machinery for enabling a few to keep the many in subjection; or whether every man shall be allotted his equal share in government. . . . In other words," he said, "is government by the people possible? And shall it prevail?"

> It is to America, and America alone, that we must look. . . . Never before has the experiment of popular government been made on so great a scale, for so long a time. . . . You have now had for more than a hundred years a government by the people. . . . But the answer to the question . . . must be based on a long experience. After two hundred years, let the world turn to America for an answer. Would that in the year 1999 or 2000 one could come back to earth . . . to hear the answer.

> May it be favorable to democracy. And may it be final.

New Year's Eve dinner in Sturgeon Bay, Wisconsin.

One minute before midnight in New York, City Hall went dark. A hush fell over the crowd of one hundred thousand people. Then the lights went back on, revealing a sign in huge electric lights—WELCOME 20TH CENTURY. Steam whistles shrieked and the crowd went wild as fifty Lyddite bombs were sent up into the sky "roaring like Niagra gone mad."

Epilogue

***

Years after the grand Century Ball in Kansas City, a woman who had attended the great New Year's Eve gala as a child remembered a terrible letdown when, after midnight, after ten thousand people had sung "Auld Lang Syne" and the electrical hourglass had marked the new century, nothing seemed to change. In truth, for most Americans the first weeks of the twentieth century were no different than the weeks that had gone before. Then late in January came the news from England that Queen Victoria was sinking. President McKinley noted that Victoria had begun her reign before most Americans were born. For many, the queen's death was the conclusive signal that the nineteenth century was finally over. For others, the century would not be laid to rest until the end of the summer.

On September 6, 1901, at the Pan American Exposition in Buffalo, New York, President McKinley, accompanied by his aides, headed for a reception at the new and ornate Temple of Music. The McKinleys had arrived at the exposition the day before and, in an era of wild demonstrations, the president had never received a warmer welcome. One hundred and sixteen thousand people had turned out to voice their respect and affection. To McKinley's amusement and the horror of his aides, thousands of people broke through the security lines to try to shake his hand. Mixing with the crowd, wearing her press badge, was Frances Benjamin Johnston. Her photographs of the president that day would soon be regarded as sad mementos.

What was evident to the press, to everyone in Buffalo, was the strong personal bond that existed between McKinley and the American people. Even those who did not share his views found the president an amiable and warmhearted man. In May, when Ida McKinley had fallen gravely ill with a blood infection and lapsed into a coma, the entire nation seemed to share his anguish. Now, seeing the president with his arm around his wife's waist, the crowd rejoiced in his obvious pleasure over her recovery.

On the morning of the sixth, the McKinleys had played tourist, traveling with friends to Niagara Falls in private parlor cars. On their return, Mrs. McKinley was placed in a carriage and sent back to the Milburn home where the presidential party was staying. The president watched her drive away, then turned and, accompanied by Secretary Cortelyou, George Foster, and two additional Secret Service men, headed for the Temple of Music. As the presidential party approached the auditorium, Cortelyou was uneasy at the size of the crowd. He had wanted to avoid this public reception, but, as so often in the past, McKinley had overruled him. As the president took his place on the dais, he nodded to those in charge and said, "Let them come," and the crowd started down the aisle, corralled into a single file.

Seven minutes later, with a Bach sonata playing in the background, McKinley stretched out his hand to greet Leon Czolgosz, a good-looking, clean-shaven man, and Czolgosz—using a short-barreled revolver covered by a white handkerchief—fired two shots directly into the president.

As McKinley was placed on a litter to be taken by motor ambulance to a makeshift operating room on the grounds, he whispered to Cortelyou. "My wife—be careful, Cortelyou, how you tell her—oh be careful." Minutes later, news of the shooting was transmitted by AP line to newspapers, government offices, and commercial centers in all the major cities. The president's condition was unknown. Czolgosz was identified as a deranged anarchist.

At the White House, at twenty-five past four, a servant cleaning in the telegraph room overheard the awful news and ran to tell Thomas Pendel. Pendel had been at the door of the White House when news arrived that Lincoln was shot and had been among those who held the deathwatch after Garfield was shot. Now, along with so many others, he awaited every bulletin from Buffalo. The physicians reported that one wound had been superficial, a gash on the ribs. The other was more serious—the walls of the stomach had been torn open—but the public was assured that the surgery had been successful. The president was resting at the Milburn home. Photographs were published of somber-looking members of the family, Vice President Roosevelt, and Mark Hanna making their way into the house. On the street outside, reporters waited for briefings from Secretary Cortelyou.

Each day the bulletins were more favorable. Over the weekend the president seemed to rally, and Mrs. McKinley was taken out for a drive. TR was encouraged to leave Buffalo and rejoin his family in the Adirondack Mountains, twelve miles from any telephone. It was important that the vice president not seem too concerned. But on the morning of September 13, a week after the attack, McKinley took a turn. Infection had set in. Physicians acknowledged the "gravest apprehensions." Park rangers were dispatched to find the vice president, who was now hiking in the mountains. In Buffalo, early evening, Mrs. McKinley was called to her husband's side; the president mustered enough strength to say, "Good-bye—good-bye all."

In the Adirondack Mountains, on a cold gray morning, a park ranger finally found TR on the summit of Mount Marcy. By a small lake named Tear-of-the-Clouds, Roosevelt was informed that the president had died. The amiable man Americans so loved had barely been allowed to touch the twentieth century. He had shaped its coming and greatly influenced the nation's future, but the future had been placed in another man's hands. As the crowds sang "Nearer My God to Thee," one writer noted that the mourners were "going back to their old beliefs in the homely virtues of a good man and tried with him to stretch out their hands to God."

They cried, "The president is dead, long live the president."

On September 22, 1901, when Theodore Roosevelt, after five days of mourning, strode into the White House, he told a friend, "It is a dreadful thing to come in this way, but it would be a far worse thing to be morbid about it." A strong, young, progressive man would now lead his nation into all the uncertainties of the twentieth century.

Sources and Notes

In writing *America 1900*, I have drawn heavily on material written or published between the closing months of 1899 and the early months of 1901. For context, as well as specific information, I am indebted to countless biographies, histories, and reference works. Below are listed those books I found most useful in trying to understand the underlying forces that made 1900 a turning point in the nation's history. Works of special interest are included in the chapter notes directly following the bibliography.

Adams, Henry. *The Education of Henry Adams*. Ernest Samuels, ed. Houghton Mifflin, 1974.

Allen, Frederick Lewis. *The Big Change: America Transforms Itself 1900–1950*. Harper & Row, 1952.

Ayers, Edward L. *The Promise of the New South: Life After Reconstruction*. Oxford University Press, 1992.

Boorstin, Daniel J. *The Americans: The Democratic Experience*. Vintage Books, 1974.

Burns, James MacGregor. *The Workshop of Democracy*. Alfred A. Knopf, 1985.

Calkins, Earnest Elmo. *They Broke the Prairie*. Charles Scribner's Sons, 1937.

Commager, Henry Steele. *The American Mind*. Yale University Press, 1950.

Crouch, Tom D. *The Bishop's Boys: A Life of Wilbur and Orville Wright*. W. W. Norton & Co., 1989.

Degler, Carl N. *Out of Our Past: The Forces That Shaped Modern America*. Third Edition. Harper Torchbooks, 1984.

Dubofsky, Melvyn, Athan Theoharis, and Daniel M. Smith. *The United States in the Twentieth Century*. Prentice-Hall, Inc., 1978.

Freidel, Frank, and Alan Brinkley. *America in the Twentieth Century*. Alfred A. Knopf, 1963.

Goodwin, Doris Kearns. *The Fitzgeralds and the Kennedys: An American Saga*. Simon & Schuster, 1987.

Hunter, Robert. *Poverty*. The Macmillan Co., 1904.

Jackson, Kenneth T., ed. *The Encyclopedia of New York City*. Yale University Press, 1995.

Katzman, David M., and William R. Tuttle, Jr., eds. *Plain Folk: The Life Stories of Undistinguished Americans*. University of Illinois Press, 1982.

LaFeber, Walter. *The American Age: U.S. Foreign Policy at Home and Abroad 1750 to Present*. W. W. Norton & Co., 1989.

Leach, William. *Land of Desire: Merchants, Power and the Rise of a New American Culture*. Pantheon Books, 1993.

Leech, Margaret. *In the Days of McKinley*. Harper & Brothers, 1959.

Lewis, David Levering. *W.E.B. Du Bois: Biography of a Race, 1868–1919*. Henry Holt & Co., 1993.

Lord, Walter. *The Good Years: From 1900 to the First World War*. Harper & Brothers, 1960.

McCullough, David. *Truman*. Simon & Schuster, 1992.

Miller, Stuart Creighton. *"Benevolent Assimilation": The American Conquest of the Philippines*. Yale University Press, 1982.

Morison, Samuel Eliot, Henry Steele Commager, and William E. Leuchtenburg. *A Concise History of the American Republic*. Second Edition. Oxford University Press, 1983.

Morris, Edmund. *The Rise of Theodore Roosevelt*. Ballantine Books, 1980.

Niven, Penelope. *Carl Sandburg: A Biography*. Charles Scribner's Sons, 1991.

Pringle, Henry F. *Theodore Roosevelt*. Harcourt Brace Jovanovich, 1956.

Roosevelt, Theodore. *The Letters of Theodore Roosevelt*, selected and edited by Elting E. Morison. Harvard University Press, 1951.

Sandburg, Carl. *Always the Young Strangers*. Harcourt, Brace and Co., 1952.

Sandburg, Carl. *Ever the Winds of Chance*. University of Illinois Press, 1983.

Schlereth, Thomas J. *Victorian America: Transformations in Everyday Life, 1876–1915*. Harper Perennial, 1991.

Schlesinger, Arthur M., Jr., ed. *History of American Presidential Elections 1789–1968*. McGraw-Hill Book Co., 1971.

Smith, Page. *The Rise of Industrial America, Volume Six*. McGraw-Hill Book Co., 1984.

Stead, W. T. *The Americanization of the World or The Trend of the Twentieth Century*. Horace Markley, 1902.

Sullivan, Mark. *Our Times, Volume 1, 1900–1904*. Charles Scribner's Sons, 1926.

Trachtenberg, Alan. *The Incorporation of America: Culture and Society in the Guilded Age*. Hill & Wang, 1994.

Wall, Joseph Frazier. *Andrew Carnegie*. University of Pittsburgh Press, 1989.

White, William Allen. *The Autobiography of William Allen White*. University of Kansas Press, 1990.

Wiebe, Robert H. *The Search for Order—1877–1920*. Hill & Wang, 1980.

CHAPTER NOTES

Prologue

The quotes about progress in the nineteenth century could have come from any of a dozen newspapers. The subject was explored at length in the closing days of 1899 and then again at the end of 1900. For references in the book see *The New York Times*, December 31, 1899, page 20, and *The Washington Post*, January 1, 1901, page 6. For examples on the debate over the century question see: *The Boston Globe*, January 2, 1900, page 3; *The Independence* (Missouri) *Sentinel*, January 5, 1900, page 4; *The Examiner* (San Francisco), January 7, 1900, page 4. The story about Mrs. Elizabeth McIntyre appeared in *The Boston Globe*, December 31, 1900. The essay by John J. Ingalls and the comments by William Randolph Hearst appeared on the front page of the special "New Year 1900" section of *The Examiner* (San Francisco), December 31, 1899.

Jack London's essay, "The Shrinkage of the Planet," can be found in a small book titled *Revolutions and Other Essays,* by Jack London (Mills & Boon Ltd., London; published in the United States by the Macmillan Co., 1910).

Chapter One: New Year's Day

The White House reception was covered at length by the national press. Most useful was the coverage in *The Washington Post,* January 2, 1900, page 2, and in *The New York Times,* January 2, 1900, page 3. There is no better source for details about the White House and the Capitol in 1900 than *Thirty Years in Washington* by Mrs. John A. Logan (A. D. Worthington & Co., 1901). The *Report of the Architect of the United States Capitol to the Secretary of the Interior for the Fiscal Year Ended June 30, 1900* is a good source for information that is difficult to come by—from the replacement of the gas lamps to explanations for the unseemly odors filtering up from the house kitchen. *Thirty-Six Years In the White House* by Thomas F. Pendel (Neale Publishing Co., 1902) is a small curious book written by one of the White House doormen.

For the portrait of the McKinleys in this chapter and throughout the book, I am indebted to Margaret Leech's elegant biography, *In the Days of McKinley.*

Boston. Details about the weather, the horses, and the electric cabs appeared in the *Boston Evening Transcript,* January 1, 1900. The story of the city without a New Year's Eve appeared on page 6 of the same issue. For more on New Year's Eve see *The Boston Globe,* January 1, 1900. Details on **Concord** came in part from a brief, informal memoir, "Concord at the Turn of the Century," written by Laurence Eaton Richardson for the Morning Study Group, Concord Antiquarian Society (May 1960). Also helpful was *Concord, in the Days of Strawberries and Streetcars,* by Renee Garrelick (The Town of Concord, 1985).

References to **Emancipation Day** can be found in many eastern papers as well as in the African-American press. The description of Franklin, Louisiana, appeared in *The Freeman, An Illustrated Colored Newspaper* (Indianapolis, Indiana), January 27, 1900, page 1. Stories about the celebration in Savannah, Georgia, appeared in *The Savannah* (Georgia) *Tribune* on December 30, 1899, and on January 6, 1900. Professor Scarborough's quote was found in *The Freeman,* December 30, 1899, page 22. Mention of W.E.B. Du Bois's appearance at services in Atlanta can be found in both *The* (Atlanta) *Constitution,* December 30, 1899, page 8, and in *The Freeman,* January 20, 1900, page 6.

Chapter Two: January

Details about **Kansas City, Missouri,** were culled from *The Kansas City Star,* January 1–9, 1900. "The Central City of the West," by Charles S. Gleed (*The Cosmopolitan,* July 1900), is an entertaining portrait of the rise of the city. "Missouri," by Charles M. Harvey (*Atlantic Monthly,* July 1900), is a look at the state's history and politics in 1900. For details about **Independence** see *An Illustrated Description of Independence, Missouri* (Press of Examiner Printing Company, 1902); *Independence and 20th Century Pioneers* by Pearl Wilcox (Wilcox, Independence, 1979); *The Jackson* (Missouri) *County Examiner* and *The Independence* (Missouri) *Sentinel.* For the tone of a small Midwest town at the turn of the century, see William Allen White's brilliant essay, "A Typical Kansas Community" (*Atlantic Monthly,* 1897). David McCullough's *Truman* also provides a superb portrait of the town that was so central in shaping Harry Truman's life.

San Francisco. *The* (San Francisco) *Examiner*, January 1–3, 1900, set the scene in the city for the beginning of the year. Details about the early settlement were found in "San Francisco's First Post Office and Its Builder," by Hester A Benedict (*Overland Monthly*, June 1900). For additional material see: "The Right Hand of the Continent," by Charles F. Lummis (*Harper's New Monthly Magazine*, January 1900); "The Vines and Wines of California," by Andrea Sbarboro (*Overland Monthly*, January 1900); *This Was San Francisco*, compiled and edited by Oscar Lewis (David McKay Co., Inc., 1962).

For over a year, *The Examiner* extolled the virtues of commerce in the Pacific. At the start of 1899, the front page of the New Year Edition carried the headline: "California's Bright New Year Outlook—Opening of Our New Oriental Possessions." Early in 1900 there were numbers of articles on America's growing commercial strength. "Our Commercial Expansion," by Frederic Emory (*Munsey's*, January 1900), is quoted in the book. For growth of rail and steamship lines, see "The Great Trade with Orient," on the front page of the *Boston Evening Transcript*, January 3, 1900.

The Philippines. Rudyard Kipling's poem "The White Man's Burden" was published in 1899. According to a note in Mark Sullivan's *Our Times*, the poem "circled the earth in a day, and by repetition became hackneyed in a week." It was still much quoted in 1900. Senator Albert J. Beveridge's speech was covered by the press and is quoted in Walter Lord's *The Good Years,* page 8. Mark Twain's comment about redesigning the American flag appeared in his essay "To the Person Sitting in Darkness" (*North American Review*, February 1901).

Andrew Carnegie's defection from the Republican party was reported by *The Kansas City Star* on January 4, 1900. The charge that the Republican administration was lying about the war appeared in the *St. Louis Post-Dispatch*, January 3, page 4. The quote by Chauncey Depew, describing the Pacific as an American lake, can be found in Carl N. Degler's *Out of Our Past*, page 510. William Jennings Bryan's speech attacking U.S. actions in the Philippines was reported at length by *The Boston Herald*, January 31, 1900, page 3.

Walter LaFeber's *The American Age: U.S. Foreign Policy at Home and Abroad* is most useful in understanding America's expanding interests in Asia.

Jack London. *The Economics of the Klondike*, by Jack London, was published in the *American Monthly Review of Reviews*, January 1900. All the London letters can be found in *The Letters of Jack London, Volume One: 1896–1905*, edited by Earle Labor, Robert C. Leits, III, and I. Milo Shepard (Stanford University Press, 1988). "Dear Miss Strunsky, O Pshaw!" is on page 144. For more about London, see *Jack: A Biography of Jack London* by Andrew Sinclair (Harper & Row, 1977) and *The Pictorial Life of Jack London* by Russ Kingman (Crown Publishers, Inc., 1979).

The House of Representatives and John F. Fitzgerald. Doris Kearns Goodwin's rich study, *The Fitzgeralds and the Kennedys*, scarcely touches on Fitzgerald in 1900 but provides essential background on his life, on Irish immigrants, and on Boston at the turn of the century. The story about "Free Bathing and Barbering for Statesmen" appeared in *The* (Louisville, Kentucky) *Courier-Journal*, January 3, 1900, page 4. The story about Speaker Henderson's new leg appeared in *The New York Times*, April 16, 1900, page 2. The interview with **Brigham Roberts** appeared in *The Washington Bee*, January 13, 1900. While the Roberts case was widely reported by the national press, the most interesting coverage appeared in *The Deseret Evening News* (Salt Lake City). Extensive articles reflecting on the anti-Mormon tenor of the debate and the "mendacious assaults upon the people of Utah" ran from December 30, 1899, throughout January 1900.

Rumors about General Arthur MacArthur appeared in *The Washington Post*, February 8, 1900. His appointment as commander of the Philippines was not confirmed until April 7, 1900.

War Veterans. The startling figures on veteran pensions appeared in *The* (Louisville, Kentucky) *Courier-Journal*, December 30, 1900, page 10. By far the most interesting writer on **Carl Sandburg** is

Carl Sandburg. *Always the Young Strangers*, a memoir of the writer's early years, is an evocative portrait of small-town life. Company C's return to Galesburg begins on page 420. The description of Sandburg's home, study area, and musings about his future appear in *Ever the Winds of Chance*, pages 8–11. Sandburg intended that this work would pick up where the first book left off. Sadly, it was never finished.

Much of the research on **Barney Dougall** and his family was provided by Rell G. Francis of Springville, Utah. The material included: "A Brief History of Springville, Utah," compiled and written by Don Carlos Johnson (Springville, 1900); "Biography of Hugh Macswein Dougall (Pioneer) Came to Utah 1849, Written by His Daughter Mary Emma J. Dougall Gardner." Rell Francis's own book, *The Utah Photographs of George Edward Anderson* (University of Nebraska Press, 1979), not only has wonderful photographs but also includes interesting material on the area and its people.

Finnish Immigration. *Boston Evening Transcript*, February 28, 1900, page 8.

Chapter Three: February

The story about **Henry Ford** can be found on page 47 in Robert Lacey's book, *Ford: The Men and the Machine* (Little, Brown and Co., 1986). The most helpful work on **Wilbur and Orville Wright** is *The Bishop's Boys* by Tom D. Crouch. Also useful: *Visions of a Flying Machine: The Wright Brothers and the Process of Invention* by Peter L. Jakab (Smithsonian Institution Press, 1990) and *The Papers of Orville and Wilbur Wright*, Marvin W. McFarland, ed. (McGraw-Hill, 1953). The Simon Newcomb quote is in Mark Sullivan's *Our Times*, page 366. **The Railroads.** Frank Munsey's article, "The Annihilation of Space," appeared in *Munsey's Magazine*, October 1900. The explanation of Standard Railway Time appears in Thomas J. Schlereth's *Victorian America: Transformations in Everyday Life, 1876–1915*, page 29. This book has a wealth of information about daily life. The Brooks Adams quote on the railroads appears in Page Smith's *The Rise of Industrial America*, page 921.

The Assassination of William Goebel. On January 13, 1900, *The Savannah* (Georgia) *Tribune* was among the papers forecasting violence in Frankfort. On January 31, 1900, the day after Goebel was shot, *The* (Louisville, Kentucky) *Courier-Journal* devoted seven pages to the story. The paper provided extensive coverage until the day after Goebel's death, February 4, 1900. The story was also covered by *The New York Times* and *The Washington Post*. For background on the controversy, see *William C. Goebel: The Politics of Wrath*, by James C. Klotter (University Press of Kentucky, 1977).

The McKinleys' social life was regularly reported in the Social and Personal column of *The Washington Post*. For a good example at this time, see February 11, 1900, page 16. *The Washington Bee*'s announcement that the president would run again appeared on the paper's editorial page, February 3, 1900. The remodeling of the McKinley home in Canton was reported by *The Washington Post*, February 15, 1900.

The Philippines. The story on the 48th Infantry appeared in *The* (Philadelphia) *Evening Bulletin*, February 22, 1900, page 4. John Barrett's article, "The Philippine Islands and Their Environment," was published in *The National Geographic Magazine*, January 1900. An equally enthusiastic article by Barrett was published by *Harper's Weekly*, July 28, 1900. A news account about the fracas involving **Senator Pettigrew** appeared in the *The Washington Post*, February 1, 1900. A story about **Fitzgerald** violating his franking privileges appeared in *The New York Times*, February 11, 1900, page 12.

Nome. *The New York Times* article on the rush to Nome appeared on April 11, 1900. Much was written about the move into the Alaskan gold fields. Tappan Adney, a journalist known for his colorful coverage of the Klondike, was now covering Nome for *Collier's Weekly*. *Harper's Weekly* also published articles and wonderful photographs of the gold seekers. The **Jack London** quotes can all be found in *Letters*. "Now I feel comfortable" is on page 161; on writing poetry and losing faith in any "cooperative commonwealth" is on page 152; " . . . your company has ever been a great delight" is on page 163.

Chapter Four: March

Axel Jarlson. Between 1902 and 1906, Hamilton Holt, editor of *The Independent*, interviewed seventy-five "undistinguished Americans," among them Axel Jarlson. These "life stories" of ordinary people were edited and republished in *Plain Folk*, by David M. Katzman and William M. Tuttle Jr., in 1982. For a sense of the sophistication of American wheat growers in 1900, see "The Movement of Wheat," by Ray Stannard Baker (*McClure's Magazine*, November 1899). Carl N. Degler's quote, "transformed raw nature," is in *Out of Our Past,* page 350.

    New York City. In 1900, the Scottish journalist William Archer wrote a short evocative book about his eight-week visit to the United States in 1899, *America To-Day: Observations and Reflections* (William Heineman, London, 1900). Among the contemporary articles about the city, see "New York at Night," by James B. Carrington (*Scribner's Magazine*, March 1900); "The Skyscrapers of New York" (*Collier's Weekly*, December 1, 1900); "A Plea for New York," by J. K. Paulding (*Atlantic Monthly*, February 1901). **The McKinleys'** visit to New York was well covered by *The New York Times* and *The World* (New York), March 1–5, 1900. Details on detectives William Funston and Henry Foye can be found in *The World*, March 4, 1900, page 2.

    Olga Nethersole. The titillating stories quoted from the *St. Louis Post-Dispatch* are both on the front page, August 16, 1900. The anti-*Sapho* campaign was begun by *The World* (New York) in mid-February; the story about "*Sapho*-crazed women" appeared February 18, 1900, page 2. *The World* carried the interview with Pastor Newell Dwight Hillis on February 19, 1900, page 8. The trial was covered by *The New York Times*, April 4–7, 1900. The reopening of *Sapho* was reported by *The Times*, April 7, 1900.

    The description of sexual attitudes in 1900 was informed by two popular marriage manuals: *What a Young Husband Ought to Know* by Sylvanus Stall (Vir Publishing, 1897) and *What a Young Wife Ought to Know* by Emma F. Angell Drake (Vir Publishing, 1901). Warning women about "men's lower natures," Drake recommended separate bedrooms as a means of helping husbands practice self-control. Drake was most concerned about young women who seemed better informed about "the methods of preventing conception, or producing abortion . . . than of any preparation for motherhood." In 1900, the birthrate among native-born Americans was being outstripped by immigrant families and Drake was not alone in her fear that "the American race is fast dying out." She urged a minimum of four children per *American* family.

    Papers given at the Sexual Hygiene meeting in Chicago were compiled and published by the editorial staff of the Alkaloidal Clinic, Chicago (Clinic Publishing Co., 1902), with the warning that "this book is written for doctors and no one else." *Women and Economics* by Charlotte Perkins Stetson (Small, Maynard & Co., 1898) is a remarkable argument on the need for women to be financially independent. *The World* (New York), February 25, 1900, published a special supplement (E5) on the "Ideals of Courtship and the Realities of Marriage." For more on the Free Love movement and the Heywoods, see Page Smith's *The Rise of Industrial America*, page 269.

    For more about Anthony Comstock's accomplishments, see "The 27th Annual Report of the New York Society for the Suppression of Vice," January 1, 1900. The report claims that by the beginning of 1900, Comstock had already traveled 497,732 miles to advance his cause.

    Jack London's quotes are all from *Letters*. The reference to moving is on page 173; "the habit of money spending" is on page 165; "Sunday evening I opened transactions for a wife . . . " is on page 178; "Dear Anna, How glad your letter has made me . . . " is on page 179.

Chapter Five: March–April

The Paris Exposition. Among the hundreds of newspaper and magazine articles published by the American press, the more interesting include *Scientific American*'s special supplement, March 31, 1900; "Paris and the Exposition," by Albert Shaw (*American Monthly Review of Reviews*, June 1900); "The Paris Exposition," by William T. Stead (*The Cosmopolitan*, August 1900). Also useful is *Harper's Guide to Paris and the Exposition of 1900* (Harper & Brothers, 1900). For **Henry Adams's** quote, see *Selected Letters*, Ernest Samuel, ed. (Belknap Press of Harvard University, 1992), page 382. The meditation on the dynamo is from *The Education of Henry Adams*, page 380. *The Washington Post* article speculating on the "awesome forces of the future" was written by Henry Litchfield West, December 31, 1900, page 3.

Details from W. T. Stead's book, *The Americanization of the World,* can be found on pages 163 and 164. The comment by the Prince of Belgium is on page 179. The quote about "the American peril" can be found on page 176.

Frances Benjamin Johnston. There is no biography of FBJ. There is an introductory essay in *A Talent for Detail: The Photographs of Miss Frances Benjamin Johnston,* by Pete Daniel and Raymond Smock (Harmony Books, 1974), that is helpful. Also see *The Hampton Album with Introduction by Lincoln Kirsten* (Doubleday, Inc., 1966). FBJ's date book and correspondence, including the May 15, 1900, letter from Thomas J. Calloway, can be found in the Manuscripts Division, Library of Congress.

Paul Laurence Dunbar's return to D.C. was reported by *The Freeman, An Illustrated Colored Newspaper*, March 10, 1900, page 4. The review by William Dean Howells can be found on page 13 in *The Life and Works of Paul Laurence Dunbar*, by Lida Weck Wiggins (Kraus Reprint Co., 1971). Dunbar's poem "Life" can be found on page 140, and "We Wear the Mask" on page 184. Dunbar's article, "Negro Life in Washington," appeared in *Harper's Weekly*, January 13, 1900. The anecdote about W.E.B. Du Bois's surprise on discovering that Dunbar was a black man can be found on page 176 in David Levering Lewis's biography, *W.E.B. Du Bois: Biography of a Race*.

For additional biographical material, see *Paul Laurence Dunbar: Poet of his People*, by Benjamin Brawley (University of North Carolina Press, 1936); *Paul Laurence Dunbar and His Song*, by Virginia Cunningham (Dodd, Mead & Co., 1947); "A Biography of Paul Laurence Dunbar," by Gossie Harold Hudson (Ph.D. dissertation, Ohio State University, 1970); "Paul Laurence Dunbar," by Doris Lucas Laryea in *The Dictionary of Literary Biography*, Volume Fifty: *Afro-American Writers Before the Harlem Renaissance* (Gale Research, Inc., 1986).

To understand the world in which black Americans found themselves in 1900, *W.E.B. Du Bois: Biography of a Race,* by David Levering Lewis, and *The Promise of the New South: Life After Reconstruction,* by Edward L. Ayers, are both important. T. Thomas Fortune's comment on the need to build schoolhouses appeared in a column entitled "Negro Education" in *Harper's Weekly* (February 10, 1900, page 120). The quote from Sutton E. Griggs is found in Edward L. Ayer's *The Promise of the New South*, page 72. For additional information on Du Bois's reponse to the lynching of Sam Hose, see Lewis's biography, page 226; the quote "What, after all, am I" is on page 172.

Opening of the Paris Exposition. The comments on the opening day speeches that appeared in the *Deutsche Tageszeitung* were republished on the front page of *The New York Times*, April 16, 1900.

Chapter Six: April

There is no better source on **Theodore Roosevelt** than his collected letters. All those quoted in this book were found in *The Letters of Theodore Roosevelt*. The letter about TR's children is on page 1,216. The description of the governor's mansion during TR's tenure comes from notes written by Richard O. Weber, supplied by Curatorial Services, New York State Executive Mansion. Background on Roosevelt's thinking and convoluted struggles over the vice-presidential nomination are revealed in his correspondence with Henry Cabot Lodge, found in *Selections from the Correspondence of Theodore Roosevelt and Henry Cabot Lodge, Volume 1* (Charles Scribner's Sons, 1925). TR's speech before the New York legislature appeared in the *Boston Evening Transcript*, January 3, 1900, page 4. William Allen White's comment about TR is found in Edmund Morris's *The Rise of Theodore Roosevelt*, page 704.

New York City. The story about dangers in Central Park appeared in *The New York Times*, March 8, 1900, page 2. The battle between Anthony Comstock and the gambling interests was a running story in *The Times*, March 8–11, 1900. "Police Betray Comstock" appeared in *The Times*, March 11, 1900, page 2. William Allen White's profile on **Richard Croker** was published by *McClure's Magazine*, January 1901. "Running a Campaign to Win," by Richard Croker (*Collier's Weekly*, October 27, 1900), is an interesting vision of a political machine from Croker's perspective. Speculation about Croker and William Jennings Bryan appeared in *Harper's Weekly*, July 28, 1900. Among the contemporary materials used in the description of the **Very Rich** are "House-keeping in a Millionaire's Family," by M. E. Carter (*Ladies' Home Journal*, January 1901); *Manners and Social Usages,* by Mrs. John Sherwood (Mary Elizabeth Wilson) (Harper, 1897); *The Wellbred Girl in Society,* by Mrs. Burton Harrison (Doubleday and McClure, 1904).

The story of **Andrew Carnegie's** mansion, the "$1,000,000 Playhouse for Baby," was reported by *The World* (New York) on March 4, 1900. For an interesting contemporary view of Carnegie, see "The Many-Sided Andrew Carnegie: A Citizen of the Republic," by Henry Wysham Lanier (in *World's Work*, April 1901). The primary modern work on Carnegie is Joseph Frazier Wall's biography, *Andrew Carnegie*. The story of the engagement of **John D. Rockefeller's** daughter, Alta Rockefeller, and the expansion of Pocantico Hills appeared in the same issue of *The New York Times*, April 13, 1900. For background on the rise of Rockefeller and Standard Oil, see Daniel J. Boorstin's *The Americans: The Democratic Experience* and Daniel Yergin's *The Prize* (Simon & Schuster, 1991). **John Fitzgerald's** speech demanding a curb on corporations can be found in the Congressional Record—House, March 31, 1900. The payments to Senator Foraker were reported in *The Rockefellers: An American Dynasty*, by Peter Collier and David Horowitz (Holt, Rhinehart and Winston, 1976).

Chapter Seven: April

The story of **M. E. Ravage** can be found in his 1917 memoir, *An American in the Making: The Life Story of an Immigrant* (Dover Publications, Inc., 1971). The description of America fever sweeping Vaslui begins on page 27. Leaving home is described in a chapter that begins on page 46. Kate Holladay Claghorn's quote on "the half-worked country" appeared in her article, "Our Immigrants and Ourselves" (*Atlantic Monthly*, October 1900). Also see "The Changing Character of Immigration" (*World's Work*, February 1901) and "Immigration to the United States," by Terence V. Powderly (*Collier's Weekly*, September 1, 1900). The story about New York as "the heathen city" appeared in *The Deseret Evening News* (Salt Lake City), January 16, 1900, page 3.

Theodore Roosevelt and Jacob Riis. The TR letter thanking Riis for the offer of pigeons can be found on page 1,237 of *Letters*. For comments by TR on the need for tenement reform, see *The New York Times*, February 11, 1900, page 6. Riis's concerns in 1900 are reflected in his "The New York Tenement-House Commission" in *American Monthly Review of Reviews*, June 1900. For more on TR's relationship with Riis, see Henry Pringle's biography, *Theodore Roosevelt*, and Edmund Morris's *The Rise of Theodore Roosevelt*. For the arrival of **Marcus Ravage** in New York City, see *An American in the Making*, page 59.

Labor. Every major newspaper beginning early in the year was reporting "labor unrest." For example, see *The New York Times*, April 3, 1900, page 1. For information on **John Mitchell** and the rise of the United Mine Workers, see *The Kingdom of Coal*, by Donald L. Miller and Richard E. Sharpless (University of Pennsylvania Press, 1985), and *Divided Loyalties: The Public and Private Life of Labor Leader John Mitchell*, by Craig Phelan (State University of New York Press, 1994). Robert Hunter's studies were published in his book *Poverty* (MacMillan Co., 1904).

The account of the strike at **Croton Dam** is based primarily on coverage by *The New York Times*, which began with a small item on April 3, 1900, page 1. On April 16, *The Times* reported that troops had been called out. The description of the militia leaving the city and the murder of Sergeant Douglas are on April 17, 1900, pages 1 and 2. The raid on strikers' homes appeared on April 20, 1900, page 2. The report on the anarchists breaking up the meeting in New York City appeared in *The Chicago Daily Tribune*, April 20, 1900, page 1. The arrival of the Hungarian workers at the end of the strike was reported by *The Times*, April 24, 1900, page 3.

Chapter Eight: May

Dewey Day. The newspapers had a field day with Admiral Dewey's presidential aspirations. *The Chicago Daily Tribune* declared, "Dewey's Bomb a Blank Shot," April 5, 1900, page 5. *The New York Times* reported that Dewey was "Willing to Run for President on Either Ticket," April 5, 1900, page 1, and thought the position easy. *The Times* followed up on April 6 and 7, 1900. On April 9, 1900, the paper observed, "Dewey an Impulsive Man." There is also an amusing account of Dewey mania in Page Smith's *The Rise of Industrial America*, page 879.

Scofield. The best account I found of the disaster is a book issued at the time to raise money for miners' families: *History of the Scofield Mine Disaster*, by James W. Dilly (Knights of Pythias of Scofield, 1900). Also see "Tragedy at Scofield," by Allan Kent Powell (*Utah Historical Quarterly*, Spring 1973).

Chapter Nine: June

Washington. Wrangling in the Capitol was described in *The Washington Post* on June 6 and 7, 1900. The description of Fitzgerald's singalong appeared on the paper's front page on June 8, 1900. Information about the founding of the Capitol came in part from "Centennial of the National Capitol" (*The Cosmopolitan*, December 1900). For details about the Federal Bureaus in the city, see *Thirty Years in Washington*, by Mrs. John A. Logan. Articles on the 1900 census include: "The Census of 1900," by William R. Merriam (*North American Review*, January 1900); "American Census Methods by Walter F. Willcox" (*Forum*, October 1900); "The Population of the United States During the Next Ten Centuries," by H. S. Pritchett (*Popular Science*, November 1900). TR's letter about Senator Platt can be found on page 1,332 of *Letters*. The story of legislators learning to use a graphophone appeared in *The Washington Post*, June 13, 1900, page 3.

The Republican Convention and the battle over Theodore Roosevelt's nomination were covered extensively by *The Washington Post*. On June 17, the paper announced that Senator Platt was blocking Senator Hanna; on June 18, the "lasso was around Roosevelt's neck." On June 19, *The Post* declared "Hanna Shows Fight" and on June 21 reported that Hanna "Bows to Party." The enthusiasm for TR—"He was all that the idolizing thousands wanted"—was described by Edward W. Townsend in "The National Republican Convention" (*Harper's Weekly*, June 30, 1900). The description of McKinley at the White House is from *The Washington Post*, June 22, 1900, page 2.

Walter LaFeber's long chapter on the "Election of 1900" in *History of American Presidential Elections 1789-1968*, edited by Arthur M. Schlesinger Jr., is a basic primer on the campaign.

Carl Sandburg's concerns about TR and the vice presidency appear in *Ever the Winds of Chance*, page 6. A description of Sandburg's trip through Bureau County, Illinois, is on pages 80–85 of the same book. The quotation about Sandburg's family album appears in *Always the Young Strangers*, page 57. For background on **Scott Joplin**, see: *Scott Joplin*, by James Haskins and Kathleen Benson (Doubleday & Co., 1978); *Dancing to a Black Man's Tune: A Life of Scott Joplin*, by Susan Curtis (University of Missouri Press, 1994); *Path of Resistance*, by David Thelen (Oxford University Press, 1986).

The most extensive coverage on the **Bubonic Plague** in San Francisco appeared in *The Examiner* in March, and then again in June. For a description of the quarantine, see March 8, 1900. For activities of the health authorities see March 23 and 24, 1900. *The Examiner* reported "tampering with bodies," on June 3, 1900. Another case of plague was confirmed by the paper on June 4, 1900. The federal quarantine was reported on June 17, 1900. The lifting of the quarantine was announced on June 19, 1900.

Key articles on the plague include: "Plague in San Francisco" (*Scientific American*, June 16, 1900); "Bubonic Plague" (*Current Literature*, Volume 29, 1900); "New Theories of Plague Propagation" (*Scientific American*, July 14, 1900); "The Plague Epidemic" (*The Independent*, July 19, 1900); "The Bubonic Plague," by Frederick G. Novy (*Popular Science Monthly*, October 1900); "The Great Mortality," by Professor Edward P. Cheyney (*Popular Science Monthly*, August 1901).

Jack London's quote on bicycling is on page 193 of *Letters*; the letter that begins "Dear Anna, Comrades!" is on page 198.

Chapter Ten: July–August

The Heat Wave was a major story for much of the country, from the end of June well into September. *The New York Times* carried a number of stories on the front page, August 12, 1900. The story about firing cannon at hailstorms in Europe was published by *The New York Times* on August 15, 1900; the *St. Louis Post-Dispatch* carried a letter on the subject, December 30, 1900, page 6. Ambrose Bierce's comments appeared in his column in *The Examiner* (San Francisco), December 30, 1900. The request for permission to distribute cool air to Washington, D.C., buildings was reported by *Scientific American*, June 30, 1900. For more about the air-cooling machine for President James Garfield, see "Cooling Garfield," by James C. Clark (*Journal of American Culture*, Summer 1990) and "The Air-Conditioned Century," by Robert Friedman (*American Heritage*, August–September 1984).

Kansas City. Governor Roosevelt's unexpected appearance in Kansas City was reported by *The Kansas City Star*, July 2, 1900. The best source for details on the **Democratic Convention**, not surprisingly, is *The Star*, July 2–6, 1900. The scenic tour of the abattoir can be found on July 5, 1900, page 12. Colorful feature material about the convention appeared in the *St. Louis Post-Dispatch*, July 4, 1900, page 4. For additional material see *The Washington Post* and *The Boston Globe*, July 5, 1900. The account of **William Jennings Bryan** receiving news of his nomination is based on a story in *The Washington Post*, July 6, 1900, page 4. For a good contemporary portrait of the Democratic candidate, see "Bryan," by William Allen White (*McLure's Magazine*, July 1900).

The report of the alienist leaving for the Philippines appeared in *The Washington Post*, July 6, 1900, page 6. Newspaper lists of casualties were regularly broken down into three categories: the ill, the wounded, and the insane. For one example, see *The Washington Post*, February 1, 1900. An extended article on "Insanity Among Our Soldiers in the Philippines" appeared in the *St. Louis Post-Dispatch*, April 15, 1900.

Governor Roosevelt's arrival in Canton, Ohio, was reported by *The Washington Post*, July 7, 1900. **Scandals.** *The Washington Post*'s report on the Chief of the Bureau of Statistics working on the Republican campaign material appeared June 15, 1900, page 3. The paper's report on illegal solicitation of Capitol employees was published June 14, 1900.

The Boxer Rebellion was a major story in the national press beginning in June. Because communications with China were poor, the newspapers were filled with speculation. Magazine accounts, often published six weeks after the fact, were more accurate. Beginning in July, *Harper's* and *Collier's* carried in-depth reports, often accompanied by remarkable photographs. Most useful are Frederick Palmer's colorful accounts published in *Collier's Weekly*. "The Taking of Tien Tsin" appeared in *Collier's*, September 8, 1900. As Americans began returning from China, personal accounts of the siege appeared in the press: "First Stories from Lips of Those Who Suffered in Pekin" (*The Examiner*, October 2, 1900); "A Woman's Diary of the Siege of Pekin," by Mrs. E. K. Lowery (*McClure's Magazine*, November 1900). "Besieged in Peking," by Cecile Payen (*The Century Magazine*, January 1, 1901), is quoted at length in the book.

For the story of **Herbert and Lou Henry Hoover's** experience in Tien Tsin see *The Memoirs of Herbert Hoover, Years of Adventure, 1874–1920*, by Herbert Hoover (Macmillan Co., 1951) and *The Life of Herbert Hoover*, by George H. Nash (W. W. Norton & Co., 1983). Unpublished notes and sketches of the siege by Lou Henry Hoover are at the Herbert Hoover Presidential Library in West Branch, Iowa. **TR on China** appeared in *The Washington Post*, July 6, 1900.

Americans Abroad. The notes about Frances Benjamin Johnston aboard the *Potsdam* are from her mother's diary (Frances A. Johnston, Manuscripts Division, Library of Congress). Instructions for travelers appeared in "When the Novice Goes to Sea," by John R. Spears (*The Cosmopolitan*, May 1900). **The Paris Exposition.** For general information, see citations, chapter five. The story about the dinner held at the U.S. Pavilion for "colored people" appeared in *The Freeman*, December 27, 1900. Du Bois's account of the Negro Exhibit, "The American Negro At Paris," was published in *The American Monthly Review of Reviews*, November 1900.

The New York Race Riot was reported by *The New York Times* and *The World* (New York) on August 16–18, 1900. On August 17, *The World* carried a roundup of comments from editors of Southern newspapers, page 2. In one way or another, most used the opportunity to make the point that the South did not have a monopoly on race problems. The editor of a paper in Birmingham, Alabama, hoped that "certain anti-Southern howlers in the North would begin their work of reformation at home." The note about Paul Dunbar was found in *The Times*, August 20, 1900. For additional material on the riot, see *Harlem: The Making of a Ghetto—Negro New York 1890–1930*, by Gilbert Osofsky (Harper Torchbooks, 1965).

Chapter Eleven: August

Lieutenant Robert E. and Josephine Peary. News of the *Windward* sailing north appeared in *The New York Times*, July 29, 1900, page 17. For magazine articles about Peary, see "The Quest for the North Pole" (*Munsey*, August 1901) and "Peary's Work in 1900 and 1901" (*National Geographic*,

October 1901). The story of the confrontation between Josephine Peary and Peary's mistress appears in Pierre Berton's *The Arctic Grail: The Quest for the Northwest Passage and the North Pole, 1818–1909* (Viking, 1988).

Among the most interesting accounts of the **Zeppelin** are: "The First Flight of Count Zeppelin's Air Ship" by Eugen Wolf (*McClure's Magazine*, November 1900); "The Ascension of Count Zeppelin's Air Ship" (*Scientific American*, August 11, 1900); "The First Two Trial Trips of Von Zeppelin's Air Ship" (*Scientific American*, October 27, 1900). H. G. Wells's comments about the use of aircraft in war appeared in the third part of a fascinating work titled "Anticipations: An Experiment in Prophecy," published as a five-part series in the *North American Review*, beginning June 1901. **Wilbur Wright's** letter to the Weather Bureau at Kitty Hawk is in Tom D. Crouch's *The Bishop's Boys*, page 182.

The Boxer Rebellion. See citations, chapter ten. On the relief of Peking, see Frederick Palmer's two articles, "The March to Pekin" and "In Pekin After the Siege," which appeared in *Collier's Weekly*, October 13 and 20, 1900. *The New York Times*'s report on the lifting of the siege appeared August 31, 1900, page 2. Also see "The Pekin Relief Column" and "The Struggle for the Pekin Wall," both in *The Century Magazine*, December 1900. The editorial in the *St. Louis Post-Dispatch* appeared on August 18, 1900.

Anarchist Plot against McKinley was front page news on August 18 and 19, 1900. *The World* (New York) reported, "Anarchists Held on Plot Against McKinley" and "Day and Night McKinley's Every Step Is Watched" (August 18, 1900). *Harper's Weekly* (August 11, 1900) warned that politicians preaching the gospel "of discontent" were contributing to the "anarchistic cause."

Chapter Twelve: September

Education. Sandburg's comment about Jon Grubb, the cow-tending professor, is on page 424, and the description of Miss Hague, the teacher "who knew her history," is on page 138, of *Always the Young Strangers*. Concern about cramming information into youthful minds, "like sausage meat into skins," was found in the article "For Character, Not Cleverness" (*Gunton's Magazine*, March 1900, page 246). Other articles reflected in this section include: "The New Spirit of Education," by Arthur Henry (*Munsey's Magazine*, May 1900); "Some Old-Fashioned Doubts About New-Fashioned Education," by L.B.R. Briggs (*Atlantic Monthly*, October 1900); "Problems Which Confront the Public School at the Opening of the Twentieth Century," by Superintendent Aaron Gove (*Education*, December 1900).

The Senate Committee hearings on Washington, D.C., public schools were reported by *The Washington Post* on February 20, 1900, page 2. A book celebrating the District school system and its modern teaching methods, *The New Education Illustrated*, by Edith C. Westcott, was illustrated with photographs by Frances Benjamin Johnston (B. F. Johnston Publishing Co., 1900). For a typical comment about overcrowding in public schools, see "A Chronic and Disgraceful Neglect" in *The Washington Post*, December 31, 1899, page 6. Mary Antin's quote is on page 186 of her memoir, *The Promised Land* (Penguin, 1997).

Football. The quote on "football slaughter" is in the December issue of *Education*, page 198. Intercollegiate football was well covered on the sports pages by the national press. Details about the evolution of football are from two issues of *Outing* —January 1900 and November 1900. Descriptions of the Harvard and Yale teams alo appeared in the January article. In November the magazine published "A Symposium of Football," a collection of essays by numbers of well-known former players and coaches, including Walter Camp. Helen Keller's description of the Harvard-Yale game in 1899 is in a letter to her sister, published in *The Story of My Life*, by Helen Keller (Doubleday &

Co., 1954, page 207). *The Boston Globe* carried a story on the Harvard and Yale teams, September 16, 1900, page 33.

Galveston. The best accounts of the disaster were published directly after the event: *Galveston in Nineteen Hundred*, edited by Clarence Ousley of the *Galveston Tribune* (William C. Chase, 1900); *The Horrors of a Stricken City*, by Murat Halstead (American Publishers Association, 1900); *The True Story of the Galveston Flood As Told by the Survivors* (American Book and Bible House, 1900). *The Examiner* (San Francisco) began extensive coverage on September 10. The paper's special correspondent Winifred Black, also known as Annie Laurie, was sent to the island by publisher William Randolph Hearst to spearhead his relief campaign. The campaign had the dual effect of providing publicity for Hearst as well as helping the people of Galveston.

The staff of *The Galveston Daily News*, in what must have been a heroic effort, published the first casualty list the day after the storm, Sunday, September 9. On September 10 and 11 the paper began to expand. The next day, readers were not only guided to free food stations but were also informed that American artists, painter James Whistler and sculptor Augustus Saint-Gaudens, had been medalists at the Paris Exposition. An article in *Harper's Weekly*, "Galveston—What It Was, and What It Will Be," October 6, 1900, argued that the city's existence was "a logical commercial necessity." The Lafcadio Hearn quote is from a *National Geographic* essay, "The Lessons of Galveston," published October 1900.

The Wrights at Kitty Hawk. The description of Wilbur's journey to Kitty Hawk is described in a letter written September 13, 1900 (*The Papers of Orville and Wilbur Wright*, page 24). Wilbur's letter to his father is on page 25. His two attempts at "flying" the glider, first with tether ropes and then without, are described on pages 189 and 199 in *The Bishop's Boys*. For additional material see *Visions of a Flying Machine*.

Chapter Thirteen: September–October

The Election Campaign. The story of the campaign of 1900 is based in large part on contemporary newspaper accounts and magazine stories. TR's appearances in Michigan were reported in *The Washington Post*, September 8, 1900, page 3. *Harper's Weekly* had a regular column called "The Progress of the Campaign," which was filled with anecdotes about the campaign and virulent anti-Bryan material. The coverage in *Collier's Weekly* tended to favor the Democrats. The article "How a President Is Elected," by A. Maurice Low, was published in *Scribner's Magazine*, June 1900. The description of Governor Roosevelt's day on the campaign trail is in Edmund Morris's *The Rise of Theodore Roosevelt*, page 730.

The United Mine Workers' Strike. From mid-September through the end of October, the eastern newspapers carried daily stories on the strike. This account primarily reflects articles from *The New York Times*, *The World* (New York), *The Evening Post* (New York), *The Washington Post*, and two Philadelphia papers, *The Inquirer* and *The Evening Bulletin*. On September 14, 1900, *The Times* reported on the "Causes of the Great Coal Miners' Strike," written from John Mitchell's perspective. The response by political party leaders appeared in *The Evening Bulletin*, September 14, 1900. There were lengthy articles in the papers the first day of the strike; see *The Evening Bulletin*, September 17, 1900, and *The Times*, September 18, 1900. *The Evening Bulletin* carried an article about the breaker boys, "Child Slaves of the Mines," September 19, 1900, page 12. The confrontation between Mitchell and John Markle was reported by the *The Times*, September 20, 1900.

The trouble in Shenandoah was a front page story in *The New York Times*, September 22, 1900. It was this same article that described the Hungarian's body abandoned in the gutter. Numbers of magazines covered the strike in depth. One of the best articles on events in Shenandoah was written by Stephen Bonsal, "The Strike of the Coal Miner" (*Collier's Weekly*, October 6, 1900). *The Times* carried stories on Mark Hanna's negotiations on September 25, 27, 29, and October 19, 1900. The end of the strike was reported in *The Times* on October 16, 1900. Also useful: "The Coal Miners' Strike" (*Outlook*, September 29, 1900); "The Strike of the Pennsylvania Coal-Miners" (*Harper's Weekly*, September 29, 1900); "The Coal Strike, The Families of the Miners," by Lillian Betts (*Outlook*, October 13, 1900); "The Great Coal Strike," by John Mitchell (*Independent*, November 1, 1900); "The Mine Worker's Life and Aims," by John Mitchell (*The Cosmopolitan*, October 1901).

For a full account of the strike, see *The Kingdom of Coal*, by Donald L. Miller and Richard E. Sharpless, and *Divided Loyalties*, by Craig Phelan. For additional background, see *The Anthracite Coal Strike of 1902*, by Robert J. Cornell (Catholic University Press, 1957).

Chapter Fourteen: October–November

The **Plot Against McKinley** was reported by San Francisco's *The Examiner*, October 3, 1900. On October 11, *The Examiner* reported that an anarchist in Italy confessed knowledge of a plot to kill either McKinley or Bryan. But up until the election, the Republican press and party leaders continued to accuse Bryan of stirring up class tensions and playing into the hands of anarchists and Socialists.

The Campaign. The reasons for McKinley's optimism are evident in a front page story in *The Washington Post*, "Betting At Long Odds, Growing Confidence Among Republicans Indicated, 5–1 Ruling Price," October 29, 1900. Detailed accounts of Croker's plans and Bryan's tour of New York City were published by *TheWorld* (New York), October 14–17, 1900. *The New York Times* published extensive coverage of Bryan's reception, October 17, 1900, pages 1, 2, 3. Bryan's comment "great is Tammany" is on page 3. Croker's fund-raising tactics were on the front page of *The Times* on September 29, 1900. The article on campaign financing, "The Cost of National Campaigns," appeared in *World's Work*, November 1900. Bourke Cockran's demand for a private parlor car was reported by *The Times*, September 26, 1900.

Voters' exhaustion with the issues was reported in "The Close of the Campaign" (*Collier's Weekly*, November 17, 1900). This unsigned article declared Bryan the winner of the campaign marathon, uttering 1,045,000 words to 2,100,000 people. The magazine noted that election night had "become a sort of Olympiad, and the newspapers are the runners in a great race for news." The quote about Governor Roosevelt's "thrasonical swashbuckling militarism" appeared in an article by Henry Loomis Nelson, "The Candidates and the Leaders" (*Collier's Weekly*, November 3, 1900).

Election Day. The story in San Francisco's *The Examiner* about its "Perfect Telephone System" appeared in a misdated issue of the paper that read October 7, 1900, instead of November 7, 1900. A description of *The Examiner*'s "bulletin service" appeared on page 20, November 4, 1900. *The Chicago Tribune*'s plans for delivering returns appeared on November 1, 1900. The telephonic system established to deliver election news was reported by *The Tribune*, November 2, 1900, page 16.

Voting. Carl Sandburg's note about voting appears on page 90 in *Ever the Winds of Chance*. For the article on William Jennings Bryan quoting Lincoln, see *The World* (New York), November 7, 1900, page 4. Descriptions of McKinley and TR at the polls were carried by many papers, including *The New York Times*, November 7, 1900. The story about the "repeaters" in New York City appeared in *The Times*, November 6, 1900. Preparations at the brokerage offices were reported by *The World*, November 6, 1900, page 2.

Election night. Stories about the McKinleys, the Roosevelts, and the Bryans appeared in *The Washington Post*, November 7, 1900. For stories on the Wall Street brokers' election night, see *The World* (New York), November 7, 1900; *The Times*, November 7, 1900; *The Evening Post* (New

York); November 7, 1900. The vote in New York City and State was reported by all the major papers; see particularly *The Washington Post*, November 7, 1900. **Post Election.** The description of the McKinleys appeared in *The Washington Post*, November 8, 1900. For Wall Street's response to the election, also see *The Washington Post*, November 8, 1900, page 2, and *The New York Times* editorial, "Wall Street Yesterday," November 8, 1900. Mr. Rockefeller's $21 million gain was reported by *The World*, November 12, 1900. For more about the stock exchange, see "Boom Days in Wall Street," by Edwin Lefevre (*Munsey's Magazine*, April 1901). According to Lefevre, for weeks "the corporate wealth of the country increased at the rate of millions of dollars an hour." The story about Croker's losses appeared in *The World*, November 8, 1900, page 4.

For an account of the president's triumphant tour through Ohio, see *The New York Times* and *The World* (New York), November 8, 1900. Andrew Carnegie's lengthy article on why he voted for McKinley, "The Presidential Election—Our Duty," appeared in *The North American Review*, October 1900.

Jack London's comment about the election appears on page 221 of *Letters*, and the letter to Anna, "I shall be over Saturday night," is on page 136. Anna's comments about Jack appear in "Memoirs of Jack London," by Anna Strunsky Walling (*The Masses*, July 1917).

Chapter Fifteen: November

The Prophecies quoted from *The Ladies' Home Journal* appeared in an article by John Elfreth Watkins Jr., "What May Happen in the Next Hundred Years," December 1900. **Automobiles.** "Automobiles for the Average Man," by Cleveland Moffett, appeared in *The American Monthly Review of Reviews*, June 1900. The New York newspapers covered the Madison Square Garden Auto Show, November 6–10, 1900, often on the sports pages. Also see: "The Automobile Show" (*The Commercial Advertiser*, November 10, 1900) and "The Automobile Show at Madison Square Garden" (*Scientific American*, November 17, 1900). H. G. Wells's comments about the future of the auto appeared in the opening section of "Anticipations: An Experiment in Prophecy," published in the *North American Review*, June 1901.

The story about the reckless Vanderbilt appeared in *The World* (New York), November 10, 1900, page 3. The demand for "man-catchers" was reported by *The New York Times*, April 12, 1900. The need for driver's education appeared in *The Times*, September 2, 1900, page 24. The demonstration of the coin-operated recharger was reported by *The Times*, November 8, page B9. The article on how to build an "auto room" appeared in *The World*, December 2, 1900, Sunday Magazine, page 4. Also see "The Place of the Automobile," by Robert Bruce (*Outing*, October 1900). "Automobile Development" by M. C. Krarup (*Outing*, February 1901) is more interesting than the title suggests. The reference to **Henry Ford** was found in Robert Lacey's *Ford: The Men and the Machine*, page 48.

The death of **Oscar Wilde** was reported by *The World* (New York), December 1, 1900, page 7. For articles about the **Pan American Exposition**, see: "All-America's Fair" (*Harper's Weekly*, January 6, 1900); "Buffalo and Her Pan-American Exposition" (*The Cosmopolitan*, September 9, 1900); "Bird's-Eye View of the Pan-American Exposition" (*Scientific American*, December 8, 1900). The article about the "sumptuous plans" for the the wedding of **J. P. Morgan's** daughter appeared in *The World*, November 15, 1900, page 7, next to the article about Bishop William Lawrence. (The bishop's conviction that "godliness is in league with riches" guaranteed Lawrence's immortality, if not in heaven then at least among historians.) The wedding was described in *The World*, November 16, 1900. For more about Morgan's distaste for competition, see "A View of Pierpont Morgan and his Work," by E. C. Machen (*The Cosmopolitan*, June 1901). Machen saw the development of the trust as "a long leap toward genuine civilization." For a more tempered and sophisticated view of the financier, see *The House of Morgan*, by Ron Chernow (Simon & Schuster, 1991).

The Harvard-Yale Game. Football "armor" was described in detail in an article in *Harper's Weekly*, October 10, 1900. The "symposium" on football, in the November 1900 issue of *Outing*, included two articles on kicking, one by George H. Brooke, the other by Percy D. Haughton. On Saturday morning, November 24, 1900, there was a banner headline on the front page of *The Boston Daily Globe* about the "Game of Lifetime." The same paper reported the appointment of Captain Daly to West Point, on page B4. In *The New York Times*, the report of Yale's triumph shared the front page with an analysis of the president's election (November 25, 1900). For additional information, see "The Close of the Football Season, With a Forecast of the Harvard-Yale Game" (*Harper's Weekly*, November 24, 1900).

Chapter Sixteen: December

Christmas. In New York City, F.A.O. Schwartz began advertising their "Grand Christmas Exhibition" in *The New York Times*, October 21, 1900. For examples of the use of the word "Xmas," see the headline in *The World* (New York), December 23, 1900, page 6, and the Huyler's Bonbons and Chocolates advertisement in *Collier's Weekly*, December 22, 1900. For information on **Frank Baum and Department Stores**, see *Land of Desire: Merchants, Power and the Rise of a New American Culture*, by William Leach, and "The Father of the Wizard of Oz," by Daniel P. Mannix (*American Heritage*, December 1964). Edna Ferber's quote is in *Land of Desire*, page 40.

The article on electrical toys appeared in *The Philadelphia Inquirer*, December 16, 1900, page 6 of the magazine section. For more about the growing American toy industry, see "Making Christmas Toys" (*Harper's Weekly*, December 8, 1900). **Marcus Ravage's** experiences as a peddler in New York at Christmas are described in his memoir, *An American in the Making*, page 95. For more about the lodging on Allen Street, see page 72; musings about holidays begins on page 118. **Mrs. McKinley's** visit to New York was reported by *The World* (New York), December 1–4, 1900.

Pennsylvania. "Christmas Joy Comes to Miners" appeared in *The Philadelphia Inquirer*, December 17, 1900. The decision not to work Christmas Day was reported by that paper on December 26, 1900. The cave-in at the Nayaug Colliery was a front page story in *The Washington Post*, December 6, 1900. News of **J. P. Morgan's** consolidation in the coalfields was reported by the *Inquirer*, December 15 and 16, 1900. The first article was headlined "Some Alarm O'er Big Coal Deal." The second declared, "J. P. Morgan and Those Associated With Him Get Absolute Control of Anthracite Output." For additional information on Morgan and **Andrew Carnegie**, see *The House of Morgan*, by Ron Chernow, and *Andrew Carnegie*, by Joseph Frazier Wall. The Kaiser's comment is in *The Americanization of the World*, by W. T. Stead, on page 172.

The **Opening of Congress** is taken from Walter Wellman's "Washington" column in *Collier's Weekly*, December 1 and 15, 1900, and from *The Washington Post* and *The New York Times*, December 4, 1900. The account of Miss Washington's funeral appeared in *The Post* on December 3, 1900. The story about John Fitzgerald appeared in *The Post*, December 4, 1900. The impact of the "white supremacy campaign" in North Carolina on **George White** and his family was reported by *The Times*, August 26, 1900, page 8.

An account of **Fitzgerald's** support of the reapportionment bill was found in "How J.F.K.'s Grandfather Fought the Grandfather Clause" (*The Negro History Bulletin*, November 1963). "The Injustice to the Colored Voter," by the Hon. George H. White, appeared in *The Independent*, January 18, 1900. White's passionate farewell to Congress was reprinted in "The Last Great Reconstruction Congressman's Plea for Racial Justice," in *Encore*, 1973.

Sadly, there is no full-length biography of George H. White. Southern historians earlier in the century dismissed White as a "race conscious, uncompromising assailant." For an interesting comment on this, see Frenise A. Logan, "Influences Which Determined the Race-Consciousness of George H. White" (*The Negro History Bulletin*, December 1950). Additional material on White can be found in *The Negro in American Life and Thought: The Nadir*, by Rayford W. Logan (Dial Press, 1954) and "Four in Black: North Carolina's Black Congressman, 1874–1901," by George W. Reid (*Journal of Negro History*, Summer 1979). White is also the subject of a Ph.D. dissertation by Reid, "A Biography of George H. White, 1852–1918" (Howard University, 1974).

The Centennial. *The Washington Post*, December 13, 1900, has a full account of the celebration, the unhorsing of General Miles, and the enthusiastic reception for Roosevelt. Governor Shaw's speech is on page 13. For additional details, see *The New York Times*, December 13, 1900, page 3. Theodore Roosevelt. The following TR quotes are taken from *Letters*: "two happy years in Albany," page 1,424; the vice presidency was like "a fifth wheel," page 1,439; feeling "old as Methuselah," page 1,427; "the rough work of the world," page 1,443; going off to hunt mountain lion, page 1,446; on Christmas, page 1,451; no expectation of going "any further in public," page 1,433. TR's comments to Philip Stewart are from letters on pages 1,446, 1,453, 1,459. Roosevelt's quote, "Black care rarely sits behind a rider whose pace is fast enough," can be found on page 273 in *The Rise of Theodore Roosevelt* by Edmund Morris.

The story of **Paul Dunbar's** invitation to the McKinley inauguration appears on page 94 in *The Life and Works of Paul Laurence Dunbar*, by Lida Keck Wiggins. For one account of Dunbar's appearance in Evanston, Illinois, see *Paul Laurence Dunbar and His Song*, by Virginia Cunningham, page 211. Dunbar's poem "Life's Tragedy" is on page 300 of *Life and Works*.

The description of **Galveston, Texas**, on Christmas Eve is based on items found in *The Galveston Daily News*, from December 23, 1900, to January 1, 1901. The most revealing: "Why Holiday Business in Galveston Is Brisker This Year Than Usual," December 23, 1900, page 8; "Night Before Christmas," December 25, 1900, page 7. A description of "The New Galveston" appeared in the paper on December 8, 1900; an editorial on December 21, 1900, pointed out "Galveston's power of recovery."

Chapter Seventeen: New Year's Eve

The literary prediction about **Jack London** appeared in the *St. Louis Post-Dispatch*, December 26, 1900, page 3. London's letter to Anna: " . . . just when freedom seems opening up," is on page 229 of *Letters*. Strunsky's comment about London appeared in an essay written after his death, "Memoirs of Jack London," by Anna Strunsky Walling (*The Masses*, July 1917). For the specifics on Jack London's extraordinary productivity, I am indebted to *Benet's Reader's Encyclopedia of American Literature*, edited by George Perkins, Barbara Perkins, and Phillip Leininger (HarperCollins, 1991).

Kansas City, the Century Ball. For details about the city and the ball, see *The Kansas City Journal* and *The Kansas City Star*, January 1, 1901. Additional material was gleaned from retrospective pieces published by *The Star* on December 28, 1930, December 29, 1940, December 28, 1947, and January 5, 1950. A good description of the fire that destroyed the auditorium appeared on the first page of *The Washington Post*, April 5, 1900. **Independence.** The quote from *The Independence* (Missouri) *Sentinel* appeared on December 28, 1900. I am grateful to David McCullough for uncovering Elmer Twyman's notes on the end of the nineteenth century and Harry Truman's admiration for the Tennyson poem about the "Parliament of man." See page 64 in *Truman* for both. McCullough points out on page 508 that President Truman was still carrying the poem in his wallet, in 1946, as U.S. Soviet relations became increasingly strained.

Boston. The retirement of the horse-drawn trolleys was reported in *The Boston Globe*, December 30 and 31, 1900, and in *The New York Times*, January 1, 1901. Speculation about Mars appeared in *The Examiner* (San Francisco), January 1, 1901, page 4, and on the editorial page that same day. Henry Litchfield West's article was published in *The Washington Post*, December 31, 1900, page 3.

The quote from the Frankfurt *Zeitung* was reported by *The Chicago Daily Tribune*, December 27, 1900, page 3. Brooks Adams's remarkable essay, "The New Industrial Revolution," was published by *Atlantic Monthly*, February 1901. The quotation about the "barbarous impulses of man" is from an editorial in *The Washington Post*, January 1, 1901, page 6. *The Courier-Journal* (Louisville, Kentucky), December 30, 1900, published an extremely interesting supplement on the century's end. The quote about Russian aggressiveness appeared in Section 3, page 1, of that supplement; the Andrew Carnegie quote appeared in Section 3, page 2; the article by Oscar Strauss is in Section 2, page 10.

Sir Walter Besant's challenge to America appeared in his essay "The Burden of the Twentieth Century" (*North American Review*, July 1901).

Epilogue

Every major periodical covered McKinley's assassination. For good contemporary accounts, see the articles in *Harper's Weekly*, September 21 and 28, 1901. "Is It All for Nothing?" by Rebecca Harding Davis, in *The Independent*, October 24, 1901, is an interesting view on the social climate in American life that led to three presidential assassinations in thirty six-years.

Acknowledgments

————◆————

This book grew out of work begun while I was the executive producer of *The American Experience*, the public television history series, produced by WGBH/Boston. Initially envisioned as a documentary film, over time the script began to expand into a book, the book took over my life, and producer-writer David Grubin took over the film. Neither this book nor the film would have been possible without the intellectual, financial, and moral support provided by my friends and colleagues at WGBH, my professional home for almost a decade.

I will always be grateful to Peter McGhee, Vice President for National Programming, for being so generous with what would be my last obsession on his watch. Margaret Drain, my closest colleague and ally from the earliest days of *The American Experience*, and now executive producer of the series, was my most constant reader and helpful critic. WGBH writers-producers Paul Taylor and Peter Cook worked on the film project in its early stages. Cook did the initial research on the mine disaster in Scofield, Utah, and I am sure there are words of his that linger still.

Three of the scholars who helped guide our thinking on the three hour film—Walter LaFeber, David Levering Lewis, and Donald L. Miller—generously agreed to serve as advisors on the book, and all three were of great assistance. Walter LaFeber is easily the best teacher I ever had—and we have yet to meet. There is no way I can express my gratitude to Don Miller, who went over the book, line by line, some chapters twice. It has been said before, but must be said again, that any errors that might remain are my own.

I am indebted to all my friends on *The American Experience*, particularly Susan Mottau, Nancy Farrell, Mari Lou Granger, and Helen Russell, not just for their help but for the warmth of their support. Christen A. Kaczorowski was the project's first researcher and put up with me before I knew what I was looking for. Researcher Heather Piggot worked for over two years culling thousands of pages of material from newspapers, magazines, and books. Every chapter is informed by her work. David Bernstein, Director of WGBH Enterprises, was remarkably imaginative in untangling a complex web of business affairs that could have strangled the project at the outset.

Much of the nineteenth century material used in the book was found at Harvard's extraordinary Widener Library. Without access to their unparalleled collection of newspapers, magazines, and books, this work would not have been possible. I am grateful to all the librarians at Widener, especially to those in the Government Document division. I also owe thanks to Lynn M. White and Stephen Sylvester of the Imaging Services at Widener for their work on the photographs.

All over the country librarians and archivists went out of their way to be helpful. Among those I am indebted to, and this list is by no means inclusive, are Verna Gail Johnson, Mid-Continent Public Library; Bob Conklin and Marcia Heise, Galesburg Public Library; Teresa L. Gipson and Bettie Swiontek, University of Missouri, Kansas City; Ron D. Bryant, Kentucky Historical Society Library; Marita Clance, supervisor of the photographic section, Library of Congress; and Anna B. Peebler, Galveston & Texas History Center, Rosenberg Library.

Some of the most stunning photographs in the book were found by Diane Hamilton, working at the Library of Congress in Washington. No one knows that vast collection any better and no one could have been more persistent. My longtime friend and assistant in New York, Ann Scott, was an early and perceptive reader who challenged every convoluted idea. In the closing months of the project, Rachel Lippman arrived to coordinate the photo research and ended up coordinating me with great good humor during a particularly harried time. Her comments on the last chapters were especially important. To Sarah Colt, my thanks for countless favors; to Lisa Ades of Steeplechase Films, I am indebted for providing me with Sir Walter Besant's essay and other interesting material. I am also thankful to Nick Katz, one of the most sophisticated readers I know, for his suggestions and help.

I will always be grateful to Melanie Jackson for encouraging me to move from one career to another. My thanks to my sister, Margot Conte, and my children, Sarah, Rob, and Jennifer, who were lured into more conversations about 1900 than they ever bargained for and remained as constant in their attentions as ever. And finally, to Sandy Katz—who did not complain as our home came to resemble that of the Collyer brothers, overwhelmed by thousands of old newspapers, magazines, and photographs—for his grace and support I am ever thankful.

—Judy Crichton
New York City, 1998

Index

Entries in *italics* refer to illustrations.

Illustration Credits

973.8 C928
                cop.1 $29.95
Crichton, Judy.

Ameri

973.8 C928
                cop.1 $29.95   12/98
Crichton, Judy.

America 1900